SELLING
THE DREAM

SELLING
THE DREAM

HOW HOCKEY PARENTS
AND THEIR KIDS ARE
PAYING THE PRICE FOR OUR
NATIONAL OBSESSION

KEN CAMPBELL WITH JIM PARCELS

VIKING

VIKING
an imprint of Penguin Canada

Published by the Penguin Group
Penguin Group (Canada)
90 Eglinton Avenue East, Suite 700, Toronto, Ontario, Canada M4P 2Y3

Penguin Group (USA) Inc., 375 Hudson Street, New York, New York 10014, U.S.A.
Penguin Books Ltd, 80 Strand, London WC2R 0RL, England
Penguin Ireland, 25 St Stephen's Green, Dublin 2, Ireland (a division of Penguin Books Ltd)
Penguin Group (Australia), 707 Collins Street, Melbourne, Victoria 3008, Australia
(a division of Pearson Australia Group Pty Ltd)
Penguin Books India Pvt Ltd, 11 Community Centre, Panchsheel Park,
New Delhi – 110 017, India
Penguin Group (NZ), 67 Apollo Drive, Rosedale, Auckland 0632, New Zealand
(a division of Pearson New Zealand Ltd)
Penguin Books (South Africa) (Pty) Ltd, 24 Sturdee Avenue, Rosebank,
Johannesburg 2196, South Africa

Penguin Books Ltd, Registered Offices: 80 Strand, London WC2R 0RL, England

First published 2013

1 2 3 4 5 6 7 8 9 10 (RRD)

Copyright © Ken Campbell and Jim Parcels, 2013

Manufactured in the U.S.A.

LIBRARY AND ARCHIVES CANADA CATALOGUING IN PUBLICATION

Campbell, Ken, 1962-
Selling the dream : how hockey parents and their kids
are paying the price for our national obsession / Ken Campbell; with Jim Parcels.

ISBN 978-0-670-06573-8

1. Hockey—Economic aspects—Canada. I. Parcels, Jim II. Title.

GV847.4.C36 2013   796.962'0691   C2012-906282-0

Visit the Penguin Canada website at www.penguin.ca

Special and corporate bulk purchase rates available; please see
www.penguin.ca/corporatesales or call 1-800-810-3104, ext. 2477.

ALWAYS LEARNING   PEARSON

TO MY SISTER DALE,
WHO FOUGHT THE GOOD FIGHT
RIGHT TO THE END

CONTENTS

INTRODUCTION

On the night of November 27, 2008, more than 6,000 fans jammed into the General Motors Centre in Oshawa, Ontario. Home of GM's headquarters since the company's predecessor, the McLaughlin Carriage Company, set up shop in 1876, Oshawa is a blue-collar town that loves its junior hockey with a passion and its tradition-steeped Generals even more—but not enough to fill the new rink to capacity on a Thursday night early in the Ontario Hockey League season for a game against the Peterborough Petes. In reality, most of those fans were there to witness the fifty-minute pre-game ceremony to honour a player who had left town more than forty years before, but who left an indelible imprint on the franchise.

Bobby Orr had finally agreed to have his No. 2 retired and raised to the rafters to join Eric Lindros's No. 88 and Albert "Red" Tilson's No. 9. Dressed impeccably in a designer suit and looking youthful enough that he could probably still play, the sixty-year-old Orr appeared a little uncomfortable with all the attention, despite being one of the most revered and celebrated players in the history of hockey. Don Cherry made a grand entrance and called Orr the greatest player to ever play the game. Former Generals teammate Ian Young was on hand, as was Wren Blair, the Boston Bruins scout who'd camped out on Orr's doorstep in Parry Sound in 1962 before getting him signed to a C Form with the Boston Bruins and started on the path to NHL stardom with the Generals, a junior team Blair was resurrecting using Orr as its centrepiece. Future NHL star John Tavares, another wunderkind who came to the Generals as a fourteen-year-old, presented Orr with a gold watch from Tiffany & Co. The choir from Bobby Orr Public School sang the national anthem.

As he took to the podium with his glasses resting on the bridge of his nose, Orr began reading from a prepared text. It wasn't long before his eyes began to well up, and his voice cracked slightly when he recalled the contribution his late parents, Doug and Arva, made to his career, telling the young players in attendance to "always appreciate the sacrifices your family members have made so you can chase your dreams."

"I know my, uh, mom and dad are watching tonight," he said. "I know they're very, very happy. Very proud. My mom and dad were perfect minor hockey parents. Their philosophy was, 'Look, go out and play, have fun and let's see what happens.' And I wish there were more parents that thought like that when it came to their kids playing hockey."

Bobby Orr brought the house down with that one. Orr has long been a critic of minor hockey in Canada, and its emphasis on structure and systems and the perceived lack of focus on fundamental skills and fun. He laments that nobody plays the way he and Larry Robinson and Paul Coffey did because nobody allows them to do it anymore. He often hearkens back to his days of playing on the Seguin River at the mouth of Georgian Bay on frigid weekend afternoons. No coaches, no parents, just get the puck and go. With no boards to make high chips off the glass, you had to stickhandle your way out of trouble.

Three months after the ceremony, Orr was back at the General Motors Centre as a celebrity coach for the Canadian Hockey League Top Prospects Game, a gathering of the best draft-eligible seventeen- and eighteen-year-olds playing major junior hockey. With two surgically replaced knees, Orr was able to get around the ice better than he had in years and seemed to be loving every minute of the experience. After the workout, he spoke to the assembled members of the media and was asked whether the experience prompted him to look back to his younger days.

"It was never a job for me. Even during my pro days, it was never a job," Orr said. "That's what these kids have to understand. Just enjoy it, keep that love and passion for the game. I think what sometimes we do ... the coaches and the parents, we just suck the love and passion from our kids. And I think that's wrong."

Not a person involved in the game today would disagree with that sentiment. And no doubt Bobby Orr meant every word of it. But Orr's world of minor hockey and childhood is a far cry from what we're seeing a half-century later. What if Bobby Orr had grown up in Parry Sound circa 2012? Would his parents still be the perfect hockey parents? Is that even possible? Orr played his minor hockey in rural northern Ontario in the 1950s and early 60s, in an era when television was in its infancy and the hockey world was small and insular. In his final season of minor hockey Orr played for the Macklain Construction Bantams, who went undefeated and won the Ontario Minor Hockey Association (OMHA) Bantam B championship. It was at a tournament that season in Gananoque that the Bruins first noticed him. Until then, the kid who would soon be called the best player ever to put on a pair of skates was a relative unknown.

But if Bobby Orr were playing minor hockey today, the world would have known about him long before he became a teenager. Teams from the Greater Toronto Hockey League would have fallen over themselves in an effort to get him to migrate to the largest minor hockey association in the world and expose himself to better competition. There's a good chance he would have been playing spring and summer hockey around the world and spending his summers working out on and off the ice. By age fifteen he would have been flooded with offers from junior teams and schools all over the United States, and he undoubtedly would have applied for exceptional player status to be eligible to play in the OHL.

He also would have been faced with an enormous life decision, since every hockey-playing school in the U.S. college system would offer him a four-year, full-ride scholarship. Media outlets from all over the country would have been dispatched to Parry Sound to chronicle every move of hockey's next superstar by the time he turned ten. As the owner of the Bobby Orr Agency, Orr is now a part of the machinery that is dedicated to finding the next NHL superstar. In fact, there's an excellent chance that Bobby Orr the agent would have been sitting in the living room of Bobby Orr the player by the time he turned fourteen, trying to convince the young man to allow the agency to represent him. That's where Orr's words ring a little hollow. The same man who thinks that young players should be left alone to play represented both Aaron Ekblad and Connor McDavid, who were both granted exceptional status to play in the OHL as fifteen-year-olds. He would have signed a multi-million-dollar contract days after being drafted first overall, and chances are that amount would at least be matched by his endorsement income. And somewhere along the line, the days of innocence playing on the Seguin River for the love of the game would almost certainly have been lost.

Now, it's not as though Bobby Orr developed in total anonymity. He had more than his fair share of admiring journalists and hockey suitors knocking on the door. He left home early to play junior hockey, and he faced the scrutiny of the media at every turn. But let's not forget, as immersed as the young Bobby Orr was in the world of hockey, it was nothing compared to what teenagers go through today. And still, for the young player and his family, it was often a wrenching ordeal.

Kids dream. That's just part of growing up. And if you're growing up in Canada, chances are good you'll go to sleep at night dreaming about hockey. It could be ballet, or lacrosse, or classical music, but chances are it's hockey. And those dreams are also what get kids out of bed in the morning. Dreams motivate us and make us better. Childhood without those dreams would be a dreary, awful thing.

But when as kids we dream—and when we dream on our kids' behalf—what exactly is it that we want? Generations of boys have dreamed of skating effortlessly like Bobby Orr, have dreamed of Bobby Orr's Norris Trophies and Stanley Cups and Canada Cup MVP award. Parents may dream that their kids will grow into someone with Bobby Orr's legendary gracious-ness and capacity for hard work. Maybe the more aspirational parents will dream that their kids will one day make headlines for their salary, the way Orr once did.

As far as realizing dreams goes, you can't do much better than Orr. And yet, even this best-case scenario is something of a cautionary tale. No parent dreams of the heartbreak of sending a kid to a far-off town to play hockey. No kid longs for the homesickness or bewilderment. No one dreams about the injuries.

So, when we talk about the dream, what exactly do we mean? We've interviewed hundreds of people in the hockey world for this book, and just about every one of them used the word "dream" in some way.

The dream takes many forms when it comes to hockey. For some, it begins almost immediately. No parent puts a child into the game—nor does a child begin playing it—thinking he's *not* going to make the NHL, despite almost insurmount-able odds. Usually the game determines the parameters of the dream. The dream might start with being identified as an elite player in one's age group. But as the dream progresses, it gets more serious and there is more at stake. Even before the player enters his teens, the pursuit of the dream becomes more methodical and things are done specifically with the dream in mind. As more and more players fall by the wayside, the dream becomes more narrowly defined—it's less about winning championships with your friends and more about career advancement. Then the bottleneck really narrows and players are filtered into different levels of junior hockey, while others chase the dream of having their education paid for by their ability to stickhandle and score. At that point, participation often becomes an "investment" for those looking to gain some kind of payback for the countless bills, early mornings, and family sacrifices. From there, the most minute fraction of players will go on to make a living from the game by playing in the NHL. Others fulfill their dreams by playing their entire careers in the minor leagues and in Europe.

And the dream often involves the entire family. In fact, when Patrick Kane was selected first overall by the Chicago Blackhawks in the 2007 NHL Entry Draft, the first thing he did was turn to his father, Patrick Sr., and say, "Dad, we did it."

Exactly what "the dream" is matters a lot, because as you'll see, kids and parents sacrifice a great deal to pursue it. If you're a hockey parent, you probably already know that. Even so, you may be surprised what sacrifices lay in store. One hockey parent reported that he is spending an average of $1,000 a week in on-ice and off-ice training—including a weekly flight from Ontario to Chicago for one-on-one skating sessions—to prepare his son for the OHL draft. Yes, the *OHL* draft. The cost of playing AAA hockey, the highest level available in any Canadian jurisdiction, is usually a minimum of $10,000 a year. The best composite graphite sticks cost north of $250. A common lament of minor hockey parents is that "you just keep paying out all this money and you wonder where it's going."

And expensive sticks are just a drop in the bucket. For example, the NHL Players' Association runs the Allstate All-Canadians Mentorship Program, of which a major component is the "National Mentorship Camp" that's held each summer for the best fourteen- and fifteen-year-old players in Canada. Every year, forty-two of the best bantam players are scouted, identified, and invited to the week-long camp, where they receive instruction from current NHL players. The camp wraps up with a game that is televised nationally on TSN2. Another showcase for young talent is the Quebec International Pee-Wee Hockey Tournament; in 2012 it had 112 teams from 14 countries (including England and Australia) and recruited 48 major sponsors, including such heavy hitters as Gatorade, Tim Hortons, Pepsi, and Reebok. A tournament pass for an adult was $50, or you could live-stream all the games for $29.99. Some games of the self-billed "most important hockey tournament in the world" are broadcast live on Réseau des sports, the French-language arm of TSN. In 2010, the sponsor of the Barrie Colts peewee team chartered a jet from Quebec City to Barrie and back in the middle of the tournament so that his team could make it for a Friday night playoff game.

It struck Buffalo Sabres GM Darcy Regier most dramatically when he interviewed Wojtek Wolski prior to the 2004 draft. During the course of the interview, he learned that Wolski had a coach specifically devoted to on-ice moves. The fact that Wolski made almost $8.5 million in his first five NHL seasons indicates that this was a wise investment. Regier also talked to a marginal prospect who required surgery on his hip, which he received in Nashville at a cost of $35,000. Tampa Bay Lightning star Steven Stamkos was working with a personal trainer when he was thirteen. In his draft year of 2008, Winnipeg Jets defenceman Zach Bogosian could do chin-ups with a fifty-pound weight attached to his feet. That's because from the age of fifteen, Bogosian spent ninety minutes in a car each way travelling from his home in Massena, New York, to Ottawa to work out with renowned personal trainer

Lorne Goldenberg, the man most responsible for extending the NHL career of Gary Roberts. He would typically wake up at 6 A.M. and return home by 3 P.M. As a youngster he played three seasons of summer hockey in Ottawa and two in Montreal, and for two years he attended Cushing Academy in Massachusetts, a prep school with an elite hockey program that charges about $45,000 a year in tuition fees. Parents intent on giving their children a leg up are willing to spend thousands more per season on one-on-one instruction—specific tutelage on everything from skating stride to shooting to stickhandling, nutrition advice, and sports psychology.

But the dream starts long before that. A hockey parent who has held scouting jobs in both the NHL and the OHL noticed during his eight-year-old son's house league game that only some of the players had nameplates on their sweaters. When he asked the coach about it, he was told that parents on the team had discovered his scouting background and wanted to make sure he knew what their kids' last names were. When the scout asked the coach whether it was a teamwide initiative, he was stunned to hear that the group of parents who decided to order nameplates wanted names on only their own children's sweaters. For eight-year-olds!

Does that sound crazy? Talk to any minor hockey coach who has been at it for any significant length of time and chances are he'll have a parental horror story. One OHL GM was confronted by a mother and father in the arena parking lot at 1:30 A.M. after a road trip, demanding more ice time for their son. It was during the 2005 NHL lockout and there was talk the NHL would cancel the '05 draft, essentially creating a double cohort in 2006. The parents of the player—a marginal

OHLer—told the GM they had been talking to people around the NHL and had surmised based on these conversations that if the draft were cancelled, their son stood a good chance of going second overall behind Sidney Crosby. Ultimately, the young man was never drafted and played Canadian university hockey after his OHL career finished.

Clearly he was a decent hockey player, but for a parent to think his kid was destined to be drafted immediately after Crosby (an honour that went to Bobby Ryan), when in fact his fate was never to be drafted at all, shows just how deluded a hockey parent can be. That may not be you, or anyone you know. But go into any hockey rink in Canada, and we'd be willing to bet you'll be able to find someone just as certain that their dream is about to come true—if only they spend a little more money, or work a little harder, or make sure their kid gets noticed by the right scout.

"Almost all the minor hockey coaches I talk to, the first words out of their mouths are, 'Boy, the parents are driving me around the bend,'" said OHL commissioner David Branch, who has also coached AAA minor hockey for the past twenty-five years.

By their very nature, the vast majority of parents want only what is best for their children, whether it's on the ice or in the classroom or any other avenue of life. We would never argue against that—and no book is going to stop parents from doing whatever they can for their kids anyway. And as we said, kids need dreams. Parents are entitled to dreams of their own as well. But a little bit of reality can be useful from time to time, especially when families are asked to make astonishing sacrifices in the name of the dream.

Maybe it's got something to with the importance hockey has in our psyche. Perhaps we've all allowed the game to become *too* important to us. In Canada, we play hockey. We do it very well. But would we attach the same kind of importance to it if Canadians were as good at sports such as football, baseball, and basketball as we are at hockey?

One example stands out. Perhaps the most cherished hope among hockey parents is that the thousands upon thousands of dollars they're spending will turn out to be a form of investment. We are reminded of an insurance advertisement that came out a couple of years ago. It depicts a couple standing in front of their suburban home. The mother says that saving for their son's college fund was getting expensive. Then the father says that in order to get around the need to save, they taught their five-year-old how to dunk a basketball. In the background, the little guy goes flying through the air and slams the ball. While their son hangs off the rim with no way down, the mother shrieks, "Scholarship!"

It seems ridiculous, of course. But is it really? In the course of interviewing scores of hockey parents for this book, we heard frequent variations of the idea that if their son could somehow pay for his college expenses with hockey, the "investment" would be worthwhile. In this book you're going to read about parents who have gone to unbelievable lengths to give their children the highest level of hockey experience possible. An owner of an OHL team reports that he often deals with parents who have taken out a second mortgage to fund their son's hockey career. Some have moved across countries and borders and quit their jobs. There are those who have been willing to drive hundreds of kilometres and sacrifice professional advancement and income to chase the dream. "I think there's a lot of parents who expect a return, no question," said OHL commissioner Branch.

Well, when you learn in later chapters just how remote the possibility of making the NHL is, even with huge amounts of money and effort devoted to a career, you'll see that what looked like an investment was little more than a game of "Canadian roulette." Yes, a few families get their money back, and fewer still get rich. But we're talking about an infinitesimal number of cases. The ones more likely to be making money are those who are selling the dream to parents who think pouring money into elite coaching and guidance is going to enhance their children's chances of making it. A hockey school in Toronto called Hockey Extreme boasts in its advertisements, "Guaranteed results every time!" How on earth can any hockey school make that kind of claim? Those parents who put tens of thousands of dollars into their sons'—and now daughters'—hockey careers in hopes of scoring the elusive scholarship would be better off taking the money and investing it in a mutual fund to cash in when their child needs the money for school.

This book is about hockey parents. But it's also about the game itself. As cynical as players and parents, coaches and agents *may* be, there aren't many people involved in the game who don't love it. We love it. We've been playing, coaching, researching, and writing about hockey our whole lives. We live and breathe the game. We love it as much as anyone else. And we have to say it: hockey needs to be protected from itself.

That may sound absurd. Our national passion for the game has not waned—in fact, it's more intense than it has ever been. NHL rinks in Canada (with the exception of Scotiabank Place, home of the Ottawa Senators) have been selling out every game since the lockout in 2004–05, and that in turn has helped create record revenues for the NHL. Canada is back to being a world-class force in the game, and the players that the minor hockey factories in this country have been producing are more skilled, better coached and managed, stronger mentally and physically, and more ready to play at the elite level than ever before. The quality of play has never been higher and it could be argued that the entertainment value never has, either. Hockey players have never been better developed, more prepared, or more skilled than they are now.

So what's the problem? As you'll see in the chapters that follow, hockey is becoming an increasingly exclusive club. And the more competitive the hockey, the more exclusive the club. As we have already seen, the sheer financial cost of the game has become an enormous barrier. The percentage of families that can afford to spend $20,000 per season per kid is painfully small. Should competitive hockey be limited to those in that tax bracket?

But finances are just one way the game is being strangled by the idea that the only reason to play it is to groom multimillionaire athletes. Even if a kid and his family had the money to play that game, would they have the time? That is, the cost of elite hockey is not just the money you spend, it's the opportunities you give up. And even if you have the time and the money, do you want to turn childhood into work? Gruelling hours in the gym may not be enough to get you into the NHL, but that sacrifice is certainly necessary.

One player who would almost certainly be excluded from the big league today is legendary playoff warrior Gary Roberts.

Remember chin-up machine Zach Bogosian? Roberts couldn't even do three chin-ups when he arrived at the Calgary Flames training camp as a rookie. Now he makes fun of the weakling he was as a kid, and everybody laughs because he's about the fittest guy in hockey these days, even though he's retired.

Today Roberts is the poster boy for extreme fitness and dietary discipline. The game's young superstars flock to him for off-season training, and pay him handsomely for it. Roberts is a true believer in the benefits of fitness. Early in his career, he had so much damage in his neck and back that he was facing the prospect of retirement at the age of thirty. It was only then that Roberts began to grasp the importance of training and nutrition, and he has been vigorously waving the flag for both ever since. As a player, he was responsible for pushing the young players on his team toward being more serious about taking care of their bodies and he managed to add eleven years—and $30 million in salary—to his career. The lesson players and parents take from this is that if you're going to play hockey, you'd better be as lean and powerful as a Greek god.

But a couple of problems come with that logic. The first is that while hours in the gym are what saved Roberts's career, they aren't what created it. Even if he was a relative weakling at eighteen, he was still a first-round draft pick based largely on natural skill with little off-season enhancement. The second is that while extreme fitness looks like a great way to improve a professional career, it is hardly necessary just to play the game, or even to play the game very, very well. So how is this bad for the game? Not only would Roberts not be picked in the first round today, he might not get picked at all. And this is a guy who played well over a thousand games in the league, and scored over a thousand points if you include playoffs. A guy who won the Stanley Cup, and went to the All-Star Game three times.

The irony is that if we think of minor hockey as a factory for turning out professional players, we may end up with fewer, not more of them. For every kid who is willing to give up nearly everything else to train for his shot at the dream, plenty more exist who love the game, but not enough to sacrifice the other things they love to do. Just ask Roberts, who spent his summers playing lacrosse, not running hills.

Bobby Orr isn't the only Hall of Famer going on record to say that "developing" kids into elite players rather than just letting their love of the game run its course is a mistake. Bob Gainey, known during his career as a thinker, didn't have to go through a program of systems to know where to be on the ice. He just figured it out somehow, and still managed to win five Stanley Cups and carve out a career as one of the greatest defensive wingers in the history of the game.

"Christ, I didn't even know what a three-on-two was until I was 19 years old," Gainey said. "You just played. You went out and played."

But how many kids are going out and playing these days? Well, the number is dropping. In fact, you might be surprised to learn that just 15.7 percent of boys, or just 1 in 6.4, play the game at an organized level in Canada. Yes, Canada, the birthplace of the game and the country where it is most woven into the national identity. The overall participation rate for children in Canada is 9.5 percent when you include female hockey, which is Canada's fastest-growing constituency. For example, Hockey Canada lost 8,000 players from 2008–09 to 2009–10, despite an increase in numbers in girls' hockey.

And changing demographics in the country certainly aren't making that outlook any brighter. For example, in 2006 there were 2.1 million children aged ten to fourteen in Canada. By 2016, that number is projected to drop by more than 300,000 to 1.79 million. If the 9.5 percent overall participation rate holds, that means Hockey Canada stands to lose 30,000 players in its most important demographic.

So it's in the best interests of everyone involved in the game to find a way to keep more children engaged and involved in it. While this book is about parents, and about the game, in the end it's mostly about the kids who play the game. In 2011, the book *Battle Hymn of the Tiger Mother* generated tempests of controversy over the question of how demanding parents should be of their kids. It's a complicated question, particularly since kids can put some pretty lofty demands on themselves, and author Amy Chua made it even more complicated by suggesting that Asian parents are demanding, while "Western" parents are not. The example most often cited of Chua's strict Chinese discipline is an anecdote about the hours one of her daughters was forced to sit at the piano in order to master a piece of music—all of which ends with the kid's delight at having finally achieved what she'd been working at so hard.

Are hockey parents "tiger" mothers and fathers? The discipline, the long hours, the insistence on ever-higher standards of excellence, the almost religious value placed on hard work certainly make it seem that parents of Chinese pianists don't have a monopoly on tigerish child-rearing. We are not here to make direct comparisons, or to say that this or that parent is doing a poor job. Criticizing parents who are as willing to sacrifice for their kids as hockey parents are is the furthest thing from our minds.

But we do want to talk about the kids. The reason parents care about things like *Battle Hymn of the Tiger Mother* is that they want to do a good job—and they'd hate to discover they're doing something wrong. Parents all wrestle with the balance between pushing their kids into new challenges on one hand, and building their self-esteem on the other. Between work and play. Between letting them be kids, and preparing them to be adults. They want to protect their kids, and they fear overprotecting them.

Sports seems to solve a lot of those puzzles. If the kids are playing sports, they're out of trouble, but they're not constrained. They're having fun and they're learning. They're playing for what seem to them like life-or-death stakes, yet they're learning to abide by rules.

Yet as hockey, like so much else, gets more structured and more results-oriented, and more about parents' expectations and less about the sheer fun, the less kids get out of it. The shortfalls of this kind of childhood become obvious even when kids succeed.

Brian O'Reilly knows all about chasing the dream. He lived it and continues to do so as both a parent and a high-performance coach. His son Ryan is a budding star with the Colorado Avalanche. Another son, Cal, has been up and down between the NHL and American Hockey League and in 2012 bounced from the Nashville Predators to the Phoenix Coyotes to the Pittsburgh Penguins, finishing the season on the Penguins' farm team. His daughter Tara was the captain of the varsity team at Carleton University before getting a degree in human rights law, and his youngest child, Shannon, was playing junior women's hockey as a sixteen-year-old in 2012. O'Reilly, whose family has had numerous foster children live with them over the years, is troubled by the psychology of chasing the dream. As a life coach, he speaks with hockey players regularly and worries about the single-minded focus that chasing the dream requires.

"All we're doing is developing fragmented people," O'Reilly said. "I see a lot of athletes that you'd be shocked how they're finished their sport and they're depressed. They're anxious. They have lots of money and they hate themselves."

In a major irony of hockey parenting, sometimes the result of all the sacrifice is that a player still just in his early teens is turned over to another authority figure for guidance. And while parents believe that the process of grooming their kid into an elite hockey player will impart important life lessons, a risk always exists that the lessons they learn will be damaging. The ranks of minor hockey coaches are filled with volunteers who love the game and are generous with their time. Without these volunteers, there would be no minor hockey. But what happens when you demonstrate to an authority figure that you are willing to do almost anything to achieve a dream—and then that authority figure uses his power to betray your trust and violate you in any number of ways?

You don't have to look much further than the lives of two troubled former NHL players—Theoren Fleury and Mike Danton—to discover the perils that come with that kind of blind faith.

Not even a Stanley Cup, an Olympic gold medal, NHL stardom, and millions of dollars could dull the pain for Fleury, who was repeatedly assaulted by his coach Graham James as a teenager. James, who led the Swift Current Broncos to the Memorial Cup in 1989, pleaded guilty in 1997 to 350 sexual assaults against former Bronco and former NHL player Sheldon Kennedy and another Broncos player. He served three and a half years in prison, but was later pardoned. Then in 2011 he pleaded guilty to sexual assaults involving two more players, one of whom was Fleury.

If there were any question whether Fleury felt beholden to James because of the older man's position and ability to affect his career, it was answered in Fleury's victim impact statement prior to James's sentencing on the second sexual assault charges in 2012. The coach–athlete relationship usually gives an imbalance of power to the coach, and that is definitely the case in hockey. The coach has the power to determine ice time and the player's role on a team, and he is often the one who advocates for a player to move to a higher level. As the handbook *Power and Ethics in Coaching*, part of the National Coaching Certification Program, explains it, "Coaches have a privileged position in the lives of athletes. The intimate nature of sport gives coaches entry into athletes' lives outside the traditions, social structures and conventions that come with being a family member or community member. This entry brings with it the potential to profoundly affect athletes' lives and, therefore, an obligation to use power in an ethical manner."

What does that have to do with dreams? Everything, according to Fleury's statement. James knew he had control over Fleury's hockey future and used that control to repeatedly sexually assault him. As Fleury explained in his victim impact

statement, James had an inordinate amount of control in his
ability to chase the dream of playing in the NHL.

"At a young and very impressionable age, I was stalked,
preyed upon and sexually assaulted over 150 times by an adult
my family and I trusted completely," the statement said. "I was
a boy with a big dream and the talent to match ... Everyone in
my life knew of my passion and my talent, including convicted
pedophile Graham James. Mr. James was a well-known hockey
coach and he zeroed in on my family and me. He skillfully
manipulated us all, and eventually my parents entrusted my
care and well being to him in order to allow me to move to
other towns and cities to advance my hockey dream ... It was
drilled into me that he held the keys to making my dream a
reality. I was just a kid. A child. I was completely under Graham
James' control."

David Frost was a minor hockey coach who later became
an agent for a number of players, including a talented but
vulnerable young player named Mike Jefferson. Frost had such
power over his young charges that they would take instruc-
tions from him in the stands rather than their own coaches.
It was a bizarre relationship to say the least, with sex and
power and intimidation at its foundations. But, like Fleury's
relationship with Graham James, it was a power relationship
based on the ability of the person who wields that power to
affect a future hockey career. Jefferson was so manipulated by
Frost that he disowned his family and changed his last name
to Danton. And in a story that made international headlines,
the former NHLer was imprisoned for more than five years for
conspiracy to commit murder. It is widely believed he plotted
to actually have Frost murdered.

In the book *The Lost Dream* by Steve Simmons, Danton's biological father Steve Jefferson recounted an incident where his son was badly hurt in a game and Frost forced him to go back on the bench.

"I just let it go. I gave [Frost] that power over my son," Jefferson said. "I let him decide. I can't believe, looking back, that I did that. I just stood there saying nothing; I got caught up in the game. I'm a victim of chasing the dream."

Theoren Fleury, Sheldon Kennedy, and Mike Danton are worst-case scenarios. In no way should their experiences be allowed to tarnish the reputations of coaches in general. But the risk of the game isn't just that devotion to it will teach young players only the very worst things about life. There is a dark side even to hockey's culture of courage. The dream can drive people to do all sorts of things against their better judgment. People such as Brad Madigan, who played minor hockey all the way to the midget AA level as a goalie.

Madigan figures that, as a youngster, he had at least four undiagnosed concussions. But he played through them, even though for weeks at a time he would suffer migraine headaches and bouts of vomiting that couldn't be explained. Madigan would be the first to call out a teammate if he felt the player wasn't "sucking it up" and playing through pain. But it all came crashing down when Madigan was sixteen years old and playing for the Aurora Tigers midget AA team. In one game, he fell and hit the back of his head on the crossbar before it hit the ice. But when the team's trainer asked him whether he could continue, he did so knowing he shouldn't have and finished the game. It was the last hockey game he ever played. In the three years that followed, he suffered from severe post-concussion syndrome to the point where he had suicidal thoughts. He still can't ride a bike for five minutes.

As a twenty-year-old part-time university student—he's unable to handle a full course load—Madigan now takes full responsibility for his actions. He knows he should not have continued playing hockey after those undiagnosed concussions, but something kept drawing him back to the game.

"I was the one being an idiot because I had this twinkling little dream in my head of the NHL," he said. "I had that NHL symbol revolving in my head. I was never going to make it, but it's what kept me going, it's what kept me playing. Now, thank God for my family or I probably wouldn't be here."

Let's not end this introduction on a bleak note, though. The reason we're writing it, and presumably the reason you're reading it, is that we know a talented, hard-working kid or two, and we want the best for him or her—the best childhood and the best future. It's probably the case that we love the same game they do. It's probably the case that we would do just about anything for them, and they would do just about anything to make the most of their lives and their many opportunities. This is hardly a terrible place to start. The fact is, if this feeling resonates with you, life is probably pretty good.

In the pages that follow, you will read some cautionary tales and some stories that will leave you shaking your head. For the most part, though, they're stories of people who mean well, who usually have a lot going for them, and who often find happy endings despite themselves.

The reason we want to share them is not to scare parents, or to turn anybody away from doing something they love. What we would like to do, though, is to inject some perspective into the debate. Is selling all your worldly possessions and living on a boat for three years in order to have your son play a higher level of hockey showing a healthy amount of perspective? Even if it results in a multi-million-dollar NHL career and not a reserve spot at a U.S. college? But how do you catch yourself before things spiral out of control? Arming yourself with knowledge and perspective will increase your chances of doing just that.

Obviously, what people call "the dream" takes many shapes. One book is not going to change parents' fantasies of seeing their kids playing in the NHL, and earning NHL dollars. But maybe it can remind us of another version of the dream, one that's more easily attainable, a lot less expensive, and probably a lot more fun for kids—the dream that Bobby Orr started with on the Seguin River. Kids out in the frosty air, chasing a puck around without refs or parents, organizing themselves and experiencing the thrill of a Stanley Cup–winning goal every time they manage to put a puck past their little brother or next-door neighbour. If it was good enough for Bobby Orr, maybe it's good enough for our kids too.

Is that a naive version of the dream? Is it unrealistic to think our kids might recapture some of the magic we knew as kids?

No more unrealistic than the dream we're already chasing.

1

TOO MUCH TOO SOON

If you ever find yourself playing the Genus V edition of Trivial Pursuit, you might be faced with the following question when you land on an orange Sports & Leisure square: Whose single-season scoring record of 104 goals in 40 games as a seven-year-old was broken by Mitchell Davis, who got 109 goals in 17 games?

The answer: Wayne Gretzky.

In the early afternoon of January 15, 2000, little No. 7 for Niroc Construction of the East Nipissing Minor Hockey Association (just east of North Bay, Ontario) scored nine goals in a game at the Astorville Arena. It was hardly an anomaly for him. Earlier that day he had scored ten, and most games he was good for at least a double hat trick. Once that season, the coach of an opposing local team had refused to play Niroc Construction in an exhibition game unless Mitchell Davis played in goal. He did, and his team won 2–0.

As the 4-foot-4, 65-pound phenom darted and weaved his way between wobbly skaters and past helpless defencemen, he continued to pour goals into the net at a prodigious rate. His fifth goal that game gave him 105, which broke the "record" for goals by a seven-year-old held by Wayne Gretzky. And that was also the precise point in time when, in the words of his father Jonny Davis, "our world turned upside down."

It's one thing to possess unique talents and show big-league potential as a seven-year-old. There are hundreds of children who do that every day in rinks all across North America and Europe. Only an infinitesimal number of them will ever come even close to playing in the NHL. Fewer will have a career that will last more than a few seasons, and perhaps one or two of them will win the lottery and become NHL stars with tens of millions of dollars in their stock portfolios.

But it's quite another thing to not only break, but shatter a scoring mark held by the greatest offensive player in the history of the game. At least on the surface. Playing for the Nadrofsky Steelers in Brantford in 1969–70, Gretzky scored 104 goals in 62 games (some records show 40 games) at the age of nine. The Great One averaged 1.68 goals per game that season. Then along came Mitchell Davis, who averaged 6.41, almost five more goals per game when he was two years younger.

Think about that for a minute. That's tantamount to a seven-year-old playing a piano recital and being deemed the next Mozart, a seven-year-old chess player winning a school tournament and being dubbed a future Bobby Fischer, a seven-year-old swimmer sweeping a regional meet and being hailed as the second coming of Mark Spitz or Michael Phelps.

A little more than twelve years after that game, nineteen-year-old Mitchell Davis sat on the couch with his feet up in the basement of his family's home in North Bay. His body ravaged by injuries and his psyche carrying the baggage of expectation and fame in the fishbowl of small-town Ontario, Davis hadn't played an organized game of hockey in more than two years. He was working at a local sporting goods store to save money for college, where he hoped to pursue a career in law enforcement. His hockey career was limited to playing the occasional game of shinny with his father on an outdoor rink on Saturday nights and exhibition games between employees of Sport Chek stores around northern Ontario.

"We had a game against a store in Sudbury and we crushed them," he said. "I got my hat trick and then I just kind of sat back and tried to set up other guys."

Severe back problems essentially snuffed out Davis's career before he even had a chance to play major junior hockey. Despite being named rookie of the year in the Great North Midget League in 2007–08, he wasn't taken until the eleventh round of the OHL draft, by the Erie Otters. Three days before his first training camp with Erie, doctors discovered a pilonidal abscess in his lower back, which was lanced. But the emotional scars Davis suffered from his early career were every bit as damaging as his physical ones.

Mitchell Davis has remarkably little to show for his achievement at age seven, save the memories it created when news of the scoring record went viral—at least as viral as something could go at the turn of this century.

It all started when Chris Dawson, then a freelance television journalist for ONtv, filed a report on Davis for the local newscast the day he broke the Gretzky mark. It was picked up by the full network that night on a news show called *Canada*

Tonight, and from there word about the prodigious young man from North Bay spread quickly.

Within days, prominent reporters from both the CBC and CTV national news were in the family's driveway in Callander, embroiled in a yelling match over which of them would have access to Mitchell first. The Sher-Wood equipment company backed a truck up to the house with more gear than young Mitchell could ever wear. Don Cherry called with congratulations, and Toronto Maple Leafs goalie Curtis Joseph—after learning he was Davis's favourite player—invited Mitchell and his parents to spend a weekend in Toronto at the Royal York Hotel and take in a Leafs game at Joseph's expense.

The Oprah Winfrey Show and *The Tonight Show with Jay Leno* both called offering thousands of dollars and plane tickets for Mitchell to come stateside to be a guest. The way Mitchell recalled it, he balked at the offers because he was too afraid to fly, but his father, Jonny Davis, said the family decided against them because everything was spiralling out of control too quickly. Mitchell recalls the money being offered by *Oprah* and *Leno* was somewhere between $5,000 and $9,000, an amount he now regrets not taking as he works his way through school sharpening skates and ringing up sports equipment.

"Things got rolling and then it just snowballed, it just went crazy," recalled Jonny. "All of a sudden, you have CTV and CBC in your kitchen and Jay Leno is calling you. It was just ridiculous. People wanted everything. If he broke a stick, I had to grab it and bring it home with me because people wanted it."

But for Mitchell Davis there was an enormously high price to pay, one he would continue to pay as long as he played hockey. Perhaps if Davis's accomplishment and the hype that surrounded it had simply represented his Andy Warhol moment, things might have turned out differently for him. But once Gretzky's name was injected into the conversation, there was no escaping the scrutiny that came with being compared to the greatest player of all time. Some of the people in North Bay certainly didn't let Mitchell forget.

"Look out, Wayne Gretzky, here comes Mitchell Davis," said a story on the website for Réseau des sports, the Quebec equivalent to The Sports Network. And CBC, which dispatched respected reporter Adrienne Arsenault to cover the Davis story, was even more effusive in its praise.

"Wayne Gretzky holds dozens of records, but he's lost one to a slick North Bay superstar—seven-year-old Mitchell Davis," CBC News wrote on its website under the headline YOUNG PLAYER SHATTERS GRETZKY RECORD. "Mitchell already has the fancy footwork and the stellar stickhandling. Now, he owns the Great One's childhood hockey record."

"Everyone wants to talk about this kid following in the footsteps of the greatest hockey player ever," the CBC website said. "Mitchell is destined for greatness, they predict."

And for quite a while, Mitchell Davis was a great player. But instead of being celebrated for the accomplishment, Davis wore the mantle of breaking the Gretzky mark around North Bay like a scarlet letter. In fact, in many ways it turned out to be the worst thing that could have happened to him. Before the end of the next season, Davis had quit the game and would sit out a season and a half before returning to play peewee. Mitchell and his father said that after one shinny game, he was verbally assaulted by the father of a child from whom Davis stripped the puck.

"I had a grown man threaten to put a stick around my neck," Mitchell recalled.

"He threatened to beat you up," Jonny interjected. "Seven years old and being physically threatened by a man. 'I'm going to punch him in the face. I'm going to wrap a stick around his head if he takes the puck from my kid again.' It was just shinny, just out on the March break playing shinny. We had to leave the rink."

Perry Olivier, whose son played for several years with Mitchell Davis, said some in the minor hockey community in North Bay displayed a rather unseemly underbelly and many were consumed by jealousy.

"It's almost as though they want people not to succeed rather than succeed. I don't know what it is," Olivier said. "It's too bad because he's a good kid. There were parents who put a bounty on him and stuff like that. 'If anybody can knock the shit out of him during tryouts, I'll pay you money.' Stuff like that. You must have heard those stories."

Perhaps the major factor that makes all of this so disturbing is that it could have—and probably should have—never unfolded the way it did, for a number of reasons. The first and foremost is that neither Gretzky's nor Davis's scoring marks were ever an official record.

First, the fact that these numbers were documented simply meant that Walter Gretzky and Jonny Davis kept close track of their sons' scoring exploits, nothing more. It's possible that hundreds of seven-year-old players have eclipsed both Gretzky's and Davis's scoring totals but were never publicly recognized for it because their parents chose not to share the information—or, even more likely, never kept track of their goals and assists that meticulously at such a young age.

Second, few of those reporters who were breathlessly rushing to Davis's door bothered to consider the ramifications of making a seven-year-old a national celebrity and comparing him with the greatest offensive player in the history of the game. That, of course, is a damning indictment of us, though, isn't it? Are we that desperate to create the next Wayne Gretzky that we don't consider the damage that could be done by making such outlandish comparisons?

Chris Dawson, who did the original television piece on Mitchell Davis, now runs a local news website in North Bay, teaches journalism at Canadore College, and is president of the North Bay Trappers Jr. A team. He said he thinks Jonny Davis contacted him about Mitchell's scoring exploits, something Jonny said never happened. In fact, Jonny Davis maintains the family never once asked for any of the attention it received.

"Back then I'm a young reporter and I'm thinking, 'This is a great story,'" Dawson recalled. "'You could be the guy filming the next NHL superstar.' You're kind of thinking back then, 'Wow, this kid's going to be something else.' I don't want you to get the impression the family is nuts or anything, but if the dad didn't bring that attention on, things probably would have been a lot better for Mitchell than having this big stigma over him at such a young age, because it was a lot of pressure on a kid who was too young to have to deal with that."

But society was fascinated with prodigies long before Justin Bieber first appeared on YouTube. In the third century,

Coa Chun served as a cavalry general under his warlord cousin Cao Cao and is the youngest person ever to fight for an army at a rank higher than major. Wolfgang Mozart learned to play his first piece of music at four, was writing his own work at five, and embarked on a three-year tour of Europe when he was seven. Shirley Temple made a total of nine Hollywood films when she was six, which earned her a special juvenile Oscar, "in recognition of her outstanding contribution to screen entertainment during the year of 1934." A couple of months before his third birthday, Tiger Woods drove golf balls and beat Bob Hope in a putting contest on *The Mike Douglas Show* in 1978.

But the pressure to live up to one's childhood exploits can be unbearable. Alissa Quart knows that as well as anyone. Quart wrote her first novel when she was seven and won a number of prestigious writing competitions through her teens. At one point, she was told she would be the next great American poet.

"It's funny because I stopped writing poetry for a long time because of that," Quart said. "Very few people are the next great American poet. No matter how exceptional people are when they are young, there is a limited number of seats in the first orchestra, right?"

Quart has since written two books, including *Hothouse Kids: The Dilemma of the Gifted Child*. She has a master's degree from the Columbia University School of Journalism, did a Nieman Fellowship at Harvard, and has written opinion pieces for *The New York Times* and *The Atlantic Monthly*. In her book, she sheds light on the downside of being prodigious, saying the effort to produce gifted children is a troubling phenomenon and places an overwhelming pressure on gifted kids to achieve. One chapter illustrates what Quart calls "the Icarus effect," profiling a number of gifted children who turned out to be depressed adults whose talents were squandered.

"Teaching kids to read in infancy, to kick a soccer ball when they're two, or to compete fiercely in spelling bees doesn't, as it turns out, mean that children's 'gifts' will ultimately be enhanced," Quart writes in *Hothouse Kids*. "Learning to read faster, or to memorize words earlier, or to play the piano with facility at an early age are not Rosetta stones for accomplished adult life."

Despite her accomplishments, even Quart struggles with self-worth. A new mother, she worries about whether she will succumb to the temptation to urge her children to overachieve and she often feels she has never measured up to her own childhood achievements.

"Oh God, yes, constantly," Quart said when asked whether she struggles with her self-worth. "It didn't even matter because winning those competitions when I was a kid and being in these gifted schools were high intensity. It sets you up for a feeling that you never quite have done what you were supposed to have done. My experience and all my research showed me, 'Wow this does not breed happiness.' It certainly can breed expertise, which can breed happiness. In the long run it might be worth it, but in itself it's not a source of joy for kids necessarily."

In other words, parents who foster their kids' desire to excel may actually be harming them, since the hunger for success will never be satisfied. Kids will perform better and better, and never experience the reward they're seeking. So the better they do, the worse they feel.

The young man who has been carrying the Gretzky label since he was seven can most certainly relate. In the fall of 2009, Mitchell Davis was faced with the choice of continuing to chase the dream of playing in the NHL in what was becoming a more difficult upstream swim or getting on with his life—essentially, throwing everything into an uncertain future or focusing on school, getting a stable job, and ultimately starting a family. He chose the latter, but instead of being liberated from the pressure of having to meet expectations, the pressure failed to dissipate.

"Ever since I broke Wayne Gretzky's record when I was seven, it's just like I've been destined for greatness and I've always just kind of put that on my shoulders," Davis said. "It's so weird. It doesn't feel like I'm just making the decision for myself because I put a lot of pressure on myself growing up and my family has sacrificed so much. My parents have done so much for me and I feel like I'm letting them down. I'm letting my family down, I'm letting North Bay down."

There was a time when northern Ontario towns such as North Bay produced a hugely disproportionate number of NHL players. Of the twenty-two players who played at least twenty-five games a season for the Toronto Maple Leafs' three consecutive Stanley Cup winners between 1962 and 1964, ten of them were from Sudbury, Timmins, and Kirkland Lake or surrounding towns and an eleventh, Dave Keon, came from nearby Rouyn-Noranda in Quebec. When the Maple Leafs were recruiting Frank Mahovlich in the 1950s, they were so intent on signing him that they purchased the rights to the Schumacher Minor Hockey Association.

North Bay itself has produced a few notable NHLers,

the most prominent among them Kenny Wharram, a former linemate of Bobby Hull who won a Stanley Cup with the Chicago Blackhawks in 1961 and the Lady Byng Trophy as the NHL's most gentlemanly player three years later. North Bay also produced defenceman Billy Coutu, a nasty piece of work who played for the Montreal Canadiens in the early days of the NHL and won a Stanley Cup with the Canadiens in 1924. Coutu became the first player to be banned from the NHL for life after he assaulted referee Jerry LaFlamme during the 1927 Stanley Cup final between his Boston Bruins and the Ottawa Senators. And Craig Rivet, Darren Turcotte, Steve Shields, Mike Yeo, Ray Giroux—all from North Bay.

Still, back when Davis was lighting up the rinks in North Bay, the town didn't have many local boys starring in the big league. So you'd think that residents might rally around a talented young player with promise such as Mitchell Davis. But to hear his father talk about it, precisely the opposite happened. Jonny Davis said rather than support Mitchell after surpassing the Gretzky mark, many people in North Bay were consumed with pettiness and jealousy and the result was both Mitchell and his family were ostracized. Friendships were irreparably damaged and the attention Mitchell received even caused a schism in Jonny's own family.

"We had friends and all of a sudden, the friendships ended," Jonny said. "It wasn't just friends, but my own family members. Some of my brothers and sisters wouldn't talk to me. I think I went back to the [family] Christmas party about two years ago. I had to skip it for about nine years. I've gone back the past couple of years because they're more satisfied now that he's not a big superstar. If he was in the NHL right now, I probably still wouldn't have a relationship with them. Not on my account, that's just the way they are."

For his part, Mitchell said he loved the attention he received for surpassing the Gretzky mark. "I don't ever wish for a second that it didn't happen to me because it was one of, if not the coolest thing that has ever happened in my life." But Jonny Davis tells a much darker story. It's clear he thinks that breaking the Gretzky mark and all of the negative attention that came with it was the worst thing that could have happened to Mitchell and his family. "Because the price we paid was so heavy, well, you couldn't live long enough to get rid of the baggage that came with it," he said. "It was terrible. Knowing inside that he could have played in the NHL—he probably still could if he wanted to—is it my desire for him to be there? No, not at all."

Both Mitchell and Jonny recalled instances during his minor hockey career that bordered on the sublime. The Davis family is devoutly Christian. In fact, Mitchell remembers the day he accepted Jesus Christ as his personal saviour because it's inscribed on his Bible—January 7, 1998. Mitchell said as a youngster, he would often get so excited before games that he would have to urinate several times. When that happened, he and his father would go to the washroom for some quiet time and to pray together before the game. It wasn't long until rumours began to circulate that Jonny was taking Mitchell into the washroom before games to vomit so his stomach would be empty and he would be able to skate faster.

Perhaps the jealousy was because Mitchell was so talented at such a young age, or maybe it was the fact that he had parents who were very involved in his life—to the point that Jonny's wife, Patty, home-schooled all five of her children. Surpassing the Gretzky mark certainly didn't help with other parents or players who were not showing as much promise as Mitchell.

"He would go to bed crying at night. 'How come I don't have any friends? How come they hate me? How come they call me these things?'" Jonny recalled. "There are so many wounds to heal. No kid should have to go through that because he was gifted."

So how did this happen? There's little doubt Jonny being a Type A personality had something to do with it. When we spoke in the winter of 2011, Jonny was holding down four jobs—doing maintenance with the school board, working for the Ontario Housing Authority, running a family-owned building maintenance business, and being the superintendent of a condominium building.

Jonny Davis was a martial arts instructor who first gained notoriety in North Bay by attempting to break the world record for push-ups. He claims to have broken the record by performing 3,612 push-ups in 1 hour and 167 in 1 minute. He also said he once was attempting to break the world bench press record by bench pressing his body weight (150 pounds) 1,000 times in 100 minutes and reached 820 before blowing out both shoulders.

"I had four world records in push-ups," Jonny said. "I would go to Walmart and people would say, 'Oh, you're the push-up guy.' Then six months later in January, 'Oh, you're Mitchell Davis's dad,' and the attention was gone from me, which was great."

"I was actually at the event where the dad broke the push-up record," said Chris Dawson. "You already knew because of his push-up record the father was into numbers. Numbers were the No. 1 thing and beating records was obviously a priority with this guy, and it started at an early age with Mitchell."

So did the weight training. Jonny always served as Mitchell's personal trainer and both acknowledge Mitchell was doing weights as early as eight years old. Jonny had built his own leg press machine for Mitchell to use. Mitchell said watching his father try to break push-up records and work out six days a week helped him stay motivated and train hard; he described his father as a workout partner. Many times, Mitchell would spend the day weight training and practising hockey before doing his home-schooling at night. Home-schooling also allowed him to play for a spring team with kids from Sudbury and Sault Ste. Marie. Jonny said that even though the home-schooling was something they did with all of their children, it would have been necessary for Mitchell after the notoriety he received for the Gretzky mark.

When it came to training with weights, Jonny said he was always careful about not overtraining any of the young people with whom he worked. "It was light, very light scale," Jonny said. "You have to watch that. I'm very particular about the weight training I give kids. Heavy lifting is totally out of the schedule. I don't do any power lifting because it's too hard on the joints. I made up homemade leg machines and stuff and would use them to work with each age group."

And when Mitchell was a young player, it seemed to work. In the years after breaking the Gretzky mark, Mitchell was meeting his goal of being the best player in northern Ontario. (It's interesting to note here that as of 2012, six players from Davis's 1992-born age group from northern Ontario attained a career in the Ontario Hockey League. Just one had an NCAA Division I commitment for 2012–13, and none of those players had been drafted by an NHL team by age 20.) Often playing above his age group, Mitchell continued to progress and, while not putting up the same kinds of offensive numbers he did as a seven-year-old, he was still considered an elite talent and compared favourably in tournaments against the likes of Tyler Seguin and Jeff Skinner of the Toronto Young Nats and Erik Gudbranson of the Gloucester Rangers, who all went on to become first-round draft picks in the 2010 NHL Entry Draft that would have included Mitchell Davis.

Mitchell recalled playing in the Bell Capital Cup in Ottawa, which bills itself as "The world's premier hockey tournament" and has the designation from the *Guinness Book of World Records* as the biggest hockey tournament in the world to prove it. Played over three days during the Christmas vacation in Canada's capital, it attracts hundreds of teams from as far as Beijing, Moscow, and Helsinki and raises about $2 million a year for local minor hockey associations. Teams that make the final in their divisions play the championship game at Scotiabank Place, the home of the Ottawa Senators.

That was the case in 2004 when the North Bay Huskies, led by Mitchell Davis, advanced to the championship final in the Peewee A division at what was then known as the Corel Centre. In the semifinal game, Mitchell led the way with a two-goal, one-assist effort in a 3–2 win over the Brampton Battalion, but was ejected from the game when he dove to backcheck an opponent and the player fell to the ice.

That meant Mitchell was suspended for the final game, the biggest of his life.

"I was crying. This was the Corel Centre," Mitchell said. "I remember just trying to feel good and my dad was telling me, 'All these kids that are on your team, they'll probably never get a shot like this again. They're not really going to go anywhere with hockey. You made this happen for them. This will probably be the best moment of their lives in hockey and you made it happen. And you're probably the only one on your team who's going to get a shot to play on this ice one day.' I looked at it from that perspective and said, 'You're right.'"

And, for much of Mitchell Davis's minor hockey career, it looked as though Jonny Davis's words were going to prove prophetic. In 2006–07, Davis was the scoring champion of the Northern Ontario Bantam Hockey League with twenty-six goals and fifty-five points in thirty-four games, despite the fact his North Bay Hilltop Variety Blades finished dead last in the league with just 100 goals. As a major bantam, Mitchell spent the next season with the North Bay Trappers midget team, and in a league that produced the Telus Cup national midget champion Sudbury Nickel Capital Wolves he was named rookie of the year and scored thirty goals and sixty-two points in thirty-four games.

Despite the scoring exploits, Davis plummeted to the eleventh round of the OHL draft that spring, going 202nd overall to the Erie Otters. It was a setback, but certainly didn't mark the end of his career. After all, a good number of players have gone on to NHL stardom after being overlooked completely in junior drafts.

True, no player selected 202nd overall in the OHL Priority Selection since 1980 has seen a game of action in the NHL. But players such as Curtis Joseph, Brett Hull, Claude Giroux, and

Martin St-Louis weren't drafted as minor midget–aged players at all. Steve Mason, the Columbus Blue Jackets goalie who won the Calder Trophy as the NHL's top rookie in 2009, was chosen 201st by the London Knights in his junior draft year. But this player, who was so dominant against his peers through most of his hockey career, was beginning to show some serious flaws.

Perry Olivier, a scout for the Otters who lives in North Bay, had to push the Otters to take Davis in the eleventh round that year. The hope was that he would go back to North Bay to play Jr. A hockey for a year and continue his development with the possibility that he would return ready to play in the world's top development league the next season. But there was a lot of room for improvement. Olivier said all the weight training Davis had done with his father made him too big and too slow to keep up in a game that had opened up offensively.

"His skating really fell off and people began to think he was really slow," Olivier said. "The West Ferris Arena [in North Bay] is really small and he could hide his skating a little bit there, but at the next level it kind of became an issue and that's when everything started to fall apart for him. When you think about it, I never would have thought he would be an eleventh-round pick myself. I thought he was going to be better than that."

And the nagging back problems that had been with Davis since he was six years old started to become too painful to ignore. After having his back troubles surgically addressed just before Erie's training camp in 2008, Mitchell went to camp and performed well, but the back pain persisted. An MRI he had done as a teenager showed signs of arthritis in his back, and even though both Davis and his father insist the weight training regimen had nothing to do with his back troubles, there was no conclusive evidence it had or hadn't been at the root of the problem.

Davis came back to play the 2008–09 season with the North Bay Skyhawks Jr. A team, but early in the season suffered a concussion after a thundering check in a game against Sudbury. He wasn't getting much ice time on a veteran team and decided to return to the midget team for his last year of minor hockey eligibility, where he scored six goals and eleven points in ten games. He hasn't played a game of competitive hockey since that season ended.

The back problems became too painful for him to play in 2009–10, and he finally had back surgery in February 2010. By the fall of that year he was ready to start working out again, and he went too aggressively and had another setback. Doctors told him he had a torn cremaster, which is the muscle that surrounds the testicle. With no cure aside from months of rest and inactivity, Davis spent a lot of time on the couch contemplating his hockey future. In the fall of 2010 Davis was considering getting back on the ice, and the Jr. A team in North Bay was hoping he would sign with them to play the season. But in an email message to Skyhawks GM Chris Dawson, Davis essentially announced his retirement. It was ironic given that Dawson was the one who had started the whole frenzy in the first place with his initial television report on Davis.

"I've had a lot of time to think about my decision after discussing my future with my family and my agent and I've decided to step away from competitive hockey permanently to pursue a career in policing," Davis wrote to Dawson. "You know as well as anybody else my decision will upset a lot of people, but at the end of the day I have to do what my heart says. Thanks again for the offer and for everything you've done for me and with me during my career. I will surely see you around the rinks for years to come."

Mitchell Davis watched the first hour of the 2010 NHL Entry Draft, which was held at the Staples Center in Los Angeles. Had everything worked out as planned, this would have been his draft year and he would have been shaking hands with the most powerful men in hockey and fashioning his new NHL sweater the way guys such as Taylor Hall and Tyler Seguin did. All that season, the two players waged a heated battle over which one would go No. 1 in the entry draft. It wasn't lost on Davis that back in 2000, there were a lot of people who thought he'd be one of the players in that battle as well.

"I watched to see who went first and I watched most of the first round," Davis said. "But all I could keep thinking was, 'What if?' There were so many 'what ifs' going through my mind. It was painful to watch." Davis said the thought of playing hockey again never leaves his mind, but he knows the dream of playing in the NHL is dead. He will always have the memories of scoring more points than The Great One did as a seven-year-old, but those can often produce as much pain as joy.

When asked whether he'd do anything differently, Jonny Davis said he would have moved his family out of North Bay after the fallout from the Gretzky mark, perhaps to western Canada where nobody would know who they were. He said as difficult as it has been for him, his wife is even more wounded about the whole affair and refused to discuss it. Patty Davis, like her son, laments what could have been and, according to Jonny, is frustrated that her son has given up on his hockey career.

After the wreckage, there's no doubt in Jonny's mind that none of it was worth the high cost.

"There's no money he could make and there are no friends he could have and no position he could be in that would be worth what he had to go through to get there, not a chance," Jonny said. "He could have been [in the NHL] and he was always the best. But to sum it up, if he was better than Sidney Crosby right now in the NHL, it still wouldn't have been worth it."

2
THE NUMBERS

A couple of summers ago, Pierre Dupuis and his wife embarked on one of the most dreaded tasks on anyone's to-do list: they cleaned out their garage. Not long after they began, they came across a motherlode of hockey trophies that were more than three decades old. Among them was the bauble he won for being the national Showdown champion in 1978. Aside from the mounds of newspaper articles and scrapbooks, the awards were the only tangible recognition of a brilliant minor hockey career that once had hockey fans agog and prompted comparisons to Bobby Orr and Wayne Gretzky.

And there they were, alongside broken toys and other useless, dust-gathering items destined for a landfill just outside of Sudbury, Ontario. Well into his forties with two teenage children, Dupuis decided to finally throw the trophies away. Looking back, he's surprised at how easy it was to part with them.

"We were just going through them and [my wife] Nicky was like, 'What are you going to do with these things?'" Dupuis said. "And I said, 'You know, I've been holding onto these things for like twenty-five years since I quit playing hockey and I started with Hydro,' and I said, 'I don't really know why I'm holding on.' I said, 'I think it's time. I'm ready to get rid of them.' And I did. It was just one of those things where I was ready to let it go at the time and I was fine."

In fact, it was almost cathartic for Dupuis, marking a triumphant end to years of self-therapy that followed an unfulfilled hockey career. Everything had happened so quickly. One moment Dupuis was a superstar earning adulation from anyone who watched him play. And seemingly the next moment, the only lofty thing about him was the fact that he was up in the air repairing power lines for Hydro, just another ordinary Joe with a nine-to-five job and a family waiting at home.

Nobody cheered his work or kept telling him how special he was. Nobody was predicting he would become the best lineman in the history of Hydro.

"I went through a mini-depression for sure," Dupuis said. "I did struggle early on and I think Nicky paid the price for that. She helped me through it. I probably took it out on her for the first five to ten years of our marriage."

Back in 1978–79, there was not a better peewee player in Ontario, perhaps even Canada, than twelve-year-old Pierre Dupuis of the Sudbury Steelworkers. The year before, Dupuis had captured the championship for eleven-year-olds in the Canadian Showdown competition, which earned him an appearance on *Hockey Night in Canada*. In the puck control competition, which required competitors to skate through a maze of pylons, the only player in Canada who beat the eleven-year-old Dupuis's time was sixteen and competing in the midget category.

Bob McKenzie, who would go on to become one of the most well-connected and respected voices in the hockey industry as the editor-in-chief of *The Hockey News* and an analyst for TSN, wrote in *The Sault Star* that "Dupuis' sole efforts made a run-of-the-mill Sudbury Steelworkers peewee team an extraordinary outfit."

In the Maple Leaf International Major Peewee Tournament in Toronto that season, Dupuis led his team to the championship in front of 1,000 fans with five goals in a 6–4 win over Wexford. After the game McKenzie quoted Frank Miller, a Toronto minor hockey official, who said Dupuis was the best twelve-year-old player he had ever seen.

"And I've seen a lot of them play, including those at the Quebec peewee tournament," Miller said. "I've never seen a kid skate so well and he showed me he is the complete hockey player. He passes the puck, backchecks, he does it all and very well."

At the 1977 Quebec peewee tournament, which bills itself as "the world's most famous minor hockey tournament" and attracts the best twelve-year-old players from around the world, Dupuis led his team to the championship final, scoring all six goals in the semifinal and five goals and two assists in a 7–0 win over a peewee team from Sweden. Meanwhile, players the same age as Dupuis—such as Mario Lemieux, Luc Robitaille, Stéphane Richer, and Patrick Roy—were playing peewee hockey in Quebec in relative anonymity. A newspaper in Quebec City gushed, "And then there was Pierre Dupuis, a hockey player with talent so remarkable that observers were comparing him to Bobby Orr and Wayne Gretzky at the same age."

And they weren't the only ones. In a story the next season in the *Toronto Sun* headlined PIERRE CAN TURN 'EM ON WITH THAT GRETZKY FLAIR, Scott Morrison wrote from the all-Ontario bantam championship in Brantford that "Perhaps it's only fitting that The Second Coming should take over the stage in the town that launched The Great Gretzky."

At another tournament that season, in Sault Ste. Marie, a team from Toronto withdrew its entry when it learned Dupuis would be playing. "The Toronto team called to tell us they wouldn't come to the tournament if Dupuis was allowed to play," tournament spokesman Gary Barbeau told *The Sault Star*. "We told them that the idea of keeping a kid out was ridiculous and the Toronto team actually backed out of the tournament."

When he was twelve years old, Dupuis was already 5-foot-4 and 140 pounds. By the next season, he was 5-foot-7 and 160 pounds. Dupuis would grow only one more inch, but continued to play above his age group. Injuries started becoming more frequent and the players he had effortlessly darted around were getting bigger and stronger and the nets he seemingly filled at will were getting much harder to find. By the time he was drafted by the Windsor Spitfires in the fourth round of the 1983 OHL draft, most of the elite players in Ontario had caught up to him.

Dupuis played just one full season in the OHL, posting modest totals of thirteen goals and twenty-six points in sixty-four games before leaving the team after being made a healthy scratch by coach Wayne Maxner in the first playoff game. It was a stressful year that saw Dupuis's father suffer a heart attack; when his future wife's mother died of cancer early the next season, Dupuis came home to Sudbury for good. A job offer at Hydro followed soon after, and by the time the 1984 Entry Draft came along everyone in the NHL had forgotten about Pierre Dupuis, distracted by the talents of players such as Mario Lemieux, Kirk Muller, Ed Olczyk, Al Iafrate, Gary Roberts, Brett Hull, Luc Robitaille, Shayne Corson, Scott Mellanby, Stéphane Richer, and Patrick Roy.

While those players found NHL stardom and the riches that came with it, Pierre Dupuis lived the anonymous life of a working man. It certainly wasn't the existence he'd envisioned when he was growing up. Back then he believed everyone who told him how special he was, and basically took for granted that he would be playing in the NHL. Even his future wife's family warned her to stay out of his way as he carved his hockey path.

But then it all fell apart so quickly, and Dupuis had a very difficult time adapting. Once you've got your sights set on the dream, everyday reality can seem pretty dreary.

"There was no abuse or anything," said Dupuis's wife, Nicole. "He just wasn't the vibrant young man that I knew. He just became very quiet and just taking the kids for a sleigh ride was a big chore."

Dupuis's story might be a little more extreme than most, but his situation is probably more commonplace than many people realize. The fact is, for every Mario Lemieux or Patrick Roy there are hundreds of guys like Pierre Dupuis doing honourable work such as being linemen for Hydro or driving delivery trucks. Some parlayed their playing careers into academic opportunities and are doctors, lawyers, and captains of industry.

But the fact remains that the ones who don't make it are in the enormous majority, particularly in Canada. Those who do and have a modest NHL career of even a few seasons have been given what is tantamount to a winning lottery ticket when you base it on the odds of making the NHL. It's a winning ticket for which they've worked incredibly hard and made enormous amounts of sacrifice, but sometimes even all the hard work and dedication a player can muster isn't enough to offer the hope of a career playing hockey.

It makes you stop to wonder whether the thousands of dollars and countless hours parents are putting into their children's hockey careers and the sacrifices they are making are worth it. In the case of Chicago Blackhawks star Patrick Kane, whose parents spent $250,000 over the course of his career in minor hockey, it was certainly a worthwhile investment—by the time his current contract expires in 2015, Kane will be just twenty-six years old and will have already made $42.7 million in the NHL. Those numbers mean his family will have earned 17,000 percent on their investment.

But all the others who have tried and failed may wish that their parents had taken the money they put into minor hockey and invested it in a GIC. For many, it would have paid out more than enough to put them through university and get a great start on their post-hockey life.

Unfortunately, that's not likely to deter anyone. Nor is the fact that the statistics you are about to read are alarming and paint a stark picture of the actual odds of making the NHL, even for a brief time. For the purposes of our research, we've based our odds on three categories: (1) the general population, (2) elite players (those who play major junior or college hockey), and (3) super-elite players (those who play for championship teams in junior or college, Canada's World Junior Championship team, or the CHL's annual Top Prospects Game).

THE GENERAL POPULATION

Every year, thousands of parents register their children for minor hockey programs in Canada. Most of them do so for the purpose of providing their children with an outlet for physical activity and competition and realize that their kids' chances of making a career in the game are infinitesimal. In reality, those children have a better chance of winning the lottery than making it to the NHL.

To measure this, we studied three birth years in minor hockey in Ontario—1965, 1975, and 1985. By the start of the 2012–13 hockey season, the majority of those players would be forty-seven, thirty-seven, and twenty-seven years old and would either be finished or well into their NHL careers. Generally speaking, by that time career paths would be determined even for the players born in 1985; if they've not played at least a game in the NHL by 2012–13, chances they ever would are extremely slim.

Ontario is Canada's largest province and has roughly 45 percent of the country's hockey players residing within its boundaries. Its expansive hockey system from house league to AAA is immense and complicated; however, it does provide a solid base to use as a sample. The methodology can then be applied—with the same results on a per capita basis—to any other Canadian province.

From any given birth year in Ontario, you can expect at least 25,000 boys to register for at least one season of minor hockey—that includes from initiation and house league level through to juvenile hockey. Some of them will drop out after a year or two, others will play until their teenage years, and some will play until their final season of midget hockey at age seventeen.

That has been the case consistently since the 1970s and continues today. The number actually is in the range of 25,000 to 30,000, but for purposes of our study we went with the more conservative number.

Of those, about twenty-five will make it to the NHL for at least one game. So, on average, the chance that a player registering for minor hockey for the first time will play even one game in the NHL is a paltry 0.1 percent.

That's a 1-in-1,000 chance. We'll discuss the costs of minor hockey later in the book, but let's say for argument's sake that it costs $100,000 for a player to play elite AAA hockey through his entire minor hockey career. If the parents of that player took that $100,000 and bought 50,000 Lotto 6/49 tickets for one draw, based on a possible 13,896,816 number combinations they would have a 1-in-300 chance of winning the lottery.

And that's just the odds for playing *one game* in the NHL!

For the purposes of our study, we broke down each birth year into players who appeared in at least one NHL game, at least 80 games, at least 200 games, and 400 or more games.

The 80-game threshold basically represents one full season in the NHL; 200 games represents the career of a solid journeyman player, one who bounces around from team to team and usually splits his playing career between the minor leagues and the NHL; and 400 games is tantamount to a career lasting five or more seasons.

Some years are more bountiful than others. Let's start with Ontario players born in 1965. The 1965 birth year produced thirty-eight players who played at least one game in the NHL. The crown jewel of that group was Hall of Famer and three-time Stanley Cup winner Steve Yzerman, who was actually born in Cranbrook, B.C., but played virtually all his minor hockey in Nepean, Ontario. Of those thirty-eight players who saw NHL action, twenty played at least 80 games, seventeen played 200 or more games, and fifteen played at least 400 games. Sixty-eight were drafted by NHL teams, and five signed as free agents without being drafted. (At that time, very few European players were being selected by NHL teams, so the total of sixty-eight draftees was the highest number of NHL draftees ever from Ontario's minor hockey system.)

From that age group, 141 players played at least one game at the OHL level and 60 played one year of Division I hockey in the National Collegiate Athletic Association in the United States. (We're presuming that virtually all of them in the NCAA played on some form of scholarship or financial assistance.)

What this all means is that based on 25,000 boys playing minor hockey in that age group, the chances of a player from Ontario born in 1965 playing in the NHL was 0.1 percent. And that's in a birth year that produced 52 percent *more* players headed to the NHL than the average hockey birth year in Ontario (1965 saw thirty-eight players see NHL action, while the average over thirty years is twenty-five players in the big show per birth year).

And we'll remind you again: that's based on playing in just one game in the NHL.

The chances of a 1965-born minor hockey player being at least a one-year wonder in the NHL was 0.1 percent. The probability of being at least an NHL journeyman was 0.08 percent. And the chances of winning the lottery and having an NHL career lasting five or more seasons was 0.05 percent, or 1-in-2,000.

Even a player's chances of an appearance in the OHL or the NCAA were slim. That year, approximately 200 players made it to those elite levels of hockey, meaning just 0.7 percent of players who played minor hockey in that birth year managed to play any meaningful hockey beyond midget. This included OHL, Jr. A, Jr. B., and Jr. C.

When you examine the overall birth rate from 1965, the numbers are even more startling. According to Statistics Canada, 72,713 boys were born in Ontario in 1965, meaning that a boy born that year in Ontario had a 0.05 percent—or 1-in-1,914—chance of playing one game in the NHL. Some of these notable 1965 NHLers, in addition to Yzerman, were Bob Probert, Dave Lowry, Todd Gill, and Peter Zezel.

Ten years later, in 1975, the mothers and fathers of Ontario produced one of the strongest crops of potential players ever seen in the province by NHL scouts. (Despite that, not one of the province's thirty-two NHL players born that year has won a Stanley Cup or an individual NHL award or earned a berth on a first or second all-star team. Notable players from the 1975 group include Todd Bertuzzi, Chris Gratton, Todd Harvey, and Ethan Moreau.) But once again, the chances of a player born in 1975 playing one NHL game was 0.1 percent—almost identical to the decade before.

The odds of playing at least a season (twenty-one players, 0.07 percent) and at least 200 games (seventeen players, 0.06 percent) remained virtually the same as well. But with just twelve players who played 400-plus games, the chances of being a long-time NHL player fell to just 0.04 percent, which is 1 in every 2,500 players.

A total of 54 players were drafted by NHL teams from the 1975 birth year, and an additional 7 signed as free agents. Of the 25,000 players who started out, 129 played at least one season in the OHL and 40 played at the U.S. Division I college level.

There was a total of 64,419 boys born in Ontario in 1975, meaning a boy born in that year had a 0.05 percent chance of playing a single NHL game—again, identical to the decade prior.

Determining the success of the 1985-born group is a little more difficult, simply because not all of their careers were over as of the 2011–12 season. But one thing we know with certainty is that the size of the Ontario contingent in the NHL went down significantly—which we expect would also be the case in the rest of Canada, with the NHL getting more of a contribution from the United States and Europe than ever before.

Of the 25,000 boys who signed up for hockey in Ontario who were born in 1985, just 25 had played at least one game in the NHL by the end of the 2011–12 season.

Since those players were at least twenty-five by that time and players overwhelmingly tend to make their NHL debuts by that point in their careers, we wouldn't expect the number to increase by more than one or two, if at all. Mike Angelidis became the twenty-fifth player from the age group to see action in an NHL game on January 24, 2012, when he suited up for the Tampa Bay Lightning. He played his first NHL game just a week before he celebrated his twenty-seventh birthday. Chances are, he'll probably be the last 1985-er from Ontario to play an NHL game as of the writing of this book.

Which means that the chance of an Ontario hockey player born in 1985 playing one game in the NHL was just 0.1 percent. As of 2011–12, eighteen of the twenty-five players who played in the NHL had played at least 80 NHL games, twelve had played at least 200 games, and five had played 400 or more. (We can probably expect that number to swell by two or three by the time all their careers are over.) What the 1985-born group lacks in quantity, however, it makes up for in quality. Among that group are Jeff Carter, Mike Richards, and Corey Perry—all of whom won a gold medal for Canada in the 2010 Winter Olympics in Vancouver—along with Nathan Horton and Brent Burns.

There were 67,715 boys born that year in Ontario, meaning those born in 1985 had a 0.04 percent chance of playing in the NHL. Dating back over the past thirty years, the average number of players from each Ontario birth year to play one game or more in the NHL is twenty-five.

So what does all this tell us? Well, one thing is that regardless of the era or the contribution from other parts of the world, the chances of a boy from any jurisdiction in Canada making the NHL are infinitesimal. The numbers have held relatively steady in terms of both minor hockey registration and production of NHL players, so there's little reason to believe they'll change anytime soon.

One of the misconceptions in minor hockey is a belief that players have to get on "big city" teams as young as possible to gain exposure when being identified by major junior clubs. For example, the Greater Toronto Hockey League (GTHL) has long been considered a strong breeding ground, with three or four elite AAA teams each year producing some of the top players for the OHL draft.

However, on the list of players from Ontario since 1975 who have made the NHL, only 16.8 percent of those players came from GTHL programs while the league itself represents approximately 20 percent of the registered players in the province—that means the league has a per capita development rate of about –3 percent.

What the research found was that players from other Ontario minor hockey leagues who elevated to the NHL actually had an edge in terms of career advancement on their GTHL counterparts by the age of nineteen.

Each year several small-town Ontario parents, some with players as young as age eight, believe it's necessary to get their kids on a GTHL superclub such as the Marlboros, Red Wings, or Jr. Canadiens. However, just twenty-one GTHL "import" players since 1997 have played a game in the NHL in the last fifteen years. This pretty much indicates that regardless of where he plays his minor hockey from the ages of eight through sixteen, a player eventually develops no matter how strong his team is as a peewee or bantam.

An excellent example comes from the Ontario players born in 1990, which featured a powerhouse team in the Markham Waxers of the OMHA's Eastern AAA League. The Waxers captured the prestigious OHL Cup and lost a grand total of two games in eight years. In 2005–06, when they were in minor midget (age fifteen), they compiled a record of 64-1-2.

The Waxers had three future NHL draft picks on their roster in Steven Stamkos (Tampa Bay), Michael Del Zotto (New York Rangers), and Cameron Gaunce (Colorado).

One Waxers nemesis in the 1990 age group was the Toronto Jr. Canadiens of the GTHL. The Jr. Canadiens were also a perennial powerhouse team and battled the Waxers on a regular basis in major tournaments and provincial championships over a seven-year period.

Like the Waxers, the Jr. Canadiens team also had three future NHL draft picks in Alex Pietrangelo (St. Louis), Josh Brittain (Anaheim), and Stefan Della Rovere (Washington).

In the same 1990 age group, a "middle of the pack" team was the Halton Hills Hurricanes (based west of Toronto in Milton). This club played in the OMHA's South Central AAA League and periodically competed with some of the top teams. Over a seven-year span, they were marginally over the .500 mark from novice to minor midget.

That Halton Hills team produced two future NHL draft picks in Mat Clark (Anaheim) and Jeremy Price (Vancouver).

Finally, the worst AAA team in the 1990 group every year was the Chatham-Kent Cyclones—a club that averaged about five wins a season playing in the Pavilion League in Southwestern Ontario. Incredibly, the lowly Cyclones also had two future NHL draft picks in T.J. Brodie (Calgary) and Jason Missiaen (Montreal).

It's a testament that regardless of where they play their minor hockey, talented players will develop at their own pace and eventually rise to the top. You don't need to be on an 85-5-1 big-city superclub to develop or get noticed.

But you'd probably expect that when you start with such a large and diverse sample group. So let's narrow it down.

General Population

Birth year	No. of boys	NHL players	Percentage
1965	72,713	38	0.05%
1975	64,419	32	0.05%
1985	67,715	25	0.04%

ELITE PLAYERS

For players with NHL aspirations, hockey resembles a pyramid. At its base is an enormous pool of players that decreases with every passing year until natural selection leaves only the elite at the top. The most dramatic narrowing of the structure occurs when players reach their teenage years and join the roster either for one of the sixty major junior teams in Canada or one of the fifty-seven Division I college programs in the United States.

For a kid to move to this level is a major accomplishment. And because it really is the only gateway to the NHL for North American players, those with dreams of playing in the best league in the world are willing to do whatever it takes to reach this stage. When a player gets to the major junior or NCAA point in his career, hockey is a single-minded pursuit and a twelve-month-a-year occupation.

For those who play major junior, it means long gruelling bus rides for fifty bucks a week and the possibility that you could be drafted at sixteen years old by a team hundreds of kilometres from home—not to mention traded or dropped from the roster at any time. For those who go the NCAA route, it means juggling the demands of elite sports with a university education. And living with the possibility that your scholarship can be yanked at any time for any reason—including on-ice performance.

But there is no doubt that major junior and NCAA represent the pinnacle for an amateur player in North America. And with these players so tantalizingly close to the pro ranks, you'd think most of them would end up in the big leagues, right?

Think again.

The reality is that only a very select few ever advance beyond this stage. For the vast majority of these players, performing in a Memorial Cup or Frozen Four tournament will represent the summit of their careers.

We examined the records of players in the CHL and NCAA for three seasons spanning fifteen years—1981–82, 1991–92, and 1996–97—to determine how many of the players at the top of the amateur hockey food chain went on to play in the NHL.

In 1981–82, there were 864 players on the thirty-six CHL teams that played major junior hockey. Of those, 281 (or 32.5 percent) went on to play at least one NHL game. A total of 186 (21.5 percent) played at least 80 NHL games, 168 (19.4 percent) appeared in at least 200 games, and 74 (8.5 percent) managed to have a career lasting more than 400 games.

CHL Stats

Season	Total players	1 game	80+ games	200+ games	400+ games
1981–82	864	281 (32.5%)	186 (21.5%)	168 (19.4%)	74 (8.5%)
1991–92	1,056	200 (18.9%)	118 (11.1%)	90 (8.5%)	63 (5.9%)
1996–97	1,176	221 (18.8%)	115 (9.8%)	89 (7.6%)	62 (5.3%)

In the NCAA that year, there were 972 players on thirty-six Division I teams. Eighty-four of them (18.6 percent) went on to play in at least one NHL game. A total of 47 (4.8 percent) played in at least 80 games, 33 (3.4 percent) had a career of at least 200 games, and 26 (2.7 percent) played 400 or more NHL games.

NCAA Stats

Season	Total players	1 game	80+ games	200+ games	400+ games
1981–82	972	84 (18.6%)	47 (4.8%)	33 (3.4%)	26 (2.7%)
1991–92	1,134	117 (10.3%)	61 (5.4%)	48 (4.2%)	31 (2.7%)
1996–97	1,134	96 (8.5%)	53 (4.7%)	44 (3.9%)	29 (2.6%)

The CHL-to-NHL numbers ten years later saw a precipitous drop, partly because the landscape of the NHL had changed and many more Europeans and Americans were appearing on NHL rosters by then.

That season, there were 1,056 players on forty-four CHL teams, 200 of whom (18.9 percent) went on to play at least one NHL game. A total of 118 (11.1 percent) played at least 80 games, 90 (8.5 percent) played 200 or more games, and 63 (5.9 percent) had a long career by NHL standards.

In the NCAA, 1,134 players played for forty-two teams and 117 of them (10.3 percent) played at least one game in the

NHL. Sixty-one (5.4 percent) played at least 80 games, 48 (4.2 percent) appeared in at least 200 games, and 31 (2.7 percent) played 400 games or more.

In 1996–97, the numbers held steady. In the CHL, 1,176 players toiled for forty-nine teams, with 221 of them (18.8 percent) playing at least one game. A total of 115 (9.8 percent) played at least one season, 89 (7.6 percent) had at least 200 games, and 62 (5.3 percent) played in 400 games or more.

In the NCAA, 1,134 players comprised the forty-two teams, 96 of whom (8.5 percent) played at least one game in the NHL. Fifty-three (4.7 percent) played at least 80 games, 44 (3.9 percent) appeared in 200 or more games, and 29 (2.6 percent) were NHLers for at least 400 games.

The numbers since then have held fairly steady, leading us to the conclusion that a junior or college career is not even close to a guarantee of a career as an NHLer. In fact, chances are overwhelmingly against a major junior playing a single game in the big league. And the chances for his NCAA counterpart are twice as bad.

Think of it this way: The next time you're at a major junior game, look down at both benches during the national anthem. Of all those players in uniform for both teams, chances are only one or two of them will have sustained NHL careers. Do the same thing at a U.S. college game and you might find one.

SUPER-ELITE PLAYERS

Every Boxing Day, millions of Canadians gather around their televisions to watch the World Junior Championship, and Team Canada responds by making it time well spent.

Super Elite

Teams	Total players	1 game	80+ games	200+ games	400+ games
Canada WJC	407	382 (93.9%)	307 (75.4%)	260 (63.9%)	201 (49.4%)
Jr. champs	1,891	691 (36.5%)	434 (23.0%)	333 (17.6%)	243 (12.9%)
Top prospects	352	239 (67.9%)	160 (45.5%)	136 (38.6%)	102 (29.0%)

Despite losing in the gold medal game in 2010 and 2011, and in the semifinal in 2012, Canada has been dominant in the tournament over the past two decades, winning exactly half the gold medals over the past twenty years thanks to two separate five-year dynasties.

Some of the greatest players in Canadian history have appeared in the tournament. In 1978, a sixteen-year-old Wayne Gretzky cemented his status as the best young talent in the world with eight goals and seventeen points in six games at the tournament in Montreal.

Eric Lindros led Canada to back-to-back gold medals, and Sidney Crosby put in a performance for the ages at the 2005 tournament in North Dakota.

It should come as no surprise, then, that the Canadian World Junior program has been the most successful factory when it comes to producing NHL players. Largely because these players represent the absolute cream of the elite, or the super-elite, their futures as NHL players are almost assured.

Almost every player here has been drafted or will be once he turns eighteen. All are star players on their major junior and college teams and, for the most part, are products of Hockey Canada's elite identification that starts at the age of sixteen.

Once they're in the program, they receive the best coaching and off-ice guidance, play in pressure-packed situations in international play with under-17 and under-18 teams, and get far more exposure to a greater number of NHL scouts.

Playing for Canada in the tournament doesn't provide an iron-clad guarantee a player will have a long career, but it's the most certain bet a player will at least enjoy a respectable run as an NHLer.

From the time Hockey Canada established its Program of Excellence in 1982 until 2005, 407 players have worn its colours in World Junior competition and almost all of them have gone on to play at least one game in the NHL.

Of the 407, a whopping 93.9 percent (382) have appeared in one NHL game. A total of 307 (75.4 percent) have played in at least 80 games, and 260 (63.9 percent) have been in the NHL for at least 200 games.

But even playing in the best tournament in the world for the best team in the world is no guarantee of NHL longevity.

In fact, 201 of those players, or 49.4 percent, had played 400 or more games as of the end of 2010–11. Although more will be added to that list, it is sobering to think that Canada's World Junior stars have only roughly a 50 percent chance of having sustained success in the NHL.

Nor does playing for an elite major junior team provide a direct route to NHL fame and fortune. Like the World Junior teams, those that win titles in the Ontario, Quebec, and Western Leagues are heavy with elite talent because they're at the top of the development cycle when it comes to building their programs. Those teams also tend to acquire many of the best talented veteran players from other teams in trades.

We took the champion from each league from 1971–72 through 1999–2000 and discovered that 1,891 players have played for those teams. A total of 691, or 36.5 percent, of the players played at least one game in the NHL and/or defunct World Hockey Association. Just 434, or 23 percent, managed to have an 80-game career in the big leagues and 333, or 17.6 percent, reached the status of journeyman with more than 200 games. What came as something of a shock was the fact that just 243, or 12.9 percent, of those players had a career lasting 400 games or longer.

No championship team has had more than six players whose career spanned 400 or more games and two teams, the 1996 Peterborough Petes and the 2000 Barrie Colts, didn't have a single player who hit the mark.

The most successful team over the twenty-eight-year period was the 1993–94 Kamloops Blazers, who had fifteen of their twenty-four roster players appear in at least one NHL game.

By far the weakest group of champions came in 1985, when the Swift Current Broncos, Laval Titan, and Peterborough Petes combined to send just twelve of sixty-five players to the NHL for at least one game.

Every year since 1992, the Canadian Hockey League has held its annual Top Prospects Game, which showcases the most coveted forty players from the three Canadian junior leagues for that year's NHL entry draft. Don Cherry and Bobby Orr have served as celebrity coaches for the event, which also features a skills competition. Although it's not seen as a make-or-break event for a draft prospect, it does provide some basis for comparison among the best eighteen-year-old players in the world.

And while the CHL bills the game as a chance to see tomorrow's stars today, fewer than one in three of those top draft prospects will have an extended NHL career.

From 1992 through 2002, a total of 352 players participated in the game and 239 of them, or 67.9 percent, saw action
in at least one NHL game.

All told, 160 (45.5 percent) were more than one-year
wonders and 136, or 38.6 percent, managed to play 200 games
or more. But when it came to careers of 400-plus games, just
102—or 29 percent—of the best draft-eligible players the CHL
had to offer managed to reach the milestone.

So whatever became of Pierre Dupuis? Well, he managed
to find happiness after all. He and his teenage love are still
married and his two children are well on their way to finding
their niches in life.

Dupuis acknowledges, though, that he discovered content-
ment only when he learned to let go of his resentments. Shortly
after joining Hydro, he was placed in the small northern
Ontario town of Verner, which is along the Trans-Canada
Highway between Sudbury and North Bay. One night, he slung
his hockey bag over his back with a couple of beers in it and
walked down the street to the local rink.

It wasn't long before Dupuis was once again leaving people
amazed with his skills—on a much smaller stage. Playing
against huffing and puffing recreational players whose best
days had passed them by, Dupuis was once again filling the net
and gaining legions of fans. People from town—and even from
other small towns nearby—flocked to the arena to watch him
play. Kids asked for autographs.

"Pierre became the little superstar all over again," Nicole
Dupuis said. "He was doing what he loved to do and I saw that
twinkle in his eye like it was when he was younger. Then Pierre

was happy. He realized, 'You know what? I've got my kids coming to see me and the kids at school were talking about Pierre Dupuis.' It was fun because people would come from all over to watch him play. It came back to what it was."

It seems kind of a shame, though, that Dupuis had to wait to be a middle-aged father before he could play hockey like a kid.

3

SIT DOWN, SHUT UP, AND GIVE ME YOUR CHEQUEBOOK

Haliburton, Ontario. It's the kind of place where they sell T-shirts emblazoned with a huge mosquito and the words HALIBURTON: LOVE AT FIRST BITE. Where the light standards downtown are adorned with flags that remind everyone to support our troops. Where the local newspaper runs headlines like REPORT: BEARS SHOT IN DEFENCE OF PROPERTY, with the accompanying story providing the following piece of advice: "Killing a bear should be a last resort and only after exhausting all options available. While landowners have the legal right to kill a bear in defence of property, it must be done swiftly, humanely and safely in accordance with local bylaws that cover the discharge of firearms." (The newspaper gives no advice for visitors who arrive unarmed.)

It's the kind of place where you can go to get away from it all—and thousands of people do just that, every summer. From the downtown waterfront you can see them tubing and water-skiing on Head Lake, one of 600 that God gave this corner of the world. People took the hint and transformed the area into a cottager's paradise.

The main drag in Haliburton is occupied by McKecks Place, a watering hole and eatery owned by former NHLer Walt McKechnie. Across the street is the Source for Sports operated by Glen Sharpley, who had a seven-year career with the Minnesota North Stars and Chicago Blackhawks. And just down the street, across from the Royal Canadian Legion, is the Dysart Community Centre. On the side of the building are murals of local hockey legends Bernie Nicholls, Ron Stackhouse, and, most recently, Matt Duchene.

Inside the arena, in the Haliburton Hockey Hall of Fame, is a picture of a young Cody Hodgson, who starred for the Haliburton Huskies novices in 1997–98 until he moved to Markham when his father, Chris, won a seat in the Ontario provincial parliament. Beside Hodgson is a picture of a beaming six-year-old with straight hair and crooked teeth, Hodgson's teammate Matt Duchene.

Duchene took his first tentative steps on skates at the Dysart Community Centre when he was just three years old. It was also around then that he began to travel with his parents to Glens Falls, New York, to watch his uncle Newell Brown coach the Adirondack Red Wings of the American Hockey League. Christine Duchene, Matt's mother and Newell Brown's sister, came from a Cornwall, Ontario, family where her three brothers had earned scholarships to Michigan State University.

"We milked cows around hockey," Christine said. "It was all I knew."

None of Christine's brothers made it to the NHL, but Newell came close. In the days when players could play both major junior and U.S. college hockey without losing out on a scholarship, Newell won a Memorial Cup with the Cornwall Royals in 1979 and was drafted by the Vancouver Canucks in 1982. Newell did reach the NHL as an assistant coach, winning the Stanley Cup with the Anaheim Ducks in 2007. It was during those trips to Glens Falls to watch Newell coach, however, that Christine and Vince Duchene realized their son had a huge passion for the game.

"We'd have to get an aisle seat so that Matt could stand on the concourse with his stick and mimic exactly what was going on out on the ice," Vince said. "If they were out there for a faceoff, he would be down for the faceoff and once they dropped the puck, he would go running all over the place."

It wasn't long before Vince Duchene, though, was the one doing all of the running around. In an effort to find better competition and more sophisticated instruction for his talented son, he began to travel to Lindsay, the nearest centre with a AAA organization, which was seventy-five minutes away by car.

It was there with the Central Ontario Wolves AAA teams that Matt Duchene would be able to take advantage of his passion to the fullest. Better coaching, more talented players, and the prospect of playing with the best in his age group in spring hockey tournaments excited Matt Duchene and his parents.

The mileage began piling up quickly and so did the expenses, which represented a significant challenge even for a two-income family. Christine is a guidance counsellor and teacher at the local high school, and Vince is a real estate agent who helps his affluent clients from the city buy and sell cottages in the area.

Let's get one thing straight right away. No hockey player—from the stars such as Duchene to the fourth liners to even the enforcers who play four minutes a game—can possibly have a chance of making the NHL without an enormous amount of natural talent, inner drive, and an ability to be so mentally focused that all other distractions are dismissed.

Players who enjoy even a brief NHL career make enormous sacrifices for the privilege, and in exchange they get an uncertain existence that can end at any moment under any circumstances. The ones who grasp that notion and are willing to go to any lengths to get it are the ones who almost always separate themselves from those who fall by the wayside in minor and junior hockey.

They're also the ones who reap the enormous rewards. In the six years after the NHL locked out its players to impose a salary cap, the average salary in the NHL rose $600,000 to $2.4 million. Star players were getting long-term retirement contracts with no-movement clauses and even the lowest-paid players were receiving an annual stipend of $500,000. With the NHL's teams being forced to pay a minimum of $48.3 million in salaries in 2011–12, it has never been a better time to be an NHL player, salary cap and cost certainty be darned.

But in what has become a growing trend, the chances of a player making the NHL are also being determined not only by talent and drive, but also by the sacrifices and challenges the people around him are willing to endure.

And the money they have.

There is a well-documented story about how the parents of Boston Bruins star goalie Tim Thomas hocked their wedding rings to pay for him to attend hockey camp one summer. Numerous others have taken on second jobs or cut corners on things such as vacations and cottages.

We saw in the previous chapter just how slim a player's chances of making the NHL are. In an effort to make those odds even a little more manageable, families are willing to spend hundreds of thousands of dollars and travel to great lengths to fully exploit their player's talents.

Matt Duchene started with the passion, talent, drive, and good bloodlines—in addition to his three hockey-playing uncles, his father's second cousin is former NHLer Andre Savard—but there's little doubt he would have made the NHL as an eighteen-year-old had his parents not been willing to pour large amounts of money into things such as spring hockey, power skating, and skill coaching.

When Vince and Christine Duchene moved into their modest starter home shortly after getting married, they planned on being in it for five years before upgrading. That upgrade took eighteen years because of the expenses associated with Matt's hockey career. Outside of hockey tournaments they never took a family vacation, and the first time Vince and Christine were on an airplane alone was to travel to Denver to see their son play in the NHL.

Only three years ago did the Duchenes move to their dream home, but Vince insists on doing all the landscaping. The four-car garage under construction will have a full gym for Matt to get his summer workouts in, and the end of the yard was being excavated to make room for an indoor shooting gallery so Matt would be able to fine-tune his shot in the off-season.

It was a long time coming, because the family had been

spending in excess of $20,000 a year on Matt's hockey, not to mention the lost income Vince suffered from having to take so much time off work during the spring.

The months between March and June are frantic for the real estate market in a place like Haliburton because that's when panic sets in for those who want to buy a cottage they can be in for the May 24 long weekend or the start of July. That time is also chock full of spring hockey tournaments, so instead of accompanying prospective buyers to cottages on the weekends Vince Duchene was taking his son to spring hockey tournaments.

Often Vince would do most of the heavy lifting for clients, only to have a colleague show them a cottage on a weekend when he was away at a tournament. So instead of getting 100 percent of the 5 percent commission on the deal, Vince would have to give 75 percent of it to his colleague and keep 25 percent for himself. He figures he missed out on at least $20,000 in commissions per year because he was at spring hockey tournaments.

Vince Duchene estimates he spent about $1,200 when composite sticks first came out and were priced at more than $300 each. In Matt's later years of minor hockey, he would go through two pairs of skates a year at about $800 each. Credit lines were almost always maxed out, as were credit card balances.

"If there was room on the Visa, you put it on and you carried on," Vince said. "And that's why we had that other house for eighteen years, because we could never catch up."

The Duchenes, like every other family of an elite hockey player, chose to spend this kind of money on their son's career.

They could have been perfectly content to have him continue to play for their local team in Haliburton.

Would it have resulted in an NHL career? Probably not. The fact is that in the vast majority of cases, a player who has NHL aspirations has to have a family that either has a lot of disposable income or is willing to make enormous financial sacrifices. Or both.

We asked Vince Duchene to estimate what he has spent on his son's career from the time he started minor hockey to when he joined the Brampton Battalion as a junior in 2007–08, and where the money went. Here is what he produced. Expenses are calculated on a year-by-year basis:

1994–95 CanSkate Learn to Skate program.	$300
1995–96 Haliburton Huskies Mite Hockey team. Registration, new hockey equipment, sticks, two tournaments, gas, food for road games	$1,400
1996–97 Haliburton Huskies Tykes program. Four tournaments, registration, new hockey equipment, sticks, gas, food for road games	$2,400
1997–98 Haliburton Huskies Novice program. Four tournaments, registration, new hockey equipment, sticks, hockey school, gas, food for road games	$3,200
1998–99 Central Ontario Wolves Minor Novice. Four tournaments, registration, new hockey equipment, sticks, hockey school, gas, food, and four spring tournaments	$13,850

1999–2000 Central Ontario Wolves Major Novice. $15,200
Four tournaments, registration, new hockey equipment, sticks, hockey school, gas, food, and four
spring tournaments

2000–01 Central Ontario Wolves Major Novice, $19,300
plus affiliation with minor atoms. Six tournaments,
registration, new hockey equipment, sticks, hockey
school, gas, food, and five spring tournaments

2001–02 Central Ontario Wolves Major Atom. $15,800
Four tournaments, registration, new hockey
equipment, sticks, hockey school, gas, food, and
four spring tournaments

2002–03 Central Ontario Wolves Major Peewee. $21,000
Four tournaments, registration, new hockey equipment, sticks, hockey school, gas, food, and four
spring tournaments; first year of composite sticks
and first year with a personal trainer

2003–04 Central Ontario Wolves Minor Bantam, $22,000
plus affiliation with major bantams. Five tournaments, registration, new hockey equipment, sticks,
hockey school, gas, food, playoffs with two teams,
personal trainer, and four spring tournaments

2004–05 Central Ontario Wolves Major Bantam. $22,000
Four tournaments, registration, new hockey equipment, sticks, gas, food, hockey school, personal
trainer, private power skating and stickhandling
development, and four spring tournaments

2005–06 Central Ontario Wolves Major Bantam and $23,000
high school hockey. Five tournaments, registration,
new hockey equipment, sticks, gas, food, personal,
trainer, private power skating development, and
two spring tournaments

2006–07 Central Ontario Wolves Minor Midget, $23,000
Major Midget, and high school hockey. Seven tournaments, registration, new hockey equipment, sticks,
food, gas, private on-ice training, and personal trainer

PERSONAL LOSS OF INCOME Missing the busy $140,000
season in the spring due to playoffs, spring tournaments, and tryouts (for under-17 team, etc.), I lost an
average of $20,000 in income per year

TOTAL INVESTMENT   **$322,450**

The thing that stands out most is the sheer size of that number at the bottom. There are a lot of things a family can buy with that kind of money.

One thing the Duchenes bought was a lot of summer hockey. At a glance, it looks as though there is an argument to be made that Matt Duchene became a super-elite hockey player and top-three pick in the NHL draft because his family contributed as much to his development in the off-season and outside the conventional game and practice situations as it did to his winter hockey career.

Which leads us to an interesting observation. It's not what a player does or what kinds of numbers he puts up or the number of tournaments his team wins from September to April that determine whether or not he is going to make the NHL someday. It's what he does with his time—and what his parents do with their money—during the crucial summer months and what kind of commitment he'll make to personal instruction that often makes or breaks a hockey career.

It was certainly that way with the Duchenes, who acknowledge their Central Ontario Wolves program was a pretty good one. But it was a small centre with a limited pool of AAA players, so the team would go to tournaments and generally be soundly beaten by teams from across the province.

But it was in summer hockey, when Matt was placed on an equal footing with many of those players from bigger cities he faced off against during the winter, that he really discovered what he needed to do to improve.

That led to the Duchenes pouring all kinds of time and money into personal training and one-on-one instruction. There are people in the tiny town of Haliburton who have no idea there were many mornings when Matt would wake at 5 A.M., travel the seventy-five minutes to Lindsay for a power skating or skill development session, then travel back home in time to be in school for his first class at 9 A.M.

Vince Duchene recalled a conversation he had with a close friend of his who told him the worst thing that could have happened for the young hockey players in Haliburton was Matt's success as a hockey player. Once Matt was drafted into the OHL (fifth overall), suddenly driving seventy-five minutes several times a week to play AAA hockey was what made the difference in the young player's career. "We were actually very private about what we did," Christine said of the sacrifices the family made for Matt, "because we really thought people would think we were loony tunes. Seriously."

The fact that Matt Duchene has gone on to stardom makes his parents' commitment to his career look like an investment. Including bonuses, Duchene earned $4.6 million in his first three years as an NHL player on an entry-level contract with the Colorado Avalanche. And despite having a disappointing third season in which he played just fifty-eight games and scored twenty-eight points, he signed a two-year deal in the summer of 2012 worth $7 million. Although his subpar third season prevented him from cashing in on a long-term, big-money deal that many of his peers signed, if he develops into the NHL talent most are expecting him to he could earn untold millions by the time his career ends. With a "return" like that, who wouldn't scrape together $322,450 to "invest"?

The thing is, while the Duchenes' hard work and sacrifice may have been *necessary* to get Matt where he wanted to go, it was by no means *sufficient*. In other words, it may be that players won't reach Duchene's sublime level of skill without all that grooming, but there's no guarantee that rigorous grooming and hard work will make any kid into Matt Duchene, no matter how much money or sweat they invest.

One thing is certain. Regardless of where a player lives in Canada or the United States, his family can expect to pay at least $10,000 a year for AAA hockey, not including the days off at least one of the parents needs to take to accompany him to tournaments and elite hockey camps. For goaltenders, whose equipment is significantly more expensive, you can expect to add $2,000 to $3,000 to that total.

Even though house league hockey is reasonably priced in most jurisdictions and lower-end and used equipment can often be purchased for an amount that won't break most families, as the level of hockey goes up, so does the price. It's expensive to be good.

Select hockey, which is basically the all-star level for house league, involves a significant extra cost. If you're from a small town with a rep program in the BB to E range, you're looking at a yearly expense ranging anywhere from $1,500 to $3,500 per year. Playing A hockey in a city will run you more than that, AA will see even more expenses, and AAA and the demands that it places on the player's family represents the platinum level of kids' sport.

Take, for example, the costs incurred for my son's Select team, the Ted Reeve (Toronto) Tornados peewee team, in 2011–12. Registration for the house league, in which the player must play if he wants to play Select, was a reasonable $350. The only problem is that in exchange for that, the player gets just one game a week and no practices. Obviously, being on the ice for one hour a week where you might handle the puck for a total of two minutes is not going to improve anyone's skill level.

Playing for the Select team costs another $600, for which players received one game and one practice per week, plus participation in two tournaments. We also travelled to an out-of-town tournament that added $300 in additional costs.

Ancillary expenses were added because our league also levied a $5 admission fee for each adult spectator plus each player participating in the game. With twenty-eight games including playoffs, that means we paid an additional $140 in gate fees, which would have been doubled had I not served as an assistant coach and thereby been admitted into the games for free.

Factor in costs for equipment, sticks, and travel and the total bill came to well over $2,000 for the lowest level of competitive hockey there is in the province of Ontario.

Hockey at almost any competitive level is an expensive sport. If you live in a city like Toronto, Calgary, or Vancouver, you pay through the nose for ice time. If you're from a small town the ice may cost less, but what you save there you're probably spending on travel.

Bob Caldwell, whose son Ryan was drafted by the New York Islanders and now plays in Europe, said that while the rink in the tiny town of Deloraine, Manitoba, doesn't even lock the doors and kids are free to simply turn on the lights and play when it isn't in use, a league that runs from Thompson in the north to Winnipeg in the south has significant travel costs attached to it.

"Our kids pay about $1,900, which doesn't sound bad, but you have to add about another $2,500 in equipment and probably another couple of thousand dollars for Mom and Dad to go along to the games," said Caldwell, who sits on several Hockey Canada boards and coaches the Southwest Cougars AAA midgets in nearby Souris. "I found the biggest expense when my son played AAA was probably me because I wanted to go see his games and my wife and I always felt one of us should be at the game."

The costs of elite hockey are astronomical to be sure, but are they any higher than those incurred in other sports or pursuits such as elite dancing or music lessons? Hockey Canada president Bob Nicholson doesn't think that's the case, but it's difficult to change perceptions. There are fixed and unavoidable costs associated with hockey to be sure, but it's when players move up the system that they get out of control—and, in some cases, unnecessary.

"The easy example is hockey costs too much compared to soccer because you can play soccer in a pair of running shoes and that's it," Nicholson said. "But where the costs really run away on you are when you have to get the track suits every year and you're doing all the trips. So you have to stay in a hotel and pay for the extra food. There are travel teams who think you have to go across the country just to get a good tournament and I'm not sure that's the case."

Greg Gamoyda can certainly relate to that sentiment, and he has personal experience with his son Luke that tells him Nicholson is onto something. Gamoyda recalls the coach of Luke's Orangeville Flyers Atom AA team declaring at the beginning of the season that the team would not be spending much unnecessary money that season. They would still go to tournaments, but close enough to home that they wouldn't have to stay overnight in hotels. Any money that would have gone into things such as new matching hockey bags, track suits, and jackets would instead be spent on extra ice time to develop skills.

With a little bit of common sense, the team managed to keep the budget significantly lower than most teams. The boys would go into rinks in more affluent centres such as Oakville wearing mismatched sweats and dragging scuffed hockey bags—and then would win by huge margins. In fact, the team finished second in Ontario that season. (And shouldn't hockey bags be scuffed and a little bit smelly anyway?)

But the return to old-fashioned hockey didn't last long. The next year, a new coach came in and dictated a new, far more expensive policy. The team would have matching hockey bags and track suits and there were more tournaments planned—including one to Ottawa and another to the United States.

"We ended up almost in last place," Gamoyda recalled, "but we looked good doing it."

In many of the larger cities in Canada, the biggest expense is the tab for ice time. It's essentially why the Greater Toronto Hockey League charges five dollars a head for everyone who enters the building, including the player who is participating in the game.

The GTHL's bill for ice time generally runs at about $4 million for roughly 12,000 games a season, and unlike smaller communities that have difficulty attracting players the GTHL has to set limits on its number of teams, largely because a publicly funded arena has not been built in Toronto since the 1970s.

GTHL president John Gardner claimed his league had to turn away fifty teams that wanted to join his organization in 2010–11 because it simply didn't have enough ice time to accommodate them.

That sort of thing has left a void in the landscape in big cities that has been filled by private arena operators. But with those private operators and their ability to rent out ice at convenient times comes a major cost difference, typically close to double what the costs are for municipal subsidized ice time. In Toronto ice time at municipally owned arenas usually runs about $150 an hour, while the private operators, who have to pay the top rate of commercial property tax on their facilities, charge up to $400 an hour.

Rep teams in Toronto, in fact, often take their

taxpayer-subsidized ice time and flip it to other organizations for a premium because they know teams are willing to pay top dollar for it.

A scan of the website www.trade-ice-time.com reveals hundreds of hours of booked ice in arenas going for anywhere from $245 for an hour at 7:15 on a Sunday morning to $645 for ninety minutes. Most of the teams, though, simply solicit the best offer.

Minor hockey groups in Calgary can rent ice time for $150 an hour, but non–minor hockey hours run about $225. Hockey Calgary president Perry Cavanaugh said with 13,000 players and 52 sheets of indoor ice, his organization is running above capacity.

Part of the problem is that aging neighbourhood rinks—which constantly need upgrading on things such as roofs, heating and ventilation systems, and refrigeration plants and are expected by the city to break even—are always trying to top up their capital reserve funds. And how can they do that? By simply offering more ice time to non–minor hockey groups that will pay more per hour, at the expense of minor hockey.

That squeezes minor hockey in two ways. First, the game-to-practice ratio, which is supposed to be 2:1 according to Hockey Canada, ends up being skewed because of a lack of ice time. Second, older age groups such as midgets often end up getting off the ice at 11:30 P.M. on a weeknight because higher-paying non–minor hockey groups have taken the prime-time ice. "The minor rates just don't cut the mustard from a sustainability point of view," Cavanaugh said.

One answer is to build new arenas, but that is far more easily said than done. Even for a barebones double rink structure, you're looking at a construction bill of about $25 million. In Alberta, for example, the funding model dictates that if a community group wants infrastructure, it must raise the first 33 percent of the capital required for a project—and no number of calendar sales and pop bottle drives is going to raise $8 million.

"Does it give me heartburn? Yes," Cavanaugh said. "Our politicians and municipalities need to get off their backsides and look at alternative ways to fund this by promoting health and wellness. As a group, we have not done a good job of positioning ourselves as a health and wellness organization and that's something we should have been doing all along. We can reduce costs by getting kids active."

Getting kids active in hockey can vary based on the damage to the pocketbook. One thing is certain, though. Hockey can be very reasonable in terms of price if expectations of what the child is getting out of it are equally reasonable.

For example, parents can equip their children with a starter kit and other equipment from Canadian Tire for less than $200. You can also buy very good used equipment at retailers such as Play It Again Sports, particularly for a growing player who might not be wearing it very long, or take advantage of equipment swaps. House league registration, as we've seen, is very reasonable.

But it's when the player gets more serious about the game that equipment prices skyrocket. Here's how it all breaks down at the absolute top end for skaters in the fifteen to sixteen age range:

Skates: $800
Helmet and cage: $270
Shoulder pads: $210
Elbow pads: $130
Pants: $250
Gloves: $250
Shin guards: $180
Stick: $300
Jock with compression shorts: $80
Dri-Fit shirt with integrated neck guard: $80
Equipment bag: $170
13% HST: $354
TOTAL: $3,074

For goaltenders, the costs at the top end are even more steep:

Skates: $600
Mask: $1,000
Chest/arm protector: $750
Pants: $350
Goalie pads: $1,500
Blocker: $400
Catcher: $550
Stick: $300
Jock: $150
Neck guard: $50
Knee pads (worn under goal pad): $150
Equipment bag: $180
13% HST: $777
TOTAL: $6,757

The price of equipment has actually not risen that much in the past decade with the exception of sticks and skates, and for both of those items the increased price is the cost of more advanced technology. It's worth noting, however, that while a space-age stick may offer a quicker release and better feel than the model a couple of price points down, there's no guarantee it's going to last any longer. As for the high-end skates that seem to weigh little more than a pair of running shoes, a heavy kid can break those down in dismayingly short order.

Hockey equipment manufacturers, who compete for a $500 million pie in the world market and $180 million in Canada, usually have five different price points for skaters and three for goaltenders. But they're also banking on the fact that some parents and players will continue to pay thousands of dollars for the best equipment in an effort to give their children an edge.

The costs of playing hockey at an elite level are astronomical to be sure. But hockey most certainly isn't alone in that regard, and in some cases those who play hockey are getting off easily.

One family we spoke to has a teenager who is the top-ranked swimmer in several disciplines and is on track to represent Canada in the 2016 Summer Olympics. This family, which requested anonymity, moved their son from their hometown in Saskatchewan to Calgary to receive the best coaching.

They purchased a condominium that runs $2,000 a month (albeit one they can later sell), employ a caregiver for $1,800 a month, and pay private school and swim and travel fees that are about $3,000 a month. Without the condo investment and the private school, that adds up to a total of $57,600 a year—and that's before the swimmer's parents fly out to see him or accompany him to meets.

Adam Svensson is a brilliant young golfer from Richmond, B.C., with a stunning list of achievements, including the 2010 Canadian Boys Championship and the Callaway Junior World Golf Championship. When he was fifteen years old, he qualified as an amateur for the Canadian professional tour and embarked on a golf scholarship at the University of Nevada-Las Vegas in 2012.

He has participated in the Callaway Junior World Golf Championship every year since he was nine and his family has accompanied him to La Jolla, California, for each event. Just one practice round at the famed Torrey Pines course where the tournament is held costs $215.

His parents are reticent to declare how much they spend on golf, but consider that they actually had to *pay* $9,000 for him to be a member of Canada's national golf team. That amount covered the cost of a number of training camps and some national team apparel. Imagine the young Canadian hockey stars being forced to pay to be part of their World Juniors team!

An elite gymnast in Toronto can expect to pay $5,300 a year just in training fees alone. In exchange, the athlete receives twenty hours of training per week, plus entrance into two meets. Extra expenses follow for big competitions such as provincial and national championships or provincial or national winter games. Uniforms for competition and travel and meals for both athletes and parents can add thousands to that total, depending on the year and how far the athlete advances.

A friend who has a child in the performing arts and high-level volleyball said she pays about $13,000 for her daughter to participate in both pursuits—$8,000 for the lessons, studio time, and travel involved in performing arts and $5,000 for volleyball club fees and travel.

It's reasonable to assume, then, that pushing to the elite level of almost any pursuit in athletics comes with a high cost, one that is not always measured in dollars. In China, children are sent away to state-run sports schools at a young age and have almost no contact with their families while they train to win gold medals. In fact, it was only after twenty-six-year-old diver Wu Minxia won her third consecutive gold medal in synchronized three-metre springboard diving at the 2012 London Olympics that she was told of her grandmother's death the year before and of her mother's battle with breast cancer. Both were kept from her to avoid distractions during her quest for a gold medal. "We've known for years that our daughter doesn't belong to us anymore," her father told the *Shanghai Morning Post* after her victory.

And Chinese swimmer Ye Shiwen, who broke the world record in the 400-metre individual medley and added a gold in the 200 IM in London, was plucked from her primary school to join the elite swim program at the Chen Jing Lun Sports School in Hangzhou after her teacher noticed she had unusually large hands and feet. "As a mother, I sometimes felt as though I had lost her," Shiwen's mother said.

So how is the Chinese Olympic champion any different from a hockey player in Canada? Well, first of all, the Chinese swimmer doesn't have many options when it comes to athletics, but Canadian parents make choices such as uprooting their children for better competition or enrolling them in sports schools to help them further their hockey career. And while the elite in sports such as swimming and diving in China is limited to a select few, the term is used far more liberally among hockey players in Canada.

If you Google the words "elite hockey," for example, you'll find 29,600,000 entries, one for almost every man, woman, and child in Canada. There are elite hockey tournaments, elite hockey training centres, elite hockey leagues, elite hockey prospects, and elite hockey consultants. In fact, the word elite fuels the dream like no other. If your child is good enough to participate in an "elite" program, then it stands to reason that you're going to keep spending to keep him or her there. There's a sports school in Toronto that you'll learn about in a later chapter called the PEAC School for Elite Athletes; it accepts AA-ranked players whose families have $15,000 a year to spend on tuition.

But we've already learned that even the supposedly "elite" athletes stand almost no chance of making it to the NHL. The *Oxford Dictionary of Sports Science and Medicine* defines an elite athlete as "an athlete who has reached the highest level of performance in a particular sport," and the *Concise Dictionary of Modern Medicine* offers the following definition: "an athlete with the potential for competing in the Olympics or as a professional athlete."

Just because a player is good enough to play AAA hockey, or even junior or college hockey, doesn't necessarily mean he's an elite player. But that doesn't stop people from spending— and others from helping them spend it.

As part of our research, we asked five Ontario families to chart their minor hockey expenses for the 2010–11 season. Of the six players involved (one family had two players),

two played at the AAA level, one at AA, two at A, and one at
AE (which, like Select, is one step above house league). The
expenses varied depending on the level played, but all were in
the multiple thousands of dollars.

In the summer of 2011, Justin Allen was one of the hottest
commodities in the GTHL.

When he decided to leave his Mississauga Rebels peewee
team, he was offered a spot by each of the other eleven teams in
the league before settling on the privately owned and operated
Vaughan Kings. Justin is a promising player who is intent on
going in the first round of the OHL draft in 2015.

"He's a big, mean kind of kid and teams like the way he
plays," said his father, Shawn. "But at this level, yesterday's
superstar is tomorrow's cut, so you have to enjoy it while it
lasts."

For the Allens, enjoying their son's hockey is not cheap.

	Justin Allen Forward Mississauga Rebels Peewee AAA
Registration	$2,000
Team fees	$3,000
Equipment	$2,400
Gas	$600
Hotels	$3,600
Meals	$3,600
Team apparel	$300
Private instruction	$3,500
TOTAL COST	**$19,900**

Moments after the Boston Bruins ended their thirty-nine-year Stanley Cup drought and Bruins captain Zdeno Chára raised the Cup over his head, Justin Allen said something that shocked his father.

"'Dad, I want to lift that Cup up and I want to lift it up for you,'" Shawn Allen recounts. "And I said, 'What? For me? What do you mean for me?' And he said, 'Well, you never got to lift it yourself.' And I thought, 'Oh man, I hope he doesn't think that's he's doing this for me.'"

But he can understand why that kind of sentiment might exist, at least in the mind of a teenager who sees his parents spending thousands of dollars and devoting so much of their energies toward his hockey career.

In fact, Allen said he knows of kids who would like to quit, but are afraid to broach the subject with their parents because they've "invested" $80,000 or more into their careers so far. Even Allen admitted himself that he's "in so deep" in terms of expenses that he would find it difficult to pull his son out.

Allen estimates his and his wife's combined income as about $150,000, but living in suburban Toronto can be expensive—particularly when 13 percent of their before-tax income pays exclusively for hockey.

Much of that total goes into the increasingly high costs associated with spring hockey, which has become a cottage industry of its own over the past decade. In fact, there are only eight weeks a year where Justin isn't on the ice and those are filled with an off-ice regimen. Allen also spends thousands on dryland training and private instruction and purchases only the best equipment.

The goal is simple—to give his son every advantage possible to exploit his talent to the fullest and see where it takes him. The spring hockey allows his son to play in tournaments with and against the best players in his age group in Ontario, which Allen believes enhances his son's development.

Allen has two sons, one who plays hockey and another who doesn't, and said that the fact one son has chosen not to pursue hockey allows him to spend more on the one who does.

"I'll tell you, I love them both, but they are totally different kids," he said. "The one who plays hockey is very structured and very disciplined and all those good attributes you get from team sports. And the other one drives me goddamn crazy. So maybe twenty grand is worth it."

Allen looks at his son's hockey like a trip to Vegas. You always go there hoping to win the big jackpot, but you usually come home with losses, money that's gone and can't be recouped. So there's no sense fretting over it, at least in the teenage years.

"People always say nobody has a chance," Allen said. "Well, somebody has to make the NHL. Why can't it be my kid? If you don't believe your kid can make it, he probably won't."

Greg Gamoyda is a customer planning manager for a major corporation. His wife runs a portrait studio out of their home. They have two children playing hockey and the following expenses:

	Luke Gamoyda Goalie Orangeville Flyers Bantam AA	Jake Gamoyda Forward Orangeville Flyers Peewee AE
Registration	$500	$500
Team fees	$1,600	$1,600
Equipment	$2,000	$900
Gas	$1,500	$1,500
Accommodations	$800	$800
Meals	$600	$600
Team apparel	$200	$200
Private instruction	$3,300	$300
TOTAL COST	**$10,500**	**$6,400**

Gamoyda has a very good job and his wife's business does well, but even he gulped when he broke down how much he spent on hockey for his two sons on a yearly basis.

In fact, it's the combination of the costs and sacrifices that have kept him from having his sons try out for a AAA team. Since Orangeville is "only" a AA centre, players wishing to play AAA have to go to the regional Halton Hurricanes based in Milton, about forty-five minutes away. Adding that extra ninety minutes of driving just to get to and from practices and home games would bump up their costs even more.

Gamoyda lives in a rural home almost a half-hour to the nearest town and spends two hours a day commuting to his job in Mississauga. The last thing he wants to do when he gets home is spend another couple of hours ushering his children to hockey practices. Gamoyda has no mortgage and his living expenses are not high, but he still finds the costs of minor hockey ghastly.

"My wife and I often sit down and say, 'How do other families do it?'" he said. "When we go into a bigger centre like Oakville and you see the cars, the uniforms, the training facilities … it's incredible to see how money-driven the sport has become. I'm not sure how an average family household can afford that. This sport is turning into a rich man's sport."

That's why Gamoyda made a very bold decision in the summer of 2011. With his older son's blessing, he pulled him out of organized hockey for a season. The purpose was to take the time and money he would have spent on playing for a team and instead direct it toward on-ice goaltending instruction and a personal trainer for off-ice conditioning.

It's an interesting tack to take with a fifteen-year-old hockey player entering a crucial time in his development in the sport, questionable even in the minds of some of his hockey friends. It's hard to believe that the best way to play hockey is not to play at all. But all Gamoyda had to do was see his son flex in the mirror—supposedly when he thought nobody was looking—to feel certain he made the right decision. He said his son felt stronger and more confident and his fitness level had never been higher. And, most importantly, he could see himself becoming a better technical goaltender.

Gamoyda sat down one day and thought about exactly what his son was getting out of playing minor hockey. First of all, he was driving to half his son's games—which is a considerable venture home or away when you live in the country—only to watch him sit on the bench. With two goaltenders on the team and a strict game-by-game rotation, he was contributing to only half the games. Then he thought about how much game action his son was actually seeing for the thirty to thirty-five games a season in which he did play, and came to the conclusion that a lot of that money was going directly down a minor hockey sinkhole.

So, he surmised, what if he took all those resources and directed them elsewhere, to someone who could actually teach his son the position and give him the on- and off-ice work he needed to become a better goalie? That's when he decided to have his son dedicate the season to becoming a better goaltender without playing a single game.

The irony is incredible, isn't it? The dream of advancing in hockey is now so far removed from actually playing the game for fun that Greg Gamoyda's son spent a year pursuing the dream by *not playing hockey*.

But why couldn't he do both, the way so many others do? Because the nearest goalie training school was an hour away, and driving to and from his training sessions would represent enough of a challenge.

"Again, we get back to family sacrifice," Gamoyda said. "If we were to do that with a regular hockey season, it would be a massive family sacrifice. Couldn't do it."

The cost of outfitting a goaltender can be high, particularly for one who isn't yet fully grown. A full set of pads can cost upwards of $2,000 and might last only one year before it has to be replaced; it can be resold for about a third of the original cost. Gamoyda has seen goaltending instructors who charge $90 per hour, but he found one in Barrie, Ontario, who charged $40 per hour. One summer of off-ice instruction added $3,000 to his costs for three training sessions a week and three one-week goaltending camps.

But Gamoyda himself is responsible for only half of those

expenses. The other half is picked up by his son, who was working three jobs in the summer to help pay for the costs. Along with working at a general store, he was also doing weeding and watering for a landscaping company and maintaining ten acres of a neighbour's property. Gamoyda said that not only helped alleviate his own expenses, but also gives his son an appreciation for how much hockey costs and motivates him to work harder at his craft.

Gamoyda said that after paying $1,000 for his part in a new set of pads, his son realized his improvement represents a personal investment, which in turn makes him want to get the most out of his training sessions. And he can do that only if he puts in his maximum effort.

"He becomes part of the decision making," Gamoyda said. "I said to him, 'If you want to get to the next level, it's going to take training and it's going to cost money. Are you willing to pay for half of it?' So since then, he has been handing over $1,000 here and $500 there. I'm starting to do the same with my younger boy as well. He's 13, but it's not a free ride. If you want to get to a higher level, you're going to have to be just as responsible for supporting yourself."

For years Joe Migliaccio billeted OHL players for the Guelph Storm, among them Ryan Callahan (New York Rangers) and Peter Holland (a 2010 first-round choice of the Anaheim Ducks). Then he saw one of his home's permanent residents become a member of the team—his son, Ryan, was drafted in the ninth round of the OHL draft by the Storm in 2011.

Migliaccio is an insurance agent for State Farm and his wife, Linda, is a CGA. Here were their hockey expenses for 2010–11 with the Halton Hurricanes AAA program:

	Ryan Migliaccio Forward Halton Hurricanes Minor Midget AAA
Registration	$2,750
Team fees	$2,000
Equipment	$1,500
Gas	$2,000
Accommodations	$4,000
Meals	$300
Team apparel	$1,000
Private instruction	$1,500
TOTAL COST	**$12,050**

Joe Migliaccio's son played for a team with a zero-based budget and he still spent $4,750 of his $12,050 on registration and team fees. But he said his son's experience a few years prior with the Vaughan Kings, a privately owned and operated GTHL team, was far more financially challenging.

Like some others, Migliaccio had put his son in the private club–based GTHL for a season, but found the costs associated with doing it were $3,000 to $4,000 higher and the experience wasn't much better than what he received in his own area.

"It was our most expensive year," he said. "It wasn't worth the cost to play in a similar league, drive all that way, and play for a privately owned organization, so he returned home to the Guelph area and had the same return."

But regardless of where his children play, Migliaccio is part of a growing number of parents who feel they're not exactly getting full value for their minor hockey experience due to limited availability of ice time and off-ice development programs.

In 2011, Ryan was drafted into the Ontario Hockey League right alongside some of his ex-teammates in the GTHL. He was picked in the ninth round of that draft by a scouting department that included his father, who has been a southwestern Ontario scout for the Storm for almost a decade.

And that is where private instructors, spring leagues, and hockey schools are finding a motherlode of potential customers.

So many games, so much travel, and an intense focus on tournaments leaves precious little time for young men to develop as players. Stepping into that breach are people who are making a very good living providing young players and their families with what they are lacking during the winter season.

Added to Migliaccio's costs, in fact, was $2,500 each summer for Ryan to work with power skating coaches and a strength and conditioning specialist starting at age fourteen.

"We had to get the extras in order for him to develop," Migliaccio said. "He needed help in those areas and it helped a lot. Due to ice limitations, associations couldn't offer the extras so [we] had to go out and get the extras like power skating and fitness on our own."

Another area where costs were substantial—and where most parents don't notice the difference until they stop to add it all up—is in travel and accommodations.

That total doesn't include the Friday one of the parents has to take off for a tournament, of which there are usually four or five per season. Migliaccio said in April 2010 his son went with Halton to the all-Ontario bantam championship held in Ottawa. For the week-long tournament it cost well over $1,000 in expenses, along with all the parents who had to book a week's vacation or miss out on a week's worth of income to share the experience with their children.

Migliaccio, though, has a point of reference when it comes to comparing costs with other avenues of extracurricular endeavour. His twelve-year-old daughter participates in competitive dance and he pays about $5,000 a year for three sessions a week at a studio, plus the costs of four or five weekend competitions.

"Hockey is twice as much money and twice the time commitment, so it's basically the same," Migliaccio said. "It's the Canadian dream to play and pursue the dream in hockey and who are we to take it away from them?"

Twice the money and twice the time commitment makes it "basically the same" as competitive dance? If parents are spending twice as much time and money on a pursuit for one child than they are for another, is that really the same thing? And yes, it is undoubtedly the Canadian dream to play hockey, but are parents who refuse to spend thousands of dollars on pursuing a dream that is so unlikely actually taking something away from their child?

In short, it's that kind of logic that inspired this book.

Brandon Grazziotto of Guelph, Ontario, is a young player who is becoming a statistic.

After playing at the more competitive A level with the Guelph Jr. Storm for the previous three seasons in novice and atom, in spring 2011 he did not make the A team and elected to play on the Additional Entry (AE) travel team for the 2011–12 campaign.

Due to a combination of factors that included size and strength, Brandon had been a victim of the numbers game as he moved to his major peewee (age thirteen) season.

Some of it also had to do with the Ontario Hockey Federation's decision to ban bodychecking at all house league and Select levels for the 2011–12 season.

The decision Brandon made was fairly typical for young players, about 40 percent of whom either drop down or out of the game due to issues surrounding size and strength around the key growth period of twelve and thirteen years of age.

Hockey Canada has been wrestling with its retention issues for some time, including examining what to do for players who don't want to be involved in contact hockey but still want to play the game at a competitive level. It's also considering the idea of offering leagues that split the season into four equal parts, with players being able to play any number of them. By playing less hockey, costs will be lowered and players will be able to pursue other winter activities without having to give up hockey.

Brandon's father, Gary, is a machinist at Blount Canada and his mother, Nancy, operates a home daycare. Here were their hockey costs for the 2010–11 season:

| | Brandon Grazziotto |
| | Defenceman |
	Guelph Jr. Storm Minor Peewee A
Registration	$550
Team fees	$1,300
Equipment	$1,000
Gas	$1,200
Accommodations	$500
Meals	$400
Team apparel	$250
Private instruction	$400
TOTAL COST	**$5,600**

Gary Grazziotto and the other parents on the Guelph Jr. Storm were able to keep their costs down by $1,500 due to a very aggressive fundraising program. But not every parent has the time and willingness to pour that much energy into raising sponsorships and selling chocolates to their co-workers.

But as the competition for the fundraising dollar gets more intense, minor hockey associations are coming up with more novel ways to raise funds. Some in British Columbia, in fact, have adopted the model that has been used in swim clubs for years. When the child registers, parents are required to sign a "commitment cheque" that guarantees they will do a certain amount of volunteer work and fundraising over the course of the season. Those who want to save the money go out and raise the funds to cover their commitment, while those who choose not to simply allow the club to cash their cheque at the end of the season. The Southwest Cougars in Souris, Manitoba, require each of their players to sell twenty hockey pools for

$10 each. The team also has a fundraiser called "Meals to the Door" in which they sell and deliver hot turkey dinners after an afternoon game on Remembrance Day.

Still, though, Grazziotto sometimes wonders where all the money is going.

"When you hear things like all the extras like name tags on the backs of jerseys, it causes some doubts," he said. "Sometimes you wonder if the dollars are allocated properly to things like ice time and coach development. He gets a lot of ice and practices, but getting quality at the practices is a different story. If it cost an extra $1,000 for a better development program, we would probably pay the extra if it was available."

Young Brock Dalley is a promising player who is intent on working his way up to the AAA level with the Nepean Minor Hockey Association near Ottawa.

That has required a significant expense—and a significant amount of travel—from his parents, Bryan and Nadene, who are both sales representatives for large companies.

Here is their expense sheet from the 2010–11 season, when Brock was ten years old (not including what they also paid for their daughter's participation in a local house league):

	Brock Dalley Forward Nepean Raiders Minor Atom A
Registration	$630
Team fees	$1,800
Equipment	$835
Gas	$1,200
Accommodations	$1,500
Meals	$1,200
Team apparel	$250
Private instruction	$900
TOTAL COST	**$8,315**

Amazingly, Bryan and Nadene Dalley could have paid for their son's entire minor hockey experience if they had only taken a fellow minor hockey parent up on his outrageous offer.

Bryan was one of the lead coaches for the Nepean Minor Hockey Association's Initiation Program, a Hockey Canada initiative that helps introduce young players aged four to eight to the game and focuses on very basic skill development with no emphasis on games or competition. It is almost always the first structured experience any player in Canada has with the game. It was after one of these sessions when the father of one of the participants approached Bryan with a preposterous proposal. If he were to give Bryan $100,000, could Bryan make his son a better hockey player?

True story.

"You're talking about a five-year-old, I kid you not," Nadene said. "It was a forty-five-minute conversation and it was crazy, it was absolutely crazy. It was mind-boggling really.

My husband told the guy, 'If this child doesn't want to do it, there is nothing you can do. There isn't enough money you can throw at it if it doesn't come from within your kid. That's the bottom line.' It's terrible. It's ridiculous. Sadly, there's always one on every team."

The Dalleys turned down the offer and are paying their own way through the minor hockey experience, about half of which they have devoted to skill development and spring hockey.

Even though Nadene was surprised at the amount when she kept track of her expenses, she believes that Brock is a good enough and motivated enough player to justify the expense. But Nadene also compares her minor hockey experience to that of the competitive soccer team for which her daughter plays—one that went to Greece for a tournament in the summer of 2010. Nadene was the manager of that team, and also collected the fees for the season.

"When you're doing it you don't realize, you just keep paying, right?" she said. "It's my joke when I was managing the soccer team, when new parents come on it's just, 'Sit down, shut up, and give me your chequebook.' You have to have it ready because you just keep writing cheques. That's just the way it is. You have to go in with your eyes open because it's going to be expensive."

For the Dalleys, much of that expense was swallowed up by travel. Including spring hockey, they made two trips to Toronto and others to Quebec City, Kingston, Syracuse, and Rochester, with each one costing a minimum of $500. Nadene sometimes wonders why a ten-year-old would have to travel so much to play in tournaments when there is so much competition close to home, just as she wonders why a girls' team from Canada would go to Greece to be soundly beaten in a tournament.

But, like others, she's willing to sit down, shut up, and hand over her chequebook.

The Dalleys did come to one realization through their involvement in spring hockey, however. And that was that they didn't feel their son improved his skills playing in the spring. It met the goal of having him on the ice a little longer, but the practice-to-game ratio wasn't enough to have him develop his skills, which will likely prompt them to pour their resources more into skill development in the spring and summer months.

And despite a trend toward twelve-month hockey specialization for elite players, the Dalleys believe giving their son a break in the summer months is more beneficial to his hockey, particularly since he plays a high level of lacrosse in the summer months. And there is certainly some credence to that notion. Many NHL players who also played lacrosse as youngsters have credited the game with making them better hockey players. Former NHLer Joe Nieuwendyk was actually a better lacrosse player than he was a hockey player growing up, one of the best in Canada. It's no coincidence that he developed into a fifty-goal scorer and elite offensive player, in large part because of the quick shot release he developed as a lacrosse player. John Tavares also excelled in lacrosse. For their part, the Dalleys believe that the physical, almost brutal, nature of lacrosse prepared their son well for the physical contact he would face in competitive peewee hockey, when bodychecking begins in Ontario.

Like most hockey families, the Dalleys see their expense in the sport as part of their lifestyle. If they weren't putting money into hockey, it would be going into other pursuits for their children. Nadene said they would almost certainly have a cottage if not for the money and the time sacrifices they make for minor hockey. And while a cottage is something tangible in which you can place financial equity, they don't look at the money they spend on hockey as a wasted expense, even if nothing further comes of the pursuit. We asked Nadene Dalley at what point the expense for minor hockey would be unacceptable and prohibitive and she wasn't able to give us a response. For the Dalleys, minor hockey is not a risk–return proposition, so there's no sense trying to get anything out of it.

"At this point we haven't thought, 'Oh my god what happens if hockey is $30,000 this year?'" she said. "He's ten and anything can happen. If you're telling me within four years I'm going to need $40,000, I'm not sure what I would do. If it's a choice between him going to university to become an engineer and playing hockey, I don't know. The best you can hope for in all reality is a scholarship. It probably won't happen, but it's the best you can hope for. Not the NHL, but if you can get a scholarship out of it, no matter how big or small it is, you're doing well."

Which brings us back to Matt Duchene and Ryan Caldwell. Duchene certainly got his payoff, but the least he would have received was a paid education out of the experience. Like his uncles, he had already accepted a scholarship at Michigan State University when he was fourteen. (For those of you who think major junior hockey is harsh for forcing kids so young to make such a pivotal career choice, and it is, remember that American colleges are pressuring some elite kids to make a binding choice of a post-secondary institution when they're barely freshmen in high school.)

When Matt was drafted fifth overall by the Brampton Battalion in 2007, he was offered the maximum education package available in junior hockey—a total of $13,000 per year toward post-secondary education for a period of four years if he did not sign a professional contract. He undoubtedly would have taken advantage of it, too; Matt is artistically gifted and likely would have pursued a career in graphic design had hockey not worked out. He was named the OHL's scholastic player of the year in 2009.

As an aside, Vince and Christine Duchene's expenses didn't come to an end when their son joined the OHL. In fact, Christine argues they were every bit as high as they were when they were driving him all over the province to tournaments and paying for high-end private instruction. That's because they tried to get to as many games as they could, giving themselves a three-hour radius in which they were willing to travel.

That meant they could go to every home game, as well as road games in Barrie, Peterborough, Oshawa, Toronto, Sudbury, Kingston, Belleville, Kitchener, Guelph, and Mississauga. They also bought their son a car in his second year of junior hockey and would often help out his billet family by supplementing their food supplies.

Caldwell got his payoff too, in the form of a four-year scholarship at the University of Denver, which he parlayed into a business degree. And even though he was a fifth-round draft pick, he got a contract from the New York Islanders that paid him a $350,000 signing bonus and a salary of $70,000 in the AHL, largely on the strength of the fact that he was

captain of the Denver team that won the national championship in 2004.

But while Duchene figures on becoming a very, very wealthy
man, Caldwell experienced the NHL lifestyle and paycheque
for a total of only four games.

His first contract, a two-year deal with the Islanders, called
for yearly NHL salaries of $500,000 and $450,000—but with
only four games to his credit, he collected only about $25,000
of that amount.

Caldwell signed two more NHL deals after that with an
NHL salary of $495,000 in 2006–07 and a $475,000 stipend
in 2007–08, but since he played exclusively in the minors he
received only his minor league salaries of $70,000 and $90,000.

Since then, it has been a whirlwind for Caldwell, who left
the AHL to chase bigger dollars in Europe—roughly double
what he made in the AHL—in an effort to have more financial
stability when he retires.

But as Caldwell has learned, an import player in Europe
is one bad season away from very quick unemployment. And
even though the Finnish Elite League where he has been playing
is a downgrade from the quality of play in the NHL, it is the
second best European league after Sweden and the physical
and mental demands are still high.

And while players such as Duchene have a strong NHL
Players' Association and a stable league to protect their
contracts, no such luxury exists in Europe. Many players
chased what seems to be terrific money in the Kontinental
Hockey League in Russia, only to go months without seeing
a paycheque.

In 2010–11, Caldwell signed with the Kassel Huskies of the German Elite League, only to see the team go bankrupt and fold after a month. Even though the players hired a lawyer because they were told their contracts were guaranteed, they didn't receive any money from the organization; early in the season, Caldwell found himself scrambling to find work before catching on as a defencemen with Assat Pori of the Finnish League. He signed a one-year contract extension in 2011–12, and at the age of thirty had one year to prove he was valuable enough to keep on the roster. In 2012–13 he signed to play with Lukko Rauma, another one of the teams in the fourteen-team Finnish League.

The future for Matt Duchene looks considerably brighter as one of the top young players in the NHL and a cornerstone for the Avalanche. And what's even better for Duchene is that instead of playing his full junior career and beginning his three-year entry-level deal as a twenty-year-old, or making far less in the minors to begin his pro career, he was able to jump into the NHL at the age of eighteen to get his relatively low-earning seasons out of the way by the time he turned twenty-one.

Both Vince and Christine remember when they started to wonder whether things had spiralled out of control. It was Matt's second-last year of minor hockey, 2005–06, and he was playing for both the minor and major midget teams with the Central Ontario Wolves and was also suiting up for the varsity team at the Haliburton District High School.

As it turned out, the high school team had qualified for the Ontario high school championship, largely because they were being led by a fourteen-year-old ninth grader in Duchene.

The Wolves had also qualified for the OHL Cup, which is the province's premier bantam tournament and one where junior scouts flock to identify up-and-coming talent.

The only problem was both tournaments were on the same weekend, with the OHL Cup in Mississauga and the Ontario high school championship in Whitby. The two cities just happen to be directly east and west of the traffic nightmare known as Toronto.

Somehow Matt managed to play for both teams, hustling off the ice at the OHL Cup and jumping into the car with his equipment still on to travel the hour across Toronto in time to help out his high school team. (A conflict in the tournaments caused him to have to miss the semifinal game for his high school team and it was eliminated.)

But it's clear that all the pressure, both financial and in terms of time, was worth it for the Duchene family. Vince still works the real estate market and Christine still works at the high school, and neither intends to retire anytime soon.

Vince does, however, work closely with Matt's wealth manager and accountant. As soon as Matt receives a paycheque from the Avalanche, which comes on the fifteenth and on the last day of every month during the regular season, all but a fraction of it is automatically deposited into an account that needs his father's signature for him to make a withdrawal. Aside from buying a new guitar and a 2003 Hummer to drive around Haliburton for the summer, Duchene is quite careful with his money thanks to his father.

"I vividly remember him asking me after he was drafted [into the OHL] and we made the decision to go to Brampton and he said to me, 'Dad, do you think I'll play in the NHL?'"

Vince recalled. "And I said, 'I'll tell you after five games in the OHL.' It was pretty obvious to me after that he would get drafted. But playing that early? No chance. Not a chance. When you look at it all, you say, 'Why the hell wouldn't we open a few more doors and spend a bit more money to see where this thing goes?'"

4
SELLING THE DREAM

Malcolm Gladwell's 2008 bestseller *Outliers: The Story of Success* featured some great news for those of us born without natural talent. Based on the work of psychologist K. Anders Ericsson, *Outliers* sets out to reassure us that the Mozarts, Bobby Fischers, and Wayne Gretzkys of the world didn't rise to the top buoyed by their natural, God-given talent. Instead, he argues, the secret to success is old-fashioned hard work. About 10,000 hours' worth.

The 10,000-hour rule—articulated by Ericsson, popularized by Gladwell, and now espoused by ambitious parents around the world—holds that while natural gifts are a factor, the true determinant of greatness is a willingness to commit to 10,000 hours of deliberate practice, over a period of at least ten years. Those hours should be enough, we read, to achieve the mastery associated with being a world-class expert in virtually any endeavour.

In 1993, Ericsson led a study that resulted in a ground-breaking article for the American Psychological Association,

"The Role of Deliberate Practice in the Acquisition of Expert Performance," which boldly stated that "many characteristics once believed to reflect innate talent are actually the result of intense practice extended for a minimum of 10 years."

It's easy to see why Ericsson's idea and Gladwell's best-seller were so welcome: the 10,000-hour rule is an invitation to all of us to join the ranks of history's great geniuses. We may have *thought* of the great composers and chess masters, surgeons and scientists as being different from us. But they're not. We too could change the world the way The Beatles did, or build a global software monopoly like Bill Gates. All it takes is 10,000 hours. "The people at the top don't work harder or even much harder than anyone else," Gladwell writes. "They work much, *much* harder."

If any one group of people already espouses the idea of hard work, it's hockey players. So the 10,000-hour rule found a ready audience among parents and coaches. One of the major factors that sets pro hockey players apart from those of us who deliver mail and write stories and teach children is their willingness to sacrifice, push their physical and mental limits, and dedicate themselves to getting faster, better, and stronger at the expense of *almost everything else*. What makes Sidney Crosby arguably the greatest player of his generation is not only his level of talent, but also his willingness to exploit his talent to the fullest by working even harder than the journeyman who is hanging onto his career by his fingernails. There's no shortage of wonderful tales of men who simply willed their way into the NHL despite facing setback after setback, finally usurping their far more talented peers through little more than hard work and unparalleled determination. It happens all the time in the hockey world.

The question is, can hard work be *bought*?

More and more, selling the dream means selling the idea of hard work to parents who think their kid won't get ahead without it. People are making a living, a very good one in some cases, with one-on-one skill development, goaltending instruction, lucrative summer hockey camps, power skating, and dryland training. A lot of people are trying to make a buck in the hockey business, including those who keep the twelve-month cycle of hockey going with spring and summer hockey tournaments, tours, and tryout camps for elite tournament teams. Remember, this is not hockey. This is not play. This is work.

Not every kid is caught up in a Spartan regimen of eating and working out like a pro. But a whole subset of players and parents out there are so consumed by the game that they want more of it than even the most elite and successful winter minor hockey associations can give them. A lot more. And the more players get caught up in the cycle, the more it plays on people's insecurities and becomes a self-fulfilling prophecy. Nobody wants to be leapfrogged at a crucial time in his development, so that means more players and more money coming into these businesses. And there's no question these people play on that sense of urgency. With slogans such as "Take your game to another level" and "Don't get left behind," there's little doubt as to the sense to which they are appealing.

"I do feel pressure that I need to do a lot of the things I am doing to keep up with the Joneses," said Shawn Allen, whose teenager is an elite hockey player in Toronto. Of the almost

$20,000 he spent on his son's hockey in 2010–11, $3,500 of it was on private instruction and dryland training.

Exactly that kind of thinking among parents of hockey players has spawned many of the cottage industries associated with the game. No longer is it enough to simply play hockey from the months of September to February if you want to be truly elite. Now, for $10,000 and another $3,000 for food, a top young prospect can go to the Gary Roberts High Performance Centre, where the former NHLer turned fitness guru will provide counsel on all things concerning conditioning and nutrition. As we mentioned in a previous chapter, when Roberts attended his first training camp with the Calgary Flames after being drafted in the first round in 1984, he couldn't complete three chin-ups. Today he's one of the most influential men in the game and is the go-to person for fitness and proper nutrition. And Roberts's business is a prime example of how much things have changed in the past twenty-five years.

But it doesn't stop there. Either in the summer or during the season, in every major city in Canada, a player can find someone to provide private instruction. And this is not just skating around pylons and skating to exhaustion. There are schools that teach specific skills such as edging, bodychecking, battling in front of the net, and shooting. In fact, former NHLer Alfie Turcotte and his father operate the Turcotte Stickhandling Hockey School, which teaches players across Canada and the United States moves such as the Gretzky, the Lemieux Flip, the Double Front Fake, the Spin-o-Rama, and the Russian Move.

Then there's the lure of spring and summer hockey, where teams of super-elite players band together from far-flung areas not only to play with and against like-minded super-elite players, but also to get noticed by scouts and college recruiters. And it's never too early to start playing spring and summer hockey. Prospects Tournaments Inc., originally established in 1995 to give young players exposure to junior scouts and college recruiters, now operates spring tournaments for players as young as eleven years old. Exactly what an eleven-year-old is a prospect for aside from junior high school is not really relevant. What is, according to company founder Bob Turow, is that it fills a need in the marketplace for parents who feel they're not getting enough out of their winter hockey experience.

"I think summer hockey is stupid, I really do," said Turow, who recently sold the franchise. "But there's a reason why summer hockey popped up and I think the reason is the people in the wintertime weren't doing their jobs. As an entrepreneur, I said, 'If these parents are going to be stupid enough to pay to have their kids play 12 months a year, I can put something together that will fulfill all the promises that are being given to them for the money they're paying.' Have I made a lot of money off this business? Absolutely. I've made a ton of money. But I did it in the right way."

And with theories such as Gladwell's 10,000-hour rule gaining so much credence in the popular media, it's no wonder thousands of parents whose children play hockey feel much like Shawn Allen does. If your child has a weakness in his or her game, likely somebody will claim to fix it. And if you're guided by the notion that all it takes is an inordinate amount of hard work … well, more than enough parents and players are willing to spend the money, make the sacrifices, and put in the time to do that.

Particularly when they read books such as *Outliers*, which talks about Ericsson's study of elite violinists in the following way: "The striking thing about Ericsson's study is that he and his colleagues couldn't find any 'naturals,' musicians who floated effortlessly to the top while practicing a fraction of the time their peers did. Nor could they find any 'grinds,' people who worked harder than everyone else, yet just didn't have what it takes to break the top ranks. Their research suggests that once a musician has enough ability to get into a top music school, the thing that distinguishes one performer from another is how hard he or she works. That's it."

But to minimize the importance of natural ability is, quite frankly, absurd. In writing about the Beatles, the book reports that the Fab Four was a struggling high school band until it was invited to play in Hamburg, Germany, in 1960, where it would often be forced to perform in clubs for eight hours a night, seven nights a week. Those many hours of playing made them more polished, to be sure. But the group's success had something to do with the musical genius of John Lennon and Paul McCartney, didn't it? And how exactly does the 10,000-hour rule explain the fact that there were countless bands playing every bit as much as the Beatles were in Hamburg that never made it big?

When Hall of Famer Brett Hull was asked to name the most valuable thing he gained from his father in terms of his game, he always quickly replied with one word—genes. Rather than teach his son how to skate as fast or shoot as hard as he did, Bobby Hull did little more than pass on his natural talents. When Bobby and Joanne Hull split up in 1976 Brett was just twelve years old, and his famous and talented father wasn't around to teach him much of anything. The fact is, Brett Hull was by his own admission overweight and lazy as a teenager and relied more on natural talent for his hockey success than any inner drive. In fact, teammates with his junior team nick-named him "Pear" for his endomorphic body type. It wasn't until he starred in the British Columbia Junior League and later at the University of Minnesota Duluth that Hull began taking hockey seriously.

So did Brett Hull put in the 10,000 hours it supposedly takes to become an expert? Probably not. And for good reason—it's almost impossible. Do the math and you'll under-stand why. Remember that deliberate practice is just what it sounds like: one of the tenets as defined by Ericsson is that it's not inherently enjoyable and it's not play. So time spent playing games, scrimmaging, and driving to the rink cannot be considered to contribute to deliberate practice.

Let's break it down, then. To fulfill the requirement of 10,000 hours over the course of ten years, a player would have to be on the ice for two hours and forty-five minutes every day, seven days a week, 365 days a year, for a period of ten years. So let's spread it over, say, a fourteen-year period between the ages of five and eighteen, which is typically the time span for prime development. That would require the player to be on the ice for almost two hours every day without missing a day for more than 5,000 consecutive days.

Where the 10,000-hour rule falls down in its application to hockey is in the logistics of it all. It may be possible to play a musical instrument, play chess, or work on computer programs for three hours a day, but it's impossible to do hockey-specific drills for that amount of time. First of all, where would you get that kind of ice time? How would you accommodate games and travel and tournaments if you're on the ice for three hours a day simply working on your skills? How could anyone possibly practise that much and do that many tedious drills— without actually playing the game—before burning out? In fact, Ericsson spells out the challenge when he writes, "Deliberate practice is an effortful activity that can be sustained only for a limited time each day during extended periods without leading to exhaustion. To maximize gains from long-term practice, individuals must avoid exhaustion and must limit practice to an amount from which they can completely recover on a daily or weekly basis."

There is perhaps no greater critic of the 10,000-hour rule than Dr. Jason Gulbin, who is the general manager of national talent identification and development for the Australian Institute of Sport. He not only refutes Ericsson's theory on deliberate practice, but also goes so far as to call it "rubbish." As the person responsible for identifying and developing athletes for international competition in Australia, Gulbin advocates a "talent transfer" philosophy. Instead of the deliberate practice model theory, where you get athletes as early as you can and train them for as long as you can, the Australians try to have their young athletes play many different sports and hold off on specialization until as late as possible.

And it works. Gulbin said 28 percent of the athletes who have competed internationally for Australia have done so less than four years after experiencing their sport for the first time. In fact, two of the athletes who represented Australia in the sport of skeleton at the 2006 Winter Olympics in Turin did so just fourteen months after hitting the ice for the very first time. Before that they were sprinters. Of course the talent pool is much smaller in a sport such as skeleton when compared to hockey, but the athletes who represented Australia quickly leapfrogged peers who had spent years training in the sport. In 2007, researchers Guillermo Campitelli and Fernand Gobet studied 104 chess masters and found the average time each spent in deliberate practice to become a master was just over 11,000 hours. But they discovered players who reached master status within 3,000 hours and those who took almost 24,000 hours to become masters.

"You know what?" Gulbin said. "I think it's unethical to peddle this nonsense that everybody's got a chance because that's complete rubbish. 'If you practice deliberately enough you will make it.' Well that just doesn't happen. Practice is important, but to achieve expertise there's a whole raft of factors that are in that milieu and these athletes don't train in a vacuum and get sucked along to the other end where they pop out as elite athletes."

Perhaps the best example of that theory in Australia is in the form of a talented young athlete named Ellyse Perry, who became the first athlete in history to represent Australia in a World Cup in two different sports. At the age of sixteen, she became the youngest athlete ever to represent Australia in the World Cup of cricket; four years later, she took the pitch as a fullback for the Australian team in the Women's World Cup of soccer. She's also a university-educated physiotherapist. Instead of forcing her to choose, the national bodies for both cricket and soccer in that country are encouraging her to pursue both sports, reasoning that having her some of the time in both sports is far better than having her

100 percent of the time in one sport and zero percent in the other.

And would anyone in their right mind suggest that Ellyse Perry, who is near the top of her age group in both sports, had anywhere close to the time to devote thousands of hours of deliberate practice in both sports *and* pursue a university education? Of course not. But the power of a snapshot is sometimes too tempting.

Well, if you want a hockey snapshot, consider the case of former NHLer Brian Savage. The native of Sudbury, Ontario, packed up his hockey bag when he was sixteen and literally did not lace his skates up even once for two full years. Savage had played AAA hockey until he was fourteen, then decided in the ninth grade to play a far lower level of competition at high school. His older brother, Mike, had played in the OHL and did not have a good experience, so Savage's father convinced him to scale back on hockey and try other sports in high school.

So instead of working toward his 10,000 hours on the ice, Savage played every high school sport he could and continued to golf, where he was one of the most promising young players in Canada. He won the longest drive competition at the Canadian Junior Gold Championship one year and participated on the Ontario Team with future Masters champion Mike Weir and his caddy Brennan Little. Savage also excelled in track and field, winning the northern Ontario high school championship in the 800-metre race despite inadvertently grabbing one shoe belonging to his brother that was two sizes too small.

It wasn't until he was eighteen years old and watched some of his former teammates in a Sudbury Wolves game that he got the itch to get back on the ice. He was still good enough to play for the varsity team at his high school that season, then spent the next season in Jr. A, where he was noticed one night by Miami University coach George Gwozdecky. After being offered a scholarship at MU, Savage played three years of U.S. college hockey and was named player of the year in 1992–93 in the Central Collegiate Hockey Association. The Montreal Canadiens selected him in the eighth round of the 1991 entry draft, and from there he went on to win a silver medal with the Canadian hockey team at the 1994 Winter Olympics in Lillehammer, Norway. He played thirteen seasons with the Canadiens, Phoenix Coyotes, St. Louis Blues, and Philadelphia Flyers.

Here's a player who basically frittered away four of his most crucial development years, with two of them spent playing a much lower calibre in high school and two of them spent not playing at all. Career earnings: $16.7 million. Hours of deliberate practice? Not even close to 10,000.

It's impossible to determine whether Savage would have made the NHL had he decided to dedicate himself to the game as a teenager, but it certainly dispels the notion that all you have to do is work hard. As is the case with music or art or any other sport, natural talent and God-given gifts have something to do with the level of success. It's no coincidence that Savage came from a very athletically talented family. His father, a high school math teacher, played university hockey; one brother played in the OHL, and another was a nationally ranked track and field athlete.

"The best decision my dad helped me make was to convince me to play high school hockey instead of AAA because I got to play other sports and develop other motor skills," Savage said. "I played football, basketball, volleyball, every sport the school had, and I really enjoyed it."

The 10,000-hour rule isn't the only place in *Outliers* where Gladwell makes a sweeping generalization. While his books have sold phenomenally well and do have their merits, he has also been criticized for cherry picking anecdotes to support complex theories. That is the case in *Outliers*, when he examines the rosters of two hockey teams—the 2007 Medicine Hat Tigers and the Czech team for the 2007 World Junior Championship—to support a theory that players born in the first six months of the year have an enormous advantage over those born between July and December. His point was that roughly half the athletes' talents were being squandered because their late birthdays put them at a disadvantage early in their athletic careers—and, because of that, they were not being pushed up the competitive ladder at the same rate as their earlier-born peers.

What Gladwell could not have known at the time was that of the six players who eventually played games in the NHL from the 2007 Medicine Hat team, three were born in the first six months of the year and three were born in the second six. The two best NHL players from that team were Darren Helm, who was born January 21, 1987, and Tyler Ennis, who was born October 6, 1989. Similarly with the Czech team, of the seven players who made it to the NHL from that squad, three were born in the first six months (all of them in February, coincidentally) and four born after July 1. That included Michal Repik, who was born on what is thought to be the absolute worst date for a hockey player, December 31.

The point is, it's impossible to determine such complex issues with snapshots because they can say pretty much whatever you want them to say. For example, of the 967 players who played at least one game in the NHL in 2010–11, just 290 of them (roughly 30 percent) were born between the months of January and March and another 249 (25.7 percent) were born between April and June. A total of 228 (23.5 percent) were born between July and September, and 200 (20.7 percent) were born between October and December.

Overall, 539 players, or 55.7 percent of those who played in the NHL in 2010–11, were born in the first six months of the year. And 428, or 44.3 percent, were born from July 1 to December 31. It's a notable difference to be sure, but not quite as stark as some would have you believe—and certainly not as predetermined as Gladwell suggests in *Outliers* when he says, "Those born in the last quarter of the year might as well give up on hockey."

But that likely won't stop those who take these kinds of things as gospel from doing what they can to give their children every advantage imaginable and going to unfathomable lengths to do it. People offering personal instruction, hockey schools, and hockey factory–type academies continue to proliferate in Canada with almost no form of regulation or licencing. Parents who put their money and trust into someone to make their kid a better hockey player are often going on little more than reputation and blind faith, all in an effort to work harder and practise more deliberately than the rest. The operators of these ventures are being kept busy, and parents believe they're giving their children the opportunity to put in the work it requires to squeeze through the bottlenecks that cull players at each next step of elite hockey.

And that's an enormous shift in paradigm in the past twenty years, even according to those who are part of the hockey factory machine. Dixon Ward is the president of the Okanagan Hockey Academy, which offers intense hockey instruction to elite hockey players in a high school setting. Ward was a talented baseball and hockey player in Leduc, Alberta, going on to get a hockey scholarship at the University of North Dakota before playing for the Vancouver Canucks, Toronto Maple Leafs, Los Angeles Kings, Buffalo Sabres, Boston Bruins, and New York Rangers, along with professional teams in Switzerland. He recalls playing minor hockey in the 1970s and 80s, when kids had fun and developed their skills. Those who were bigger, stronger, faster, and had a better skill set moved on and the others were weeded out.

"What's happening now, though, is we're trying to manufacture those guys," Ward said. "We just played and the best guys moved on and the others didn't. Now we're trying to make them all and manufacture them and see who the best players are. But there's no such thing as manufacturing a pro hockey player. If they are somehow manufactured, most of them are by accident."

That hasn't stopped Ward and others, however, from charging parents thousands of dollars a year to provide them with elite-level hockey instruction. They are simply responding to a demand in the market, and nothing is necessarily wrong with that. Ward points to the fact that he uses hockey and the lessons gleaned from it to make kids better students and people—because even with the extra work, the chances of

them having a career in professional hockey remain remarkably small. That's all true, but the real problem is created when
parents and players, guided by notions such as the 10,000-
hour rule, have expectations that are not in line with reality.
Even by Ericsson's admission, deliberate practice is a long and
arduous process. It's not inherently motivating or enjoyable,
and it carries heavy costs in terms of both lifestyle and finances.

"Deliberate practice requires available time and energy for
the individual as well as access to teachers, training material
and training facilities," Ericsson writes. "If the individual is a
child or adolescent, someone in the individual's environment
must be willing to pay for training material and the time of
professional teachers, as well as for transportation to and from
training facilities and competition."

There was a time when anything outside of the regular
season came in the form of a one-week summer hockey school.
Most of them were essentially mom-and-pop operations run
by professional players who, at the time, needed to supple-
ment their incomes, which were significantly less than the
multi-million-dollar salaries players make today (even when
you adjust for inflation). Many would lend their name to the
school, hire instructors, and show up for a day or two, and
everyone would be happy. When the week ended they went
home and continued to play baseball or golf until the calendar
turned to August or September and the hockey cycle began
once again. Kids finished playing hockey in April and threw
their equipment in the basement until hockey camp, which
would create a frenzy of activity because half of the gear didn't
fit anymore. It's a way of life that is extinct for today's serious
hockey player.

Former NHLer and TSN analyst Ray Ferraro said shortly after he retired in 2002 he was offered $100 an hour by the parent of a player in Vancouver to teach the boy how to score goals. He couldn't have sought out a much better teacher than Ferraro if he wanted his son to have good hands and moves around the net—108 goals in his last season of junior hockey and 408 career goals despite being only 5-foot-10—but Ferraro declined. But then he got to thinking, if one person was willing to pay him $100 an hour to work with his son with no advertising, how many people out there would be willing to do that if he promoted himself as a skills coach?

"Honestly, the only thing similar to the way I played as a kid to today is that we wore skates, and that's it," said Ferraro, whose son Landon is a prospect with the Detroit Red Wings. "The chase of the dream for the kids, I believe, is still pure. For the parents, though, I think it's different."

And that's where the hyper-parenting comes into the picture. The same instinct that drives parents to Baby Mozart and Baby Einstein is what drives them to seek out private instruction, hockey schools, and summer tournaments. The result—aside from a bulging trophy mantle in the family rec room—is to give their children a leg up on all the others who are doing the same thing or less. And it's certainly not confined to hockey. Promising golfers aged thirteen to eighteen are eligible to compete in the Jr. PGA Tour, which culminates in the PGA Jr. Championship every summer. For those who would rather wear fire-retardant suits, a number of driving series in NASCAR country allow children as young as five to race up to fifty miles per hour.

And according to Harvard University sociologist Hilary

Levey Friedman, all of it is doing little more than widening the gap between the haves and have-nots in society. She points out that a century ago it would have been the lower-class children competing under adult supervision while the upper-class kids were participating in non-competitive activities that centred around the home. And how many times have we seen that in hockey? During the 1950s and 60s, the NHL was chock full of kids from northern Ontario and the prairies who came from working-class families hit hard by the Depression. But now the model has been turned upside down, in part because the families with more money have created an enormous advantage for their children by exposing them to programs that cost a lot and require a huge commitment.

"If the playing field was ever level, it certainly is no longer," writes Friedman, the author of *Playing to Win: Raising Children in a Competitive Culture*. "The orientation toward success and achievement in childhood reinforces inequalities, like those based on class ... The forces that have led to increasing inequality in other spheres—education, the workplace, wages—have all come to the world of play."

Perhaps it's time to stop focusing on players' birthdays and look at their parents' bank accounts when we're trying to project which ones will thrive and which ones will fall through the cracks in hockey. And that's where those who sell the dream really come into focus. They provide the avenue for improvement, and as they build up more and more graduates who go on to become professional hockey players, they create more demand for their services.

On the surface, Jari Byrski and Colin Chaulk could not be more different. Byrski came to Canada from Poland with a background in child psychology and has since established himself as one of hockey's top skills coaches. Chaulk started his hockey career at the Ted Reeve Arena in Toronto, moving into AA and AAA hockey and then the OHL. Starting in 1998, he played in twelve different cities in seven different minor leagues, finding a home with the Fort Wayne Komets in the Central Hockey League. At different times in his career he has been an Ice Bat, a Lizard King, a Tiger Shark, and a River Otter. He has played in Europe, won championships, and even lasted a couple of days on a tryout in training camp with the Pittsburgh Penguins.

But what unites Jari Byrski and Colin Chaulk is that they are both vendors in the selling of the dream. They're just doing it on different levels. Byrski operates a hockey school called SK8ON with a list of graduates that would make a formidable NHL team. Chaulk, on the other hand, works his instruction between trips to such locales as Wichita, Evansville, and Dayton. He charges $75 for a minor hockey practice in Fort Wayne and uses the summers to build his Hockey House business, which he hopes will provide him with a living once he retires as a player.

Both have come a long way. Byrski rose out of a life of poverty in Poland to become university educated in psychology. When he came to Canada, he worked odd jobs on a cleaning crew at a funeral home and as a painter and landscaper. That all changed one day when he took his son to a public skating session and began teaching him. A woman whose son was also on the ice offered him $20 if he would teach her boy as well.

Before long, Byrski was working with Dr. Yasha Smushkin at Smushkin's renowned skills hockey school in Toronto before going out on his own. When he runs a session, every inch of ice is in use all the time. The skill work he does is truly mind-boggling—and it not only has his classes for youngsters running at capacity, but also has him in demand by NHL players during the off-season. When we spoke in the summer of 2011 while he was preparing to travel to Vancouver to work with Manny Malhotra and some of his Canucks teammates, Michael Cammalleri, then of the Montreal Canadiens, called to see whether he could get in one more skills session with Byrski before leaving for training camp.

Byrski doesn't profess to be a student of game strategy, and marvels at how dedicated Canadian kids are and how much they're willing to sacrifice for hockey. He doesn't claim to be a genius, but there's little doubt he has a gift for teaching individual offensive skills. He remembers Chris Stamkos, the father of NHL star Steven, once challenging him to a skating race around the ice, confident he'd be a better skater than Byrski. But Stamkos also acknowledged Byrski had an ability to teach that he simply couldn't pass on to his son.

"He would say to me, 'I want you to teach my boy because he won't listen to me as much as he will listen to you,'" Byrski said. "'But I will tell you what to teach him because I know the game better.' It was in a very nice way, and it was so true."

That philosophy, centred around teaching skills and allowing others to do the coaching, has made Byrski a wealthy and busy businessman. He said he once was offered a ten-year contract worth more than $1 million from a parent in Toronto to work exclusively with his son in the hopes the young man would develop the skill set needed to play in the NHL. Byrski turned down the opportunity because, he says, it would have robbed him of the satisfaction of having so many former students achieve success. In his Toronto office are the sweaters of such NHL stars as Steven Stamkos, Jason Spezza, Wojtek Wolski, Brent Burns, and Alex Pietrangelo—members of SK8ON's Hall of Fame.

But Byrski has never forgotten his humble roots. He remembers the early days in Toronto when people laughed at him because he would sing and joke with the children on the ice. He remembers the petty jealousies that resulted in his car insurance being cancelled because of the number of times he would come out of the rink to see the windows of his car bashed in. But most of all, he remembers being a small boy with little confidence or self-esteem, living on a farm with his grandparents on the outskirts of Posnan, Poland.

"I wouldn't invite friends to come to my place because I was embarrassed," Byrski said. "When they would ask me where is the washroom, I've got to show them the outhouse. But the outhouse in the summertime, holy shit, it stinks. We had no toilet paper, so when you wiped your ass you did it with the newspaper and the newsprint was left on your ass. I swear. If there was snow, you wiped your ass with the snow."

Chaulk didn't face quite the same financial obstacles, but he does come from a working-class background in the east end of Canada's largest city. He remembers improving his skills by playing on open-air rinks in a time when the winters seemed to be a little colder and a little longer than they are now. He would play until the rink was closed down and the lights were turned off, then would move the net to an area where he could get some of the residual light from the street lamps and play well into the night. He sees kids now who skip practice if they have too much homework. In his day, he would go to practice and report to school without his homework done and deal with the consequences.

And he did remarkably well. He played four seasons with the OHL's Kingston Frontenacs, and after posting just eleven points as a rookie went on to lead the team in scoring for three straight years. Despite being ranked ninety-first among North American prospects for the 1995 NHL entry draft, he was never selected. But he did receive one pro offer when he graduated from junior hockey, and he was more than happy to accept it.

"I got my first contract offer [in 1998] and it was for $35,000 with the Utah Grizzlies of the IHL and $25,000 with the Tallahassee Tiger Sharks in the East Coast League," Chaulk said. "I had come off leading the Kingston Frontenacs in scoring three years in a row and I was fifth in OHL scoring and that was all I could get. My dad said, 'If you're going to play at that level, you might as well not even play.' And I was like, 'What are you talking about? I have to start at the bottom and work my way up,' ... because I was so focused and all I wanted to do was play pro hockey."

Instead of working his way up, Chaulk had to explain to his family members why his peers were continuing to get called up while he was stuck in the lower tiers of the minor leagues. Players at that level don't make very much money, most likely in the $500-a-week range during the season and nothing in the summers. He has seen a lot of players come and go, most of them because they can no longer take the hassles that come

BioSteel camp that has become a magnet for NHL players in the summer.

"Not too many people realize when you go to the [arena] manager's office, you have to pay $350 an hour for the ice," he said. "I have a lot of clients who come to me and say, 'That many students, that much money, you must be wealthy.' But I found that if the main motivation is for you to become rich, it wouldn't have the same kind of results for me. I'm 50 years old and I still get excited."

Lindsay Hofford once coached the London Knights in the OHL and the Lethbridge Hurricanes of the Western Hockey League, but has moved on to far bigger and more lucrative endeavours. Unlike most coaches who measure their success by how they do in the junior and professional ranks, Hofford has made his living by stepping back into minor hockey. He no longer dreams of coaching in the NHL, largely because he doesn't have the time or the inclination, but also because he's doing so well on his own. The joke around the OHL is that Hofford will never coach in that league again because none of the teams would be able to afford him.

Hofford is the founder and chief executive officer of the Pro Hockey Development Group, an all-encompassing organization that has tentacles in almost every aspect of elite minor hockey. For $1,000, Pro Hockey Development will conduct thorough on- and off-ice testing for a minor hockey team, including an evaluation of off-ice fitness, a musculoskeletal assessment, and computer stride analysis. Hofford's company also organizes tours to tournaments in Sweden, Finland, and Russia, and operates a number of tournaments of its own, including its Original Six three-on-three tournament, a one-day affair open to individuals for about $100 and teams for $640. Its Ponytail Hockey Challenge is a spring weekend tournament for elite girls that costs $1,100 per team to enter.

Hofford is asked about creating expectations. After all, his company is called Pro Hockey Development, when he could have easily called it Total or Ultimate Hockey Development. Surprisingly, Hofford doesn't see it that way. In fact, he said when he established the business he simply thought Pro Hockey Development "had a nice ring to it." But almost immediately, Hofford's company began churning out players who would make it to the NHL. When he started the company in 1992 along with Bob Turow, the first elite tournament for players born in 1978 and 1979 had fifty players who ended up playing in the NHL. And the factory has continued to produce elite players through its tournament teams and instructional sessions.

And make no mistake, there is definitely a pro element to Pro Hockey Development. Take, for example, its Brick Evaluation Camp, which is used to select the team that will play in the annual Brick Invitational. Parents pay $700 for a week of hockey, but they get much more than just hours of drills skating around pylons. In fact, kids as young as nine and ten basically get treated like pros. One component of the school is the on- and off-ice testing. There are also—remember, this is for ten-year-old kids—age-specific lectures on nutrition, off-ice training, and sports psychology. Six years before they'll have to choose where they want their hockey path to go if they're good enough to continue, the kids are provided with an overview of U.S. college, major junior, and professional hockey. The final game of the camp is scouted by college and junior coaches, who provide a computer evaluation of each player and an unbiased opinion of his strengths and weaknesses.

"With this company, I wanted to give people an opportunity to have the channels to get advice and programs that could get them to a level where they could at least feel they were doing everything in their power to get to the National Hockey League," Hofford said. "It can sometimes be as simple as identifying a player and saying to the parent, 'Your son has the capability to play in the National Hockey League.' They may have never heard this before, but then he understands, 'OK, what do I have to do?'"

Well, since you asked … seems pretty easy to manipulate credulous parents, doesn't it? After all, that's exactly what Bob Turow said he did with spring hockey. He made no secret of the fact that he discovered there are a lot of "stupid" (his word) parents out there, so why not capitalize on that stupidity yourself because someone else will if you don't? On one hand, Hofford admits that sometimes all that's needed is telling parents their son might have what it takes to play in the NHL. What parent doesn't want to hear that? And once they do, who can blame them for doing everything within their power to get them there?

This is not an indictment of people like Hofford. It's an indictment of *us*. Lindsay Hofford is simply responding to a niche in the hockey market—an enormous one.

When Hofford isn't running the affairs of Pro Hockey Development, he's serving as the hockey director for The Hill Academy, a sports school in Vaughan, Ontario, that's home to an elite hockey program, and he's also the director of scouting for the OHL's London Knights. By his count, he watches more than 400 games a year just for scouting purposes, and hundreds of others at lower levels of minor hockey. In 2011, Hofford's company began hosting winter tournaments for hire. Basically, a team or organization will get sanctioning to host a tournament, which is a major revenue producer. But instead of running it themselves with their core of volunteers, they'll turn it over to a company such as Pro Hockey Development, which runs the event and splits the profits with the host organization.

"I work seven days a week, about sixteen hours a day," Hofford said. "I'll go for four weeks in a row and then I'll take a bit of time off for four or five days to recharge. I'm not a guy to sit around. I'm not a big TV guy. My brain is always going so I have to keep it occupied."

Like most other coaches, Hofford aspired to work behind an NHL bench and seemed to be on that trajectory. He was named coach of the year four times in the Ontario provincial Jr. A league before moving to the major junior ranks, but that's where his coaching aspirations ended. Hofford was a good coach, but he wasn't a very good self-promoter—ironic, since he has done such a good job as a businessman in the hockey world. He was still running Pro Hockey Development while he was coaching, but once he quit working with teams and turned his full attention to his business it began to flourish.

Hofford wasn't about to open his books for us, but he said with the tournaments, hockey schools, tours, and spring teams, at least 10,000 players come through his business each year. In addition, he has sponsorship agreements with Bauer, Adidas, and BioSteel, and revenues have grown every year. In 2010 the company had five teams tour Europe and forty boys' and girls' teams that played in spring tournaments.

"We're probably a little bit more expensive than some of our competition," Hofford said, "but I think on our tours and our tournaments, they may be a little more higher level. Family and personal experiences is what we want them to get most out of it."

The crown jewel of Pro Hockey Development's program is its entry into the Brick Invitational Super Novice Hockey Tournament. Established in 1990 by Bill Comrie, the Edmonton-based billionaire who founded The Brick chain of furniture stores and the father of former NHLer Mike Comrie, the three-day summer event is held at the West Edmonton Mall and gathers the best nine- and ten-year-old players in North America. Pro Hockey Development holds a summer evaluation camp for the tournament, which costs $700 per player; those who are selected for the team can expect to pay about another $2,500 for the tournament. Among others, the tournament has featured the talents of future NHLers such as Steven Stamkos, Dion Phaneuf, Dany Heatley, Dustin Byfuglien, Logan Couture, Tyler Seguin, and Alex Pietrangelo.

It also featured Matthew Cimetta and Bo Horvat, two players we will meet in a later chapter. Horvat, who was the London Knights' first-round pick in 2011, was playing AAA for the Elgin-Middlesex Chiefs near his hometown of Rodney, Ontario, until he came to play with Pro Hockey Development's team and ended up being the MVP of the tournament. Part of the reason both players went to Pro Hockey Development was they weren't seeing the commitment level for summer hockey with their peers at home that they could find among the best nine- and ten-year-olds in Toronto. They went there looking for a higher level of commitment to the game and they found it. That's why both of them decided to travel every weekend to Toronto to play in the Greater Toronto Hockey League and why Horvat's parents were willing to allow him to leave home and play in Toronto at such a young age.

Talk about separating the wheat from the chaff. When you see children that young whose parents can afford that kind of travel and competition, it's hard to argue that the playing field is remotely level. It's not level because of economics, but also because these young people come from families where a high level of commitment is imperative. Most of that comes from the parents, of course. After all, what nine-year-old kid is going to go looking for something like Pro Hockey Development to advance his career? These hockey schools and spring tournament teams are driven largely by parents who, in an effort to give their children every advantage they can, are the ones driving all over the province and paying for these opportunities. And kids who miss out on them when they are ten years old generally don't start getting them later in life. You're either born into what one hockey coach called the "lucky sperm club"—or you're not.

So, if you want to make it as a professional hockey player you're going to need parents who pass down the athletic ability and, increasingly, you're going to need parents with the time and money to put into giving you a head start on other players. Of course, minor hockey is hardly the only place in the world where money brings advantages. If money didn't offer advantages, it would be worthless. The top schools in the world are chapters of the lucky sperm club, as are corporate boardrooms and many other places that are pinnacles of achievement. If you're not born with talent and the money to exploit it, you're probably out of luck. That's just one of the cruel truths about life. Life is unfair. No point complaining about that.

On the other hand, we might want to pause and ask ourselves whether we really want to deliberately model our kids' novice hockey leagues on the injustices of the world. Hockey Canada's mission statement promotes the values of "fair play and sportsmanship," so to try to justify the fact that wealthy kids have an unfair advantage over kids of more modest means kind of misses the point. Hockey is not going to make the world fair, but it may be a clue that something has gone wrong when we celebrate the unfairness by privileging those with the time and money to pull away from their rivals. You can't pay your way into the NHL—it's always going to be a lottery. But the thing is, the lottery tickets get more expensive all the time. That means that only the privileged kids get their names in the hat.

Spring and summer hockey don't just give some kids an edge by making them better players—they have the added advantage of making the pool of competitors smaller. They've created a whole new level of hockey that essentially caters to those parents who think their children are not being challenged enough at even the highest levels of winter hockey. Because Hockey Canada isn't involved there are no arcane residency rules to deal with, so people such as Carlo Cimetta are free to have their sons play where they want without having to get releases from thirteen different minor hockey associations. That allows teams to cherry-pick the elite of the elite for spring and summer hockey—and as much as they benefit from the competition, they also reap the rewards of soaking up an environment where everyone has the same approach they have to the game.

The way Shawn Allen sees it, even in what many parents see as the most competitive minor hockey league in the world, the GTHL, his son's top-ranked team will do little more than break a sweat against seven of the twelve teams in the league and will get competitive games against the other four. But summer tournaments are now offering a new division called Super Elite AAA, which essentially has created a new Quadruple-A division filled with players who are the best players on the best AAA teams.

"So now you're playing in tournaments against Montreal's best team, Winnipeg's best team, and then you bring in the Chicagos, Detroits, and Bostons of the world," he said. "The reason we do it is to play literally the best of the best and that's what my son gets in the spring. I really view the spring as more valuable than the regular season. There are other people who think their kids are getting better by riding their bike or playing lacrosse. Well, that's their opinion. I put value on my son competing against the best of the best and I don't get that in the regular season."

Do we need any more proof that all of this is parent driven? Consider Shawn Allen's last comment. "I don't get that in the regular season." Notice the subject of that sentence? It wasn't his son, it was Shawn. And he isn't the only one who thinks that way.

In 1977, the summer before he embarked on an NHL coaching career that led to the Hockey Hall of Fame, Roger Neilson started a small summer hockey camp in Peterborough. Neilson didn't have children, but he did have a passion for developing character through hockey. His vision of hockey camp was to provide players with a strong base in the fundamentals, but also to allow them to share their passion for the game and meet people from around the world. It may sound a little too altruistic, but Neilson wanted his campers to see as much value in being a good teammate and family member as being a good hockey player. Neilson really cared about making kids into better citizens.

But he could afford to be that altruistic—Neilson never found himself out of work. Despite being fired as an NHL coach countless times, and even though he never won a Stanley Cup, he was always in demand as a head coach and, later in his career, as an assistant. His camps were successful because of the name association and the NHL players he could attract as instructors. But the hockey camp was never a make-or-break proposition for Neilson, who died in 2003.

It is one now, though. In fact, it's the primary source of income for director Marshall Starkman and associate director Mike Shiner. Both started with the camp as children and have been affiliated with it for decades. They are undoubtedly passionate about keeping Neilson's legacy alive, but for them it's also about making money. It has to be, because if the school isn't successful, they won't have a business and those who rely on the camp for employment won't have jobs. Without Neilson promoting the camp and without his ability to draw in kids from the many cities where he coached, Starkman and Shiner have to work that much harder just to keep things status quo. When Neilson's camp started more than three decades ago, the competition for the hockey camp dollar was far less intense.

"It's changed," Starkman said wistfully between sessions of the camp on a sunny afternoon in 2011. "We've never lost sight of Roger's legacy, but the legacy loses some of its steam because people forget who Roger is. We're at a transition point because most of the kids coming into our camps were little babies or weren't even born when Roger died. We've recognized that in order for this to function and support people, you need to make it more of a business. It's not a wonderful livelihood, that I can tell you."

The days of the hockey camp lasting a pure and uncomplicated week, tops, are over. Former NHLer Ray Ferraro remembers digging through his hockey bag in the days before camp started to make sure all his equipment still fit him. Not much of a chance of that happening with elite players now, because even in the off-season they don't go long stretches out of their skates to discover they suddenly don't fit. Hockey has become a twelve-month-a-year pursuit, and all over Canada hockey schools have sprung up to respond to the growing demand.

Starkman has found that for many parents, the sizzle is just as important as the steak. In other words, it doesn't matter the quality of your program as much as it does how you market it. Marketers have known for decades that the higher the price for a product, the more consumers gravitate to it. It's a concept called premium or prestige pricing, and it involves charging at the high end of the price point to attract status-conscious consumers. On a rational level, it makes little sense. But when you're dealing with a group of people who have a lot of disposable income and are accustomed to paying premium prices for their children's hockey experience, a high price is often enough to attract them.

Starkman and Shiner are no marketing experts, but they've certainly stumbled upon the concept in their time running the Roger Neilson Hockey Camp. They long eschewed the notion of having a spring program or running revenue-producing tournaments, but those are now part of the business plan. So is offering a premium-priced program with little more than additional trimmings.

"We've already been working on a program that caters to, for lack of a better term, kooky parents who are looking for the absolute Cadillac of camps," Starkman said. "We've actually started calling it the Bentley of camps because Cadillac is not good enough. It doesn't differ significantly from what we do. It's largely marketing because in many ways we already offer it. What we'd be doing, essentially, is emphasizing some things and hammering people over the head a little more with what we do through smoke and mirrors."

Back at the Prospects Tournament, the 1996-born College Cup is a roaring success. The parking lot of the suburban Toronto rink is overflowing with SUVs and a smorgasbord of licence plates from just about every northern state and a surprising number of southern ones as well. Teams with names such as Regional Express, Canadian Future Pros, Bauer Selects, and East Coast Selects are teams in name only. What they really are is a collection of individuals who need a team around them to showcase their talents to the U.S. college scouts in attendance. Even though they're only fifteen, the battle for the hearts and minds of the players between the U.S. college game and major junior is fierce. Actually, very few agents are in attendance, largely because most elite players that age already have either an agent or a "family adviser." Curiously, there are no scouts at the tournament from the OHL, which banned its scouts from attending several years ago.

The teams playing in the tournament come from nowhere in particular. They're an assembled hodge-podge of elite players picked from a number of places and their allegiance is fleeting and short-lived. This is a prospects tournament, and the goal is to get noticed. Being a good team player is nice, but being a shining star is what's going to set you apart from the crowd.

The players are largely in it for themselves and themselves alone. And there's nothing wrong with that, because it's why everybody is here. The players are playing to get offers, the college recruiters are here to get access to players before they get into the clutches of major junior operators, and Bob Turow and his partners are here to make money. Everybody here is making money. The restaurant and bar in the arena is seeing a steady stream of adults and hungry young men. The East Coast Selects, run by Gordie Howe's grandson Travis, are making money.

Turow points to minor hockey associations in Toronto that sell for hundreds of thousands of dollars. He does the math on Hockey Canada's insurance plan and sees that it's about $40 per player multiplied by 600,000 players. That's $24 million. The Canadian Hockey League and Hockey Canada split millions of dollars in revenue from the World Junior Hockey Championship, which Turow claims encourages Hockey Canada to give all kinds of unfair advantages to the CHL. There's a lot of money in the hockey world, and if people are willing to spend it at a prospects tournament in the middle of May, Turow is willing to take it.

"Hockey Canada and [the Canadian Hockey League] will point their finger at people like me or one-on-one guys or the hockey school guys, but believe me it's big business here and it's big business there," Turow said. "This is a business. Yes, we're selling the dream."

The thing is, he's selling what can't be bought.

5

THE HOGWARTS
OF HOCKEY

In a portable classroom behind an arena in suburban Toronto, Peter Merrill is teaching his business leadership class to a small group of boys at The Hill Academy. Most are hockey players; others excel at lacrosse and volleyball. But they're all athletes. You can tell as soon as they walk in the door—not an ounce of fat on any one of them. They come in gulping sports drinks with the flush look of a group of young men who have just worked out. At one point during the class, a student pulls out a piece of cold pizza and nobody in the room, including Merrill himself, so much as bats an eye.

Merrill sits on top of his desk, not behind it. The banter is light, but there is a sense of purpose. He's grilling his students on the progress they're making on their term projects. Two boys stumbled upon a couple of washers and dryers in the basement and hope to have a laundry service up and running by the next school year. Another is planning to sell lanyards with the school logo. Without question, Merrill hands his credit card to the student so he can punch the number into the order on his laptop. Another is hard at work on a brochure to advertise a summer sports camp. After less than fifteen minutes, Merrill dismisses everyone so they can go and cheer on the girls' hockey team in the arena nearby.

Not far away, in another makeshift school in another part of the city, a French teacher at the PEAC School for Elite Athletes is conducting her lesson on the floor of an all-purpose room, oblivious to the grunts and strains of the young athletes working out around her. In what was once an aircraft hangar when the surrounding park was a Canadian Forces base, still with a temporary banner at the entrance, it looks like a typical high school with errant shoes, hoodies, and books strewn on the floors around the columns of lockers. "You do not pronounce the 'ent' at the end of 'jouent,'" the French teacher explains. On the other side of the parking lot, older students are doing sprints. Buses sit ready to take students to a nearby arena for their daily hockey practice.

Thousands of kilometres to the west, young hockey players leave a $90 million facility at the Okanagan Hockey Academy to attend Penticton Secondary School, a high school that was rebuilt in 2008 at a cost of $55 million. Within the public school, the Okanagan Hockey Academy has teachers, guidance counsellors, and tutors who cater exclusively to the needs of the hockey players. The head guidance counsellor, head of the English department, and head of the math department all work for the hockey academy. They run private study halls and provide extra help to young people who are dismissed at 1:00 P.M. so they can do ninety minutes of hockey practice and dryland training that includes fascial stretch therapy to increase connective tissue flexibility.

"This," says Okanagan Hockey Academy vice-president and former NHL player Dixon Ward, "is Disneyland for hockey players."

Like Disneyland, though, there is an admission price. A steep one. Parents of aspiring young players are increasingly sending their children to "sports schools" or "hockey academies" that blend high-level academics with elite hockey—and spending, in some cases, hundreds of thousands of dollars for the privilege with no guaranteed return. Hockey Canada recently estimated there are about eighty such schools in Canada, with no sign that number will shrink anytime soon. In fact, the industry has been growing by leaps and bounds in recent years as those with both pedagogical and entrepreneurial strengths realize there is a void that needs to be filled.

Unlike baseball, football, and basketball in the United States, hockey has never been a key component to the public school system. Basketball, for example, was being played in American high schools as early as 1895 and in universities by the turn of the twentieth century. The first recorded football game took place in 1869 between Rutgers and Princeton and the game was the driving force behind the formation of the National Collegiate Athletic Association, the leviathan organization that is now a multi-billion-dollar industry. Football, in particular, was established at the college level long before it ever became a sport played by professionals.

Hockey, by contrast, was first played by college students, but professional leagues began forming as early as 1904. Junior leagues followed and minor hockey associations started forming as early as 1911, leaving schools in Canada largely out of the business of producing elite hockey players and teams.

The result has been that, almost from the beginning of time (at least from a hockey standpoint), players have had to pursue almost all their hockey opportunities outside of the structure of school, which adds both cost and time to the equation. Instead of Canada's outdoor rinks and arenas being filled with games during school hours or just after school, most minor hockey players in Canada over the years have had a clear delineation between their schooling and their pursuit of hockey.

And this is where the hockey academies and sports schools— which are, of course, top heavy with hockey players—have found their niche. Many of them present an option in which the player can balance a high level of hockey and academics equally. For the most part, students are completely immersed in the school/hockey experience because they live together either on campus or in billeted housing, practise and play together on school teams, and study together under supervision in a private-school setting.

If you are trying to engineer a particular outcome for a kid, there's no substitute for surrounding him with like-minded, driven, and motivated peers, particularly for students who are at an age—typically, middle and high school—when peer pressure is intense and the need to be accepted is high. After all, it's a crucial time for many teenagers, a time when their social relationships are just as important to them as their rela-tionships with family members. Those who run hockey and sports academies report that even if their students don't turn out to be professional athletes, almost all go on to be high achievers. Merrill pointed to The Hill's first graduating class of fifteen students: all but one went on to post-secondary education. He also noted that the class of 2011 produced twenty-two athletes who went on to the NCAA in the next season.

"We've never had a person that I can recall come back after and criticize us for not making their kid a successful hockey player," says Ward of the Okanagan Hockey Academy. "But we have a lot of people sitting in my office telling me two or three years after, 'You saved my kid's life. He could have gone one way and he's gone another way and he's not a hockey player, but he's going to university.'"

Mihaly Csikszentmihalyi has been described as the world's leading expert on happiness, creativity, and positive psychology. He is the author of a number of books, including *Talented Teenagers: The Roots of Success and Failure* (along with Kevin Rathunde and Samuel Whalen), and he argues that talented adolescents spend significantly less time socializing with peers, including talking to friends and going to parties, than their less talented peers.

This prompted renowned educational psychologist Helen Patrick to write, in a 1998 study on the role of peers in continued motivation in sports and the arts, that "the increased time commitment needed for talent development, coupled with the increased desire for peer relationships that is typical during adolescence, has led Csikszentmihalyi to argue that adolescence is a time of potential conflict between the necessary conditions for talent development versus maintaining satisfying peer relationships, and to speculate that talented adolescents' concerns for their peer group may interfere with the dedication necessary for continued talent development. Talent requires high level of practice and commitment and decisions about one's commitment are often made during adolescence."

So it's quite obvious that hothousing that kind of talent and dedication in an atmosphere where those distractions don't exist would tend to bring out the best in young hockey players. It's much more than the ubiquitous "falling into a bad crowd" concept that every parent dreads. It's a matter of ensuring the impressionable young person is thriving and, perhaps more importantly, staying a step ahead of the competition. For example, the motto for the Harrington College of Canada, a hockey prep school located just outside Montreal, is, "Where the serious hockey player goes to school." At the Banff Hockey Academy in Alberta, "Goals for education, hockey, life" are the words by which they operate.

Nick Bollettieri has certainly seen the effects of positive peer pressure in the thirty-plus years he has run the world famous Nick Bollettieri Tennis Academy. A former U.S. paratrooper who celebrated his eightieth birthday with a jump, Bollettieri opened the world's first live-in sports academy in 1978 in Bradenton, Florida, when he bought the Colony Beach Hotel and its twenty-one tennis courts and started his academy with ten local players and one from out of town. In the years since, Bollettieri not only has churned out a bevy of top-ten players and Wimbledon champions, but also has provided the template for the sports academy. The Nick Bollettieri Tennis Academy was the linchpin for the monolithic IMG Academy, which now includes golf, football, soccer, baseball, basketball, and lacrosse academies along with a high-performance institute. While the institute attracts more than 10,000 aspiring athletes year-round, about 1,000 full-time students, some as young as twelve years old, pay up to $50,000 to attend school for roughly four and a half hours a day, with the rest of the day spent immersed in their sports.

The roster of players who have passed through the academy, either as full-time students or in summer camps run by Bollettieri, reads like a professional tennis hall of fame— Venus and Serena Williams, Andre Agassi, Pete Sampras, Jim Courier, Boris Becker, Bjorn Borg, Tommy Haas, Martina Hingis, Brad Gilbert, Aaron Krickstein, Monica Seles, Jimmy Arias, Maria Sharapova, Tommy Haas, Jelena Jankovic, Anna Kournikova. In 2009, students at the Bollettieri Academy won the junior boys' title at the Australian Open, the junior girls' title at the U.S. Open, and both men's and women's singles champions in the NCAA. It also produced the No. 1 ranked junior player in the world. (An interesting note: Carling Bassett-Seguso, the daughter of Canadian billionaire and media mogul John Bassett, was an early student of Bollettieri and went on to establish her own tennis academy with husband Robert Seguso, which is now the Chris Evert Tennis Academy in Boca Raton, Florida.)

And while the singular focus on the game and the instruction are integral, Bollettieri said the most prominent factor in his students' success is the motivation that comes when like-minded young people are placed in the same environment.

"A couple of years ago at the U.S. Open somebody was asking what was wrong with American tennis," Bollettieri said. "And Jim Courier said, 'Well, back in the 80s and 90s, Nick gave us the balls and racquets and we went to the back courts and we beat the shit out of each other. We raised each other's level.' This is not a guarantee, but usually when you put talent together and let them duke it out, they'll take each other to greater heights. You can talk all day long, but the greatest advantage of the academies is they gather talent in the same place. You can have the best instructors and the best facilities, but baby, one person pushing another person is the best thing."

Bollettieri had the academy idea long before anyone north of the 49th parallel had the same thought for hockey players, so it probably bears some examination for purposes of comparison. It has experienced enough success that there are those in tennis who believe Bollettieri should be inducted into the International Tennis Hall of Fame in Newport, Rhode Island. One of those people is Agassi, the winner of eight grand slam singles titles and an Olympic gold medal, and himself a 2011 inductee into the International Tennis Hall of Fame.

When he was inducted, Agassi posted an open letter to Bollettieri on his foundation's website thanking him for his counsel and saying, "There were days that I felt it was just you and me against the world. I'll never forget that."

But in his 2009 book *Open: An Autobiography*, Agassi paints a much darker picture of the academy, writing that he actually dropped out of the high school component in the ninth grade, with Bollettieri's blessing. "People like to call the Bollettieri Academy a boot camp, but it's really a glorified prison camp," Agassi wrote. "And not all that glorified. We eat gruel—beige meats and gelatinous stews and gray slop poured over rice—and sleep in rickety bunks that line the plywood walls of our military-style barracks ... Like most prisoners, we do nothing but sleep and work, and our main rock pile is drills." He went on to write, "The constant pressure, the cutthroat competition, the total lack of adult supervision—it slowly turns us into animals. A kind of jungle law prevails. It's

Karate Kid with racquets, *Lord of the Flies* with forehands." He also talked about the academic life at the academy, saying, "The system is rigged, guaranteed to produce bad students as quickly and efficiently as it produces good tennis players."

In Bollettieri's defence, much has changed at the academy in the years since Agassi played there. Now owned and operated by the worldwide sports juggernaut International Management Group (IMG), the campus now sits on a 350-acre site that has its own school. But those who believe that the hundreds of thousands of dollars parents invest in their children at academies like this one provide an unconditional pass to the professional ranks are mistaken—and disappointed. After all, do the math. Thousands of players have passed through the Nick Bollettieri Tennis Academy over the years and no more than a couple hundred have gone on to the ATP Tour.

Even Bollettieri himself is loath to give any guarantees about what kind of tennis player will emerge from his school. Perhaps the ones who do are such phenoms that they would have found a way to be stars anyway. Bollettieri acknowledges that a "very, very, very, very small percentage" of those who go through the doors of his academy will find themselves playing at Flushing Meadows or Centre Court at Wimbledon.

"Most of them will get a partial or total scholarship," Bollettieri said, "and that's what we strive for." In other words, this elite school is not designed to churn out stars, though that happens. And it's not even designed to pay players and parents back with scholarships. In fact, parents should expect to *lose* money sending their kids to the academy. So if they aren't there to be turned into stars or scholarship athletes, what *are* they there for?

The New York Times provides an answer: "Give them a child with a bagful of tennis racquets, sign a yearly cheque ranging from $25,000 (no frills) to $50,000 (for the personal touch of an industry icon like Nick Bollettieri) and, in the best and rarest of circumstances, the academies hand back a teenage phenom. At the very least, they vow to produce an adolescent with the solid strokes that earn tennis scholarships to the college of his choice and can later function as passports in corporate life."

That is, they're not training privileged kids to be great tennis players. They're training privileged kids to be privileged—just what we saw in the previous chapter. The only difference between expensive supplementary hockey training and all-day hockey training in an academy is that the latter is even more exclusive.

That's not quite fair to rich kids or the people who teach them. All parents want to do everything they can for their kids, no matter how rich they are. You can't fault parents with resources for lavishing them on their sons and daughters. And you can't fault the kids for being born into advantages. There's no reason a wealthy young boy or girl wouldn't be driven by the same kind of passion as the kid on the other side of town whose parents struggle to make ends meet.

And it's not as though academies groom their students to be showboaters and preening superstars. Instead of professing themselves to be hockey factories churning out future NHL players, they emphasize the importance of quality education, character development, and overall wellness as much as they do hockey. None does this more than the Athol Murray College of Notre Dame in Wilcox, Saskatchewan. Located in the breadbasket of Canada and surrounded by grain elevators, Notre Dame and the college epitomize the romantic Canadian vision of hockey. In their book *The Rink,* broadcasters Chris Cuthbert and Scott Russell write, "The only red lights in Wilcox are located behind the hockey nets."

Father Athol Murray came to Wilcox on loan from the Archdiocese of Toronto in 1927, seven years after the Sisters of Charity of St. Louis opened the Notre Dame of the Prairies Convent and St. Augustine's Elementary and High School for boys and girls. Father Murray, who had spent five years in Regina before moving to Wilcox, started a boys' athletic club called the Argos, named after the renowned Argonauts Rowing Club in Toronto that was co-founded by his father.

Murray took over the school in 1933, during the depths of the Depression, and set about to build the foundation on the Greek philosophical principles of building the mind, body, and spirit, envisioning an institution that could produce athletes and scholars through an emphasis on academics, athletics, and faith. Eighty years later, almost two-thirds of the 300 students at Notre Dame play for one of the ten boys' and girls' teams the college has in minor hockey leagues in Saskatchewan. Those who have graduated from high school and play for the Jr. A team in the Saskatchewan Jr. Hockey League live in a separate dorm and are required to take either two university courses or classes to upgrade their high school marks. Costs for that team are covered by fundraisers and sponsors.

Those at Notre Dame often face a daunting task in convincing people they're not running a hockey factory, but both the quality and quantity of the finished products are impressive. Former NHL goalie Curtis Joseph played three years of Jr. A in Ontario without even a hint of a scholarship to an American university, but received an offer from the University of Wisconsin after his first week in Wilcox. Joseph has often said if not for Notre Dame, he'd have been the best beer league goaltender in the world. Other Notre Dame alumni include former Toronto Maple Leafs Wendel Clark, Gary Leeman, and Russ Courtnall; Stanley Cup winners Rod Brind'Amour, Vincent Lecavalier, and Brad Richards; and young NHL stars Jordan Eberle, Braydon Coburn, and Teddy Purcell.

"We don't use that hockey factory term because I always feel it reduces the athlete to almost a machine status," said president and director of education Rob Palmarin. "Our philosophical point of view is you're a person and you have dignity."

You get the distinct impression the other hockey and sports academies in Canada want to be like Notre Dame when they grow up. Because of the Hounds' long tradition and the fact they were part of minor hockey leagues around Regina long ago, their participation in Hockey Canada leagues has essentially been grandfathered while most other specialty schools have found it near impossible to get around Hockey Canada's residency rules. Because they attract students from all over the country and in fact the world, they often find themselves frozen out of local leagues that require players to live locally either permanently or with a guardian.

Having kids play in a high-level league as a part of their school experience, instead of in addition to it, gives Notre Dame a big advantage. It's much easier for the Notre Dame experience to work because parents aren't driving children to and from arenas well into the evening.

"There is a small group of people who would sooner have Notre Dame go elsewhere because in some of our leagues, we might win too much," Palmarin said. "But on the other hand, that's a challenge for them to ask themselves how they get more competitive. The majority of people want us here. They work with us, they cooperate with us, and they beat us sometimes and we beat them sometimes."

As is the case with the other sports and hockey academies, there's a major cost for that kind of experience—$19,000 a year for students who live in Saskatchewan and $26,000 a year for those from outside the province. Palmarin estimates that 40 to 50 percent of the students in the school are on some sort of financial assistance, thanks to tireless fundraising efforts and a very generous alumni association. But it's certainly not an insignificant amount of money for any prospective player. For every captain of industry and millionaire who sends his child to Notre Dame, there are people such as Yvon and Christianne Lecavalier, who sent their two sons. It was at Notre Dame at the age of fourteen that Vincent Lecavalier met Brad Richards, the son of a lobster fisherman from Prince Edward Island.

Yvon Lecavalier worked four jobs in order to pay Notre Dame tuition for Vincent and his elder son, Philippe. But the investment paid the family back a hundredfold—Philippe earned a hockey scholarship to Clarkson University in Potsdam, New York, and went on to become a certified agent with the NHL Players' Association. Vincent, meanwhile, cut his stay at Notre Dame short when he was drafted first overall by the Rimouski Oceanic of the Quebec Major Junior Hockey League in 1996, two years before he was drafted in the same spot in the NHL by the Tampa Bay Lightning. Lecavalier is currently in the middle of an eleven-year deal that will pay him $10 million a season through 2015–16.

Notre Dame does not deny its hockey program is a top-notch operation. After all, it has hockey coordinators for both the boys' and girls' program, a goaltender coach, a strength and conditioning coach, and even a physiotherapist. Most students come to Notre Dame for the hockey, but Palmarin maintains they end up getting much more out of the experience. Hockey players are encouraged to try other sports, or even the drama club or choir, and exploring their spirituality is a constant based on the school motto *Luctor et Emergo* (Struggle and Conquer).

"We want kids to ask those deep questions that sometimes get avoided," Palmarin said. "Is there a God? Does He have a plan for your life? What do you do when you're struggling, when you're suffering? When a lot of hockey players get here, they fall in love with the other stuff besides hockey. They realize, 'Hey, I'm a hockey guy, but it's more than that.' We're not a hockey school—we're not *just* a hockey school. I'll word it that way. And we're certainly not a factory and we don't like to call ourselves an academy. We're just a school."

Neil Doctorow sits in a boardroom at the PEAC School for Elite Athletes with the air of a person who always has to be somewhere. At thirty-three he's tanned and fit, looking far more like one of the students than the school's managing director, spokesman, and tireless salesman. Even Doctorow sees the irony in his involvement in education. The son of two teachers with PhDs who espoused Trotskyism, Doctorow and his older brother, Cory, were both products of the alternative school system.

Neil Doctorow was identified as a kinesthetic, or tactile, learner—a style in which learning takes place when the student does physical tasks rather than listens to a lecture—and something of a behaviour problem with anger management issues. The public and alternative school systems did not serve him well, while his brother Cory excelled and went on to university, but did not graduate. Cory is a well-known blogger and science fiction writer who is an activist for more liberal copyright laws and has written several books. One of them, the bestselling *Little Brother,* is used in the Grade 10 curriculum at PEAC.

Neil Doctorow, on the other hand, was an athlete who persevered and managed to get a teaching degree. After teaching in the public system, he had the idea to establish a sports school for elite athletes, largely because he didn't see their needs being responded to in the public or private school systems, both in his academic and teaching careers. As a student, Doctorow said, any success he gained in athletics came because he worked out and had more drive than anyone else.

"I feel like if you set up not only the environment, but the standards for training, for everything, then you can actually create an environment where kids are academically successful and athletically successful," Doctorow said. "You have kids here who have similar ethical and moral standards as a result of just trying to be excellent in their sport. So the default here is you don't have kids smoking in front of the school, you haven't got kids who are showing up to class high."

They do, however, often show up to class tired, largely

because of the physical demands that are placed upon them. The programs vary from school to school, but most of the sports/ hockey academies operate on similar principles and schedules. The school day is split between academic and athletic, with equal emphasis, time, and importance placed upon each. Most academies will offer a strength and conditioning program in the morning, then between sixty and ninety minutes on ice, almost always strictly devoted to skill development. That is supplemented by about the same time devoted to sport-specific dryland training, along with occasional sessions breaking down video or dealing with nutrition or the psychology of sport.

And all of that is accomplished in the context of an academic atmosphere where the students learn in small groups—student-to-teacher ratio is typically under fifteen to one—for between four and a half and five hours per day. All schools are required to meet the curriculum requirements for their province's ministry of education standards. After all, there wouldn't be much point in grooming students for scholarships at American universities if they're going to flunk their SATs or not make the grades to get into university in the first place.

And that appears, above all, to be much of the end game here. Students, regardless of their abilities or standing prior to entering the academies, are all directed through the academic stream of high school learning as opposed to the applied stream, which is geared more for students who are bound for community college or the workforce. Some students end up leaving early to pursue major junior options. Brothers Brett and Nicholas Ritchie are two such examples. Both attended The Hill Academy in Toronto until Brett, a second-round pick of the Dallas Stars in 2011, joined the Sarnia Sting in 2009.

Despite being offered a full scholarship by the University of Notre Dame, Ritchie went the major junior route after two years of high school. His younger brother, Nicholas, was one of the top fifteen-year-old players in Canada when he was drafted second overall by the Peterborough Petes in 2011. Already at 6-foot-2, 205 pounds, Ritchie would have been the first player taken had Aaron Ekblad not been designated as an "exceptional" underage junior player and selected first by the Barrie Colts.

In 2012, PEAC had its first-ever No. 1 overall pick in the OHL draft in teenage phenom Connor McDavid, who was taken by the Erie Otters after being granted exceptional status by Hockey Canada. His teammate on the Toronto Marlies midget team, Joshua Ho-Sang, went fifth overall to the Windsor Spitfires, and attended PEAC alongside McDavid.

But most players at hockey academies are pursuing a hockey scholarship at an American university—even though, like the odds of playing junior hockey, it's a long shot. In 2010–11, of the 1,568 players who played Division I hockey at American universities, just 481 (or 30.7 percent) were Canadians. Each year, hundreds of thousands of players pursue a total of 822 full scholarships. Those can be broken up into partial scholarships any way a school sees fit, and some players can make up the difference with financial aid (based on need) or merit (based on academic standing). But the reality is that even when it comes to having your university life paid for on the basis of your athletic prowess, the pickings are slim indeed.

It should also be noted that Canada's three junior leagues—the Ontario Hockey League, the Quebec Major Junior Hockey League, and the Western Hockey League—all have scholarship programs for players as well. The top prospects for each league customarily get a "schoolboy package," which guarantees their tuition and living expenses will be paid for four years after they graduate from junior hockey. Lesser players receive somewhere in the neighbourhood of $5,000 for each year they play in the league.

But there's a catch. When a player signs a professional, not an NHL, contract, the education money is revoked. (Though the player does have eighteen months to take advantage of his scholarship.) So what that means is the junior operators typically don't have to worry about paying out too many of the schoolboy packages because those players are top NHL prospects who will almost certainly turn pro. But it also affects the player who might sign a professional contract in the minor leagues or Europe in hopes of working his way up to the NHL someday.

That, however, does not deter a number of players and their parents from looking at academies as an opportunity to get a leg up on all those other kids seeking scholarships. And why wouldn't they? In most cases, they get upwards of 140 more hours of ice time just in instruction and practice each season, not to mention the dryland training and the other off-ice enhancements. And that's before they finish their school day! Many players then take to the ice with their AAA club teams for more high-level instruction and competition, the way Nicholas Ritchie did when he established himself as a star with the Toronto Marlboros, a midget juggernaut in the GTHL that counts young NHLers such as Rick Nash of the Columbus Blue Jackets, John Tavares of the New York Islanders, and Jason Spezza of the Ottawa Senators among its alumni. In

2010–11, the Marlboros won every tournament they entered, including the prestigious OHL Cup, which essentially serves as the all-Ontario midget championship. (Incidentally, Ritchie's teammates and future OHL stars Jordan Subban and Joshua Ho-Sang were students at PEAC the same season.)

So you can see what a competitive advantage being immersed in this kind of atmosphere can offer a player. There's the burden of cost, but there's also the very large pot of gold of a professional career—or the significantly smaller but still lucrative pot of gold in the form of a scholarship—waiting for those whose talents allow them to rise to the upper crust of their age groups.

"You get one Division I scholarship, that's 40-grand a year," said Peter Merrill of The Hill Academy. "That's a pretty strong payback. If we can get it to the point where a kid comes here for a few years and if we can help them out [with post-secondary education], make it a little bit less, then there's a pretty good payback that way."

All right then. Let's examine this solely from a financial point of view, not taking into account what the student gleans from the experience and the character development that each of these institutions prides itself in promoting and grooming. From strictly a financial standpoint, the outlay can be staggering. And parents who are cutting those cheques in the hopes of at least seeing the money come back in the form of a free or subsidized university education could be setting themselves up for a very expensive disappointment.

Take Merrill's Hill Academy as an example. For the 2011–12 academic year, the cost for a Grade 11 or 12 hockey player was $33,750. That included tuition fees, room and board (subtract $12,500 for those not requiring room and board), and fees associated with playing hockey. Costs are slightly lower for Grades 6 through 10.

Now, assume that an aspiring hockey player begins attending an academy such as The Hill in Grade 6 and continues through high school. If that player is from outside Toronto and requires room and board, his parents will pay a total of $95,250 for Grades 6 through 8; $66,000 for Grades 9 and 10; and $67,500 for Grades 11 and 12. That comes to a grand total of $228,750 without taking into account things such as travel for visits or discretionary spending. (That total would be $141,250 for students who did not require room and board.)

Let's say the student simply limits his experience at The Hill to the high school years. If he were an out-of-town student, the fees would be $133,500 ($83,500 for those who don't require room and board). With a four-year undergraduate degree at an American university costing anywhere between $160,000 and more than $200,000, all costs included, those few who earn them will have indeed paid back their parents' investments. (We'll explore in a later chapter the financial aspects of the American scholarship and the price people pay for their children's educations.)

Fees at The Hill are typical of those from around the country. Students at the PEAC School for Elite Athletes in Toronto can expect to pay about $31,500 per year if they are living away from home and $21,500 if they live in Toronto. Included in that is a $6,500 fee to play hockey. Those at the Ontario Hockey Academy in Cornwall, Ontario, pay about $35,000 per year, and those at the Banff Hockey Academy pay $28,000 per year. But because the government of Alberta recognizes the right to choose a private school and covers 60 percent of the base instruction rate for private schools, the Banff Hockey Academy receives about $7,000 per student from Alberta.

The fees at the Okanagan Hockey Academy, meanwhile, are higher than most others in Canada. A student from outside British Columbia can expect to pay $44,000 with a billet and $39,000 without a billet. Those from British Columbia pay $33,500 with a billet and $28,000 without.

But the high costs of an elite education are hardly exclusive to hockey. At the IMG Academy, which features instruction from, in some cases, former major league coaches, they are astronomical. Tuition and boarding fees—and there are thousands of dollars in other fees attached to each sport—are $50,135 for one year for the Madden Football Academy, as well as the basketball, baseball, soccer, and IMG Performance Institute. The Bollettieri Tennis Academy costs $53,535 per year and the Leadbetter Golf Academy costs a whopping $60,210 per year.

And the parents of those students can at least hope their kid gets a chance at an athletic scholarship after graduation. But there weren't many universities handing out, say, ballet scholarships the last time we checked. If your son or daughter is an aspiring dancer or musician, with probably an even more remote chance of ever making it big in his discipline, you're also going to pay big for a specialized high school education.

Take, for example, the National Ballet School in Toronto, which offers academic and dance instruction for students from Grades 6 through 12. Including the mandatory summer school sessions, parents of students who attend for the entire seven-year cycle can expect to spend a total of about $143,000 if their child requires residence. That does not include the thousands spent each year on school uniforms, dancewear, or physiotherapy.

The Interlochen Arts Academy high school in Michigan attracts 500 students per year from all over the world who display an aptitude for creative writing, dance, motion picture arts, music, theatre, and visual arts—and offers a comparative arts program for those who specialize in more than one area. Tuition and boarding fees at Interlochen run at $46,540 per year. At the Idyllwild Arts Academy in California, students pay about $55,000 per year.

If parents have money, they will spend it on their kids. The difference between these schools and the hockey academies is that, like the Bollettieri Tennis Academy, the arts schools are investments in only a very indirect way. Parents aren't looking for a financial return. If they never see a penny from a scholarship, they won't deem the years of grooming a failure. That's a big difference from Merrill's suggestion that graduates can reasonably expect scholarships valued at $40,000 a year.

And it's one thing for the rich to pay handsomely for a platinum-plated education. But it's something entirely different for a family of more modest means to compromise its financial future in the hope of a payoff that may never come. "You get the people with Escalades and you get people in minivans," Doctorow said of the parents who drop their children off at PEAC. "We have families that take out a second mortgage, sometimes downsize to one car." He means to illustrate that his academy is not only for the "one percent," but the implication is that the minivan people risk a lot more sending their kids to his school.

Here's how Doctorow, whose father was born in a refugee camp in Azerbaijan, sees it. If you want to take yourself out of the regular stream of anything, unfortunately it's going to cost you money.

"Socio-economic limitations exist in all spheres of life," Doctorow said. "Our system is designed such that we will service people with money and people without money will continue to be in the same socio-economic class they will always be in. That's how our system is created. If someone is an earner of minimum wage or less, it's in the best interest of the government and in society's best interest to keep them in that role so other people can get rich. That's the premise of capitalism, right? Some people get more and others get less and the people who get more capitalize on the people who get less. It's an unfortunate reality.

"If you look at what happens when people become marginalized," Doctorow continued, "and they become part of a socio-economic standard that's lower than what I would consider to be the middle class, then what happens is they become almost pigeonholed into this lifestyle of limited educational opportunities. And once you're in that kind of bracket and in that environment, it's very hard to break out of it."

So there you have it. His school is not there to help kids get to the top. It's there to help kids stay at the top.

Doctorow counts the children of former NHL stars Doug Gilmour and Brian Bradley among his students, as well as Malcolm and Jordan Subban, the brothers of talented Montreal Canadiens defenceman P.K. Subban. Former Toronto Raptors

GM Glen Grunwald sent his child to The Hill. A decade before winning the Calder Trophy as the NHL's top rookie, Tyler Myers moved with his father, Paul, an oil and gas executive, from Houston to Calgary and spent time at the Banff Hockey Academy. Joe Colborne, who was selected in the first round of the NHL draft by the Boston Bruins and was later traded to the Toronto Maple Leafs, is the son of well-known TriStar Oil and Gas executive Paul Colborne and attended the Edge School for Athletes in Calgary, then went to the University of Denver for one season before turning pro.

"A lot of people don't think I have much to do with it," Colborne told the *Calgary Herald* just prior to the 2008 NHL draft. "But they haven't seen how hard I have worked. I had the chance to see how hard my dad had to work to be successful and I know what it will take to reach my own goals."

Absolutely no doubt exists that any player who reaches that tier of hockey has to possess a level of commitment that goes far beyond what most people are willing to endure. As the bottleneck gets smaller and more players are competing for fewer spots on elite-level teams in junior, college, and the professional ranks, the more determination, sacrifice, and effort it takes to be included in that minute group of players who have reached the top of their craft. No player, particularly in this day and age, makes it on natural talent alone. That talent must be nurtured, developed, and perfected with thousands of hours of practice, even if a player hopes to be a fourth-line checker at the NHL level.

But it's also true that, in an increasing number of cases, those who are exposed to the highest level of instruction and competition are going to be the ones who rise to the top. And how does a player do that? Well, having parents with a lot of disposable income and the time to devote to a young player's career gives that player an enormous advantage. And that's the case even with hockey academies. First of all, as we've established, players wanting to pursue a hockey-heavy schedule in a private school setting, or any other specialization for that matter, require access to an enormous amount of money.

Remember, just getting into these schools is competitive, even for those with the resources to pay. The academies attract players who are already at an elite level by the time they get to the sixth or seventh grade. To be sure, the Okanagan Hockey School in Penticton is not taking garden-variety house league players and turning them into highly skilled star players. Typically, hockey academies hold tryouts every year where sometimes hundreds of kids are vying for spots on prep teams. In 2010–11, for example, The Hill had eighty players trying out for twenty-three available spots.

So naturally these spots are going to the better players, many of whom are already at the AAA level. And what is one of the reasons they're already at that level? Because their parents have the $10,000 a year it takes to keep a child in AAA hockey. So, what happens in many cases is the children whose parents have money end up being able to afford exposure to the best competition and training, thus becoming better hockey players. Because they're better hockey players whose parents have money, they have the added advantage of being able to play at a sports or hockey academy, where they spend hours per day on the ice and in the gym. They get physically stronger and their skills increase, thus putting them into an even more advantageous position when it comes to competing for those spots on major junior and college teams. They're training more often at the precise time in their lives when their bodies are maturing and one that is most crucial to overall skill development, they're playing against better competition, and they're largely shielded from the distractions that can derail a career when a player is most vulnerable to them.

Viewed this way, hockey academies begin to look like bastions of inequality. They reinforce privilege. And while they can't guarantee that any of their students will make it as a professional or a collegiate athlete, they do render it much harder for the unprivileged to make it because they raise the standards of commitment to a level that very few can hope to afford. That doesn't mean the students who go to these schools are bad kids, or even pampered kids—in fact, they work like fourth-liners desperate to hold on to a roster spot. It doesn't mean their parents are bad people—in fact, not giving your kid everything you can is probably more blameworthy than using your resources to improve your child's future. It doesn't mean the schools are bad, either—they're not run by cynical profiteers. Peter Merrill founded The Hill Academy not to fleece credulous parents but because he'd seen what sports academies had done for his own kids, who had struggled in the public system but went on to academic (and athletic) success at an academy.

But something is wrong if good people doing the right thing for the right reason still end up doing something that hurts the game and stifles other people's kids.

It comes back to the dream, and the high expectations that keep both parents and students investing more and more. And how can parents who put, in some cases, more than $100,000 into giving their children every advantage in sport not have some level of expectation that it's going to result in something tangible for them and their kids? So many of the schools find one of their most important jobs is managing those expectations. Adults will almost always talk a good game when it comes to their children's athletic pursuits, but how many times have we seen a parent get caught up in the high stakes that seem to be getting higher all the time? Keep in mind that success in athletics doesn't just mean good things for the young player involved—some of that glow tends to shine on the adults in their lives as well.

For Bollettieri, it's a quagmire that often results in disappointment for parents of young tennis prodigies. Some of the students at his IMG Academy come from across the country with at least one parent, largely because they're arriving at an age as young as thirteen. The stress of paying for the academy and the split of the family often creates a discord that is too much for many families to bear.

"I've had people say to me—and the baby isn't even born yet, the poor son of a bitch—they think their kid is going to be the next Agassi," Bollettieri said. "The problem multiplies when the family splits up—when the father stays and the mother goes or vice-versa—that puts on more pressure. Daddy has mortgaged the home, we're away from Mommy and Daddy. All that shit puts more pressure on the student."

John Walters knows all about expectations. He had them himself. He was a AAA goaltender throughout his minor hockey career and said he missed thirty-three days of school when he played peewee, including more than a week to play in the world-renowned Tournoi International de Hockey Peewee de Quebec, a tournament that has seen hundreds of future NHL players and is essentially hockey's equivalent to the Little League World Series. Walters said he missed so much school that he almost failed the eighth grade.

His expectations were high, but they were never realized beyond a brief stint as a professional player in Italy in his late teens. As the director of hockey at PEAC, he sees parents and players with high expectations all the time. He also coached the Toronto Red Wings, including a young man by the name of Tyler Seguin, who was drafted second overall by the Boston Bruins in 2010 and won a Stanley Cup in his rookie season. He has coached Jr. A and along with being director of hockey at PEAC works as a recruiter for NHL agent Ian Pulver, so he has seen the weight of expectations from almost all sides of the equation.

And Walters doesn't like what he sees. He understands that parents want what's best for their children and he knows the stakes are high. As an agent, he meets with the parents who have remortgaged their homes or maxed out their lines of credit to keep their sons playing at an elite level. For parents such as that, it seems that building a successful life and being able to perhaps contribute to their children's school-ing isn't enough. These parents, to use a poker term, are "all-in." And they are despite the odds against their sons ever repaying that investment. Some of them realize it, but many of them don't. And most of them, Walters said, are normally level-headed, hard-working people who simply get caught up in a web from which they feel there is no escape. After all, once you've paid so much money to get to a certain point in hockey, some parents feel they need to see it through.

To give up after all that expense and effort would feel like a waste.

That's a phenomenon sometimes called the "psychology of previous investment"—the thing is, it's hard to stop doing what you're doing, especially if you've ploughed a lot of money into it, even if you know that it has stopped making sense. Sometimes when people realize that the amount they owe on their mortgage is more than the house's market value, they walk away from the property. But most people stay in the house and keep paying the mortgage, even though it means they're losing money. Maybe the house is important to them. Maybe they have nowhere else to go. Maybe they believe it's the right thing to do. There are many reasons to do things that don't make financial sense.

But to do things that don't make financial sense for no good reason? That's harder to defend. And hockey parents all too often put down their "investments" with blinders on, when only a few minutes of homework would show them the odds they face. Let's assume that of the 822 scholarships that are available in U.S. colleges, 25 percent are destined for freshmen players. And let's assume that 25 percent of the spots on the sixty teams in the Canadian Hockey League are set aside for rookies. That means that 205 full scholarships and 300 roster spots (based on a roster of twenty players per team), for a grand total of 505, would go to players who are not already established in either U.S. college or major junior hockey. To suggest there are tens of thousands of players chasing those spots would probably be a low estimate.

"I encounter people every day, parents not only at this school, but everywhere every day who are unrealistic about the end game of why their children play hockey," Walters said. "A lot of them are just uneducated about the realities of making it. I've had numerous parents say to me, 'At least if he can get a scholarship or go to the OHL and get a school package, then it's all worth it.' But what if they don't? What if they're just not good enough?"

Walters sees it both ways. Players who excel as young teenagers often peter out and those who are gangly and awkward and growing into their bodies sometimes emerge as the ones who rise to the top. When he was coaching the Red Wings team with players born in 1992, there was no room for a young defenceman who was tall and skinny and not a particularly graceful skater, and Walters decided to cut him. In the summer of 2011, all 6-feet-8 of Jamie Oleksiak was drafted out of Northeastern University by the Dallas Stars; Oleksiak then left school and his full scholarship to sign an entry-level contract with the Stars. He played the 2011–12 season with the Niagara IceDogs of the OHL and received a signing bonus of $92,500.

A new parent himself, Walters hasn't been in the position of wanting what is best for his child but having invested huge amounts of money, time, and family resources to make the dream a reality. He doesn't know how he would act with so much on the line, but he hopes he would have a more level head than many of the people he sees in minor hockey.

"I wish at some point somebody could educate people on the realities of making it," Walters said. "It gets tough sometimes because this minor hockey thing, it's almost a cult. And it gets nasty sometimes. I've seen it get completely nasty. Most of these people are good people. It's not like they're bad people, but they just fall into this minor hockey trap with all the hoopla and hype."

Paul Ritchie is one of those parents, but both his kids were good enough to make it. Both Brett and Nicholas attended The Hill Academy in suburban Toronto and played in the Greater Toronto Hockey League, despite the fact they lived about eighty kilometres from the city in the small town of Orangeville. Both of Ritchie's boys were able to immerse themselves in the sports academy situation and play a high level of hockey with the best players in their age groups. And while both are still working through the ranks and have yet to completely realize their dreams, things are looking promising.

As a twelfth-overall OHL pick by the Sarnia Sting in 2009, Brett Ritchie received the same full education package his younger brother Nicholas received when he was selected second overall by the Peterborough Petes two years later. The prospect of paying for private schooling and to play at the highest level of arguably the most expensive minor hockey league in Canada was something Paul, who owns and trains standardbred horses and played three years in the OHL himself before going on to Brock University, saw coming. His sons both began their education at The Hill in Grade 9 and went full-time for two years. Brett returned to The Hill for the end of Grades 11 and 12 after his junior hockey season ended, something Paul expects Nicholas will do as well when his seasons wrap up in Peterborough.

"The way I saw it, you either spend your money early or you spend your money later," Ritchie said. "It costs money to go to these places, right? You spend money early, you might get a scholarship. If you don't spend money early, you might not get anything and then you've got to pay your own education. And that's the chance you take sometimes. You have to have the right type of kid."

It's no secret that success and athletics go together. The kids who thrive on the ice or the pitch are often the kids with drive and discipline. They love the rewards of applying themselves. So the idea of a hockey academy is not bizarre at all, and neither is the idea that young men and women might excel both academically and athletically. It's not a zero-sum game.

But neither is it a simple matter of putting like-minded kids together and allowing them to spur each other to new heights of achievement. There is the question of what people expect as the outcome of the experience. Ritchie says you need the right kind of kid to make the academy experience work, but what if it's the other way around?

In other words, why do we look for the right kind of kid to turn into a hockey player? Why don't we take hockey players, and develop them into the right kind of kid?

That was the approach of the godfather of today's academies: St. Michael's College in Toronto. Like Notre Dame, St. Mike's was born out of the Roman Catholic tradition. Also like Notre Dame, St. Mike's was once a hockey powerhouse. The school first opened as a private all-boys college in 1852, but it wasn't until 1906 that the hockey program began. Since then, it has produced more than a hundred NHL players and thirteen Hall of Famers, including Frank Mahovlich, Dave Keon, Turk Broda, Tim Horton, and Ted Lindsay. In the late 1920s, Maple Leafs owner Conn Smythe sponsored the hockey program at St. Mike's, effectively making the school the pipeline for all of the Catholic hockey talent in Ontario.

And players, particularly from northern Ontario outposts, came to St. Mike's in droves in the 1940s and 50s. Horton hailed from Copper Cliff (near Sudbury), Mahovlich from Schumacher (near Timmins), Dick Duff from Kirkland Lake, and Keon from nearby Rouyn-Noranda, Quebec. Broda hailed from Brandon, Manitoba, and Lindsay from Renfrew, Ontario.

Not surprisingly, St. Michael's was the class of amateur hockey, winning Memorial Cups in 1937, 1946, 1947, and 1948 before taking home its last in 1961. After that, they shut the program down. Shortly before, the future Hall of Famer Father David Bauer wrote a letter to the Toronto Maple Leafs' Smythe (who had fostered the St. Mike's team as a development program) explaining why St. Mike's would have to pull out of junior hockey. "My opinion is that sooner or later [the college] will see fit to discontinue the Jr. A series because of its growing professionalism, its long schedule and rough play which so often results in unfavourable publicity difficult for the educational institution to handle gracefully."

Of course, that was a different time, and Father Bauer had a pretty high standard for doing the right thing. First, he gave up a chance to play for the Memorial Cup because he felt that enlisting to fight for Canada in the Second World War was the more important thing to do. Then, when he later had the opportunity to play in the NHL, he chose to join the priesthood instead. He would go on to found the Canadian national team, and today Hockey Canada's Olympic-sized rink in Calgary is named after him. His legacy earned him a spot in the Hockey Hall of Fame.

The St. Michael's Majors, the team he disbanded because it didn't reflect the values of the school, resurfaced as an OHL team in 1996 and until 2012 played in nearby Mississauga but had no formal affiliation with the school. During the 2010–11 season, when the Majors were romping through the playoffs, one of the team's major sponsors and rink-board advertisers was a business called Aren't We Naughty. The store had rink-board advertising in the Hershey Centre and often was the title sponsor for the three-star selection after the game. Somehow, a team whose roots go back more than 150 years to the teachings of the Basilian Fathers of the Roman Catholic Church was partially propped up by a business that claims on its website that "we offer thousands of choices in sex toys from vibrators to penis rings to masturbators. You won't find a larger selection of adult toys at a better price anywhere else in Canada." So it looks as though Father Bauer's concerns that it would prove impossible for the school "gracefully" to combine a high standard of education with elite hockey were justified.

6
CRAZY IS LIKE CHOLESTEROL

Near the end of their three-year adventure, Max Strang and his family experienced the quintessential idyllic Canadian evening. Max had played a great game, his team had won, and as they left the arena that night the snow was fluttering to the ground in thick, heavy flakes. It was a beautiful scene to be sure, and if any member of the Group of Seven had been there to see it he would have immediately pulled out his palette and canvas.

Max was hungry from playing. His father, Scott, and his mother, Shirley, were ravenous from watching. Even the Strang family's ninety-five-pound chocolate lab and constant companion, Gus, was feeling rather peckish. (Don't ask. They just knew.)

With traffic crawling and their home base possibly hours away, a cheap, quick meal at McDonald's was looking like a very tempting family dining option until everybody came to the realization they had no money. A stop at the bank machine revealed that the third-last payment on Scott's truck had been withdrawn earlier that day. Unfortunately, it also revealed there were no funds remaining in the account.

Feeling desperation set in, the Strangs combed the truck for loose change, jamming their hands between and under the seats and rummaging through the glove compartment searching for hard currency. Miraculously, their quest produced a grand total of three dollars, enough to take advantage of a promotion that offered two hamburgers for a dollar.

"So we got our six hamburgers," Scott recalled. "We each had a hamburger-and-a-half and volunteered half a hamburger to Gus."

Hockey stories are almost always stories of sacrifice. The long drives through blizzards on prairie highways, the gruelling routine of early-morning practices. The realization that your family is so "hockey-poor" (yes, there's a term for the special kind of poverty that descends on a household that includes hockey players) that you find yourselves sharing burgers with a dog.

Every family has a story of the crazy things they've done. That means every kid who makes it to the NHL can look back at all the things his parents did to make his dream come true.

Take Carey Price of the Montreal Canadiens. Price grew up in Anahim Lake, a remote village in northern British Columbia that is barely a dot on the map. But that didn't prevent his father from doing everything to make his NHL dream happen. Living in the town where Carey's mother, Lynda, was the chief of the Ulkatcho First Nation, Price would fly—yes, *fly*—in to practices and games 320 kilometres south in Williams Lake. Jerry Price, Carey's father and a former minor league goaltender in the Philadelphia Flyers organization, bought a plane and flew it himself solely for that purpose.

Most parents hear stories like that and think their hours in the car and their dwindling bank accounts don't seem like much of a sacrifice after all. Maybe, they tend to think, they could do a little more. They'll also tell you they see it as their parental duty to open as many doors and to provide as many opportunities as possible to give their children the chance to take their passion as far as their abilities will allow. They would do the same, they say, if their child exhibited an exuberance for music, dance, art, or any other athletic endeavour. And the common theme for all of them is that their enthusiasm for advancing their children's opportunities in hockey knows no bounds.

The effect might be called "sacrifice inflation." The more extreme the stories that circulate about the lengths to which parents have gone, the more parents feel they're expected to do. We don't want to contribute to that by mentioning Carey Price's bush-pilot father. And we don't want to make things even worse with the stories you're about to read. The last thing we want anyone to think is that if they're unwilling to match the sacrifices of these parents they are somehow shirking their parental responsibilities. We're all for parents doing everything they can for their kids.

But there is such a thing as going too far.

Whether the parents in this chapter have gone too far is a question we will leave open for now. But of all the tales you'll ever hear about the sacrifices players and families make to pursue the dream, and the lengths to which they will go to make it happen, there's a good chance none will be as extreme as the yarn the Strang family from Gilbertsville, Pennsylvania, can tell. Or not. Perhaps you might be more blown away by the Zucker family from Las Vegas. Then there's always the Cimettas from Sarnia, Ontario.

Regardless, there are hundreds, perhaps thousands, of families in North America that will seemingly stop at nothing to give their children the opportunity to play at the highest possible level they can handle. The remarkable thing about it is the end game is not necessarily a career worth millions of dollars in the NHL—or at least that's what they say for public consumption. The goal seems to be the still-very-difficult-to-attain hockey scholarship at an American university, or in most cases, the opportunity to teach life lessons that it seems cannot be learned without overcoming a series of enormous obstacles for the privilege of enjoying hockey.

Families have taken minor hockey organizations to court and spent thousands of dollars in litigation fees for the opportunity to travel thousands of kilometres a year to play hockey. Countless players and their parents have moved to a different city—or even country—to expose their children to the most ice time, the best competition, and expert coaching. And there are parents who have been willing to allow their children to move hundreds of kilometres from home and be cared for by a guardian at an age as young as ten just so they can play hockey in an organization such as the Greater Toronto Hockey League (GTHL), which is billed as the largest hockey league in the world and carries the perception from those on the inside and the outside that it's an assembly line for pro talent. And the thing is, many of these families know what they're doing is crazy.

"To me, crazy is kind of like cholesterol, there's good and bad," said Carlo Cimetta, a Sarnia-based lawyer who spent a year travelling between Sarnia and Toronto so his son could play in the GTHL, then spent two years renting a home in Port Huron, Michigan, so his son could play with the renowned Honeybaked organization in Detroit. "I was willing to do the good crazy, but I'm not prepared to do the bad. And I take some pride in that."

Much of this is undoubtedly driven by a new kind of parenting. With this generation having fewer children, parents have more time and financial resources to devote to their kids' pursuits. Without a doubt, the stakes for success have been driven higher and the need to get an early start on establishing successful habits is more important to this generation of parents than any other before it. Generally speaking, there are more demands on parents professionally than ever before, and in spite of that they continue to pour enormous amounts of financial, time, and emotional resources into their children.

In fact, some would argue they do exactly that *because* of the unprecedented professional pressures. You're dealing here largely with Type A personalities who have displayed the same kind of drive in their own lives. But probably an element of guilt to all of it exists as well, says Dr. Richard Ginsburg, one of the foremost sports psychologists in the United States and the author of *Whose Game Is It Anyway?* There's no one typical profile, Ginsburg says, but there is something about athletic pursuits that seems to bring out the fanaticism in many parents.

"You don't have a bunch of parents sitting around a table watching their children solve math problems," Ginsburg said.

"So we're spending lots of time on our weekends, dropping a lot of cash to do this. There are certainly examples of parents who are so engaged in their work and their lives that there's a sense of guilt that they have to do everything for their children because they're missing out in other areas. As parents, we're thrown into a current that's pretty fast. It's seductive and sometimes it just picks you up and carries you. It even happens to me. I have a son who's pretty athletic and I'm like, 'That's my boy!' I see it coming and even then I'm powerless to stop it."

Some of it, though, has to do with the unique nature of hockey in the sports landscape. Although you can probably find similar examples in every sport, hockey displaces more young people than any other. For the most part, young people can play baseball, football, or basketball in the United States very close to home because of the emphasis on sports being part of the school system. Even in small towns, the high schools have programs in those sports that are good enough for a player to be able to stay home until he graduates and then, if he's good enough, move on to the collegiate ranks. Baseball and basketball do draft players right out of high school, but the vast majority of players can stay in the watchful eye of their parents until at least the end of Grade 12.

Hockey is different in many ways. As young Max Strang discovered in eastern Pennsylvania, not a lot of American centres have elite hockey programs, so a kid may have to either travel long distances or move to another city to play with teams that offer him enough of a challenge and opportunity to advance. Even players in large American cities such as Los Angeles find they outgrow the quality of hockey and have to move north. As far as Canada is concerned, in small towns often there aren't enough players to form a AAA team—and even if there are, the issue is that travel to larger cities where the best competition resides is oppressive, so players often find themselves moving for that reason as well.

And while there are no quasi-pro major junior leagues in football, basketball, and baseball, the Canadian Hockey League is the premier development league for any player over the age of sixteen. So even if a player is from a city or town where he can play good hockey, he'll quite likely have to move when he's sixteen years old to play in one of the Ontario, Western, or Quebec Major Junior Hockey Leagues.

A player wanting to pursue a scholarship at a U.S. university faces the choice of either playing a lesser calibre of hockey at the Jr. B or Jr. A level for two years of high school, or joining a major junior league and forfeiting his opportunity to compete for a U.S. scholarship. (More on that in the next chapter.)

The other factor that often forces such radical behaviour is the current residency rules that cover minor hockey, which come down from the governing body for the game, Hockey Canada.

Although the rules are currently subject to reform and Hockey Canada is finding itself under pressure to give players more choices over where they will play, they basically state that a player must play AAA hockey either in the town in which he resides or in the nearest geographical centre that offers AAA hockey.

That means if a player wants to play in a minor hockey association outside his jurisdiction, he must either secure a waiver from his home AAA organization and each AAA team between home and where he wants to play, or move with at least one parent to the other centre. The family must establish a residence in that city and the child must attend school there.

The minor hockey residency rules in Canada have been legally challenged a number of times and the courts have sided with Hockey Canada on each one. So when Ontario players Christopher Beauchamp of Penetanguishene and Mitchell Lebar of Aurora mounted their challenge to the Ontario Hockey Federation's residency rules in an effort to play for the Toronto Young Nationals minor bantam team in 2004, they did so by taking a very unique approach.

Instead of issuing a challenge to the residency rules founded on human rights legislation such as the Canadian Charter of Rights and Freedoms or Ontario's Human Rights Code, Beauchamp and Lebar argued—through prominent attorney Brian Greenspan—that minor hockey in Canada is a business enterprise and restricting their ability to choose where they could play was contrary to the provisions of the Discriminatory Business Practices Act and in violation of the United Nations' Convention on the Rights of the Child.

At the time, Lebar and Beauchamp were two of the top thirteen-year-old players in Ontario and were being recruited to play for the Toronto Young Nationals of the GTHL. Until that time, Beauchamp had played for the North Central Predators (based in Orillia) and Lebar for the York-Simcoe Express (in the Newmarket area).

Both teams were members of the Ontario Minor Hockey Association's Eastern AAA League—a league that has developed top players for several years, including Steven Stamkos, Corey Perry, Adam Foote, and Keith Primeau.

Both boys felt that moving to the GTHL would be better

for their development as players. In their statement of claim, Beauchamp and Lebar argued that by refusing them the chance to play for the team of their choice, "the respondents have improperly interfered with the parental right to determine what is in the best interest of their children. The respondents have interfered with Beauchamp's and Lebar's finite window of opportunity to develop their skills and have denied them the opportunity to maximize their potential."

During the trial, Greenspan compared residency rules to child labour laws in Great Britain in the 1820s and portrayed minor hockey as a business operated under the guise of a non-profit organization.

"These so-called not-for-profit clubs are being bought and sold for hundreds of thousands of dollars," Greenspan told the court. "AAA hockey in this province has become a business and people are in the business of producing a product and selling that product to the public. It looks like a business, it acts like a business and it operates like a business and it can't camouflage itself from being a business simply because it is incorporated under the Corporations Act as a not-for-profit entity. [Minor hockey associations] see themselves as protectors, but these protectors have a monopolistic control over elite hockey. This control is being exercised with unfettered discretion, without any rules, without any fairness, without any particular guidelines."

Greenspan eventually lost the case, but his argument has a lot of merit. Big money does rule minor hockey, and one of the most blatant examples of that is the Greater Toronto Hockey League. To be sure, Frank Smith, the seventeen-year-old goaltender who founded the Toronto Hockey League with a hundred players and five teams in 1912 would not even remotely recognize the monolith that his creation has become a century later.

Teams in the GTHL are non-profit, but owned by private individuals. One of them was Stuart Hyman, who at one point owned ninety-two teams in Toronto alone. He paid hundreds of thousands of dollars for some of the organizations he purchased, and in a number of them the costs were passed on to parents who saw their registration fees double and were faced with unexpected payments in the middle of the season.

"Some guys collect art and put it on the wall," Hyman told the *Toronto Star* in 2004. "I collect hockey clubs."

Hyman divested himself of most of his teams after an investigation by the *Star* and the GTHL tightened its rules concerning non-profit status and auditing. But there are still teams that pay coaches for positions that were once occupied by volunteers. The GTHL has major sponsorships with heavy-hitting companies such as Scotiabank and Canadian Tire.

Most AAA and AA organizations in the GTHL are privately operated. Of the twelve AAA organizations that exist in the league, only two have changed ownership since 2001. One was Hyman, who was essentially forced to sell. The other owner died.

And while they may be non-profit for the purposes of bookkeeping, huge money is involved. Most players who have played AAA hockey in Toronto have played under a coach who has been paid. Most have played on ice that has been marked up. Most have been forced to buy new equipment, jackets, and sweatsuits ordered by the team. Toronto is the only place in Canada where this happens.

Even though Greenspan was able to successfully point out to the court that the GTHL had revenues in excess of their expenses, that minor hockey associations have major sponsorship agreements, and that teams in the GTHL had been bought and sold for profit, the court ruled in favour of the Ontario Hockey Federation and, by extension, Hockey Canada. It declared that minor hockey associations in Canada are not engaged in business, largely because their primary goal was neither profit nor material gain.

"The residency rules have been put in place by the respondents based on what they believe best promotes the goal of providing opportunities for minor hockey players," Justice Guy DiTomaso wrote in his decision. "The courts have long held that it is not their role to get involved in running the affairs of non-profit organizations or athletic associations where they have acted in good faith, lawfully and in accordance with natural justice."

The presiding judge even went so far as to say that he "accept[s] and understand[s]" that the parents of Lebar and Beauchamp believed playing for the Young Nationals was in their children's best interests, but it was not for the court to determine what the best interests of the children were. And he made it clear that the residency rules governing minor hockey in Canada were necessary for the good of the game.

"In this case, the 'best interests' of Beauchamp, Lebar and their respective families must be considered within the context of what is best for thousands of other children and their families who participate in minor hockey in Ontario governed by the respondent hockey organizations under well established rules," the judge ruled. "I find that the 'best interests' of Beauchamp and Lebar do not trump or override the residency rules."

In addition, Justice DiTomaso awarded costs to the respondents, meaning Lebar, Beauchamp, and the Young Nationals had to pay not only for the services of one of the most expensive and high-profile litigators in Canada, but also for those of the party they were taking to court. "As you can imagine, when you get down the line that far, the costs are pretty significant," said Thane Campbell, an NHL player agent who at the time was one of the lawyers for the respondents. "It was well north of $100,000."

Beauchamp ended up playing the next season for the Young Nationals anyway. But instead of living at home and driving ninety minutes one way for every game and practice, he moved to an apartment in Toronto for his first year of high school to play with the Young Nationals.

His father, a registered nurse, and his mother, a volunteer coordinator at a mental health facility, kept their jobs and took turns staying in the apartment with their son so he would never be alone.

Beauchamp's father, Bill, had played in the OHL with future NHLers Brad Marsh and Rob Ramage in the 1970s and was playing in the Pittsburgh Penguins farm system until serious knee injuries in back-to-back years forced him to retire. Like his father, Beauchamp had his sights set on playing in the OHL, a dream he realized when he was drafted forty-fifth overall by the Brampton Battalion in 2007.

Beauchamp thought playing in the GTHL would give him the best chance to be drafted by an OHL team, but ironically he left the GTHL after one year and was drafted largely because of his performance while playing minor midget hockey for the OMHA's Eastern AAA Barrie Jr. Colts, which is an hour north of Toronto.

"There was always talk about the GTHL and all the great players who come out of there," Beauchamp said. "But if I were to do it again, I don't think with all the trouble I went through, I probably wouldn't do that. You play against GTHL guys in tournaments and you say, 'Oh gee, look at them,' but we had a great team here at home anyways. I don't think I would do it again."

Beauchamp did end up playing in the OHL, albeit sparingly. In his first season with Brampton, he spent most of the year playing for their Jr. A affiliate (the OJHL Brampton Capitals) and was dealt to the Sarnia Sting early in his second season, which was 2008–09. Despite what he thought was a good playoff, two days before the home opener the next season he was dropped by the Sting; he jumped to the Quebec League Rouyn-Noranda Huskies for a brief stint before finishing his career again playing Jr. A hockey, this time for the Trenton Golden Hawks of the OJHL.

These days, he's a special constable with the Midland Police Department after being hired at the tender age of nineteen.

It looks as though Lebar won't realize the NHL dream, either. He was drafted in the first round, seventeenth overall by the Barrie Colts in 2007 and bounced around the OHL for four years, finishing his career with the Kingston Frontenacs before going on to play for the varsity team at Wilfrid Laurier University in Waterloo, Ontario.

Despite his high selection, Lebar never established himself as an impact player in the OHL, with his best season coming in 2009–10 when he scored seventeen goals and thirty-nine points for the Frontenacs.

About four hours into their trip from Pennsylvania to Canada—somewhere around Buffalo, Max Strang reckons—his father received a call on his cell phone. It was the coach of the Toronto Red Wings peewee team calling. More precisely, it was the former coach. He had just been fired by the organization and was calling to inform them that the commitment he'd made to Scott Strang's son for a goaltending spot on the team was being withdrawn.

By this time, Scott had already sold his stake in a successful medical market research business he had built from the ground up. His wife, Shirley, a corporate travel agent, would spend the first year travelling from Pennsylvania to Toronto before quitting her job to join them permanently. Scott had also sold the family home, and the twenty-eight-foot sailboat that was going to be their fixed address for the foreseeable future was already well on its way to the Port Credit Harbour Marina just west of Toronto.

Scott turned to his twelve-year-old son and asked him what he wanted to do. Max Strang told his father to keep pressing on, that everything would work out and he'd find a team that would want him.

And thus began a three-year stint in which Strang, his parents, and the family dog lived on a sailboat in the harbour, and Scott and Shirley spent their life savings in order to give their son a chance to play in the GTHL.

For three winters and three summers they lived on the boat and Max played for three teams: the Brampton Jr. Battalion of the OMHA's South Central AAA League; the Don Mills Flyers of the GTHL; and, in his last season of 2004–05, a Markham Islanders GTHL minor midget team that included a very raw but talented defenceman by the name of P.K. Subban.

Life was difficult at times, but it was also exhilarating. During the winter when the Lake Ontario water in the harbour turned to ice, Max and his new friends would play outdoor hockey for hours when they weren't at the rink practising with their team. Max was home-schooled on the boat and managed to finish his high school equivalency by the time he was fifteen with a grade point average of 3.8 (out of 4.0).

Outside testing revealed he was an exemplary student, one who would have easily made the honour roll had he attended a traditional school, and academically gifted enough to receive an academic scholarship at a school with high standards.

On the ice there were obstacles, but for the most part it was positive. Even though he bounced from team to team each season, Max revelled in being immersed in a culture where hockey is an almost maniacal obsession.

His skills were improved to be sure, but he also learned the dedication it takes to become an elite player at the AAA level. Even though he has played in front of as many as 8,000 fans in a U.S. college game, for Strang it has never equalled the atmosphere at the tiny arena in suburban Toronto when his Markham Islanders team defeated a squad led by future NHLers John Tavares and Sam Gagner in the championship final of the Toronto Marlboros Christmas tournament.

"Back home, the nearest arena was thirty minutes away," Max said. "There's not a lot of good players, there's not a lot of good skill coaches. The whole atmosphere is all wrong. There's no TSN with thirty minutes of continuous hockey coverage and two minutes of basketball. It's just not the same, it's special and I really do miss that."

Special, but with a number of challenges. Life on the boat was not easy. The Strangs thought Max would be playing in Toronto for at least three years, and neither Scott nor Shirley was able to work in Canada because they were here on visitors' permits. With no money coming in and thousands going out so their son could play elite hockey, the family needed to keep costs down. And there was no better way to do that than to live on the sailboat Scott had spent five years building from a hull, where they could keep their living expenses down to about $450 per month, a fraction of what they would have had to pay in rent for an apartment or a house in Toronto. (The boat was 28 feet long by 10 feet wide, but Scott points out that since it was tapered at both ends the family somehow managed to survive with about 150 square feet of living space.)

But in exchange for the low rent came a lot of inconveniences. There were times on particularly cold days when the water would freeze up against the side of the boat and had to be chipped away with an ice pick. To do that, Scott would tie Max to the dock and have him hanging over the boat, with others ready to pull him out of the water if he fell in once the ice cracked. They had racks installed in their van where they would hang Max's wet hockey equipment after games and practices. During the winter the equipment wouldn't dry, and sometimes would even freeze solid, which forced Max and Scott to air-dry it under the blow dryers at the marina.

Scott said because quarters were so cramped, the family also had to adopt a "no-look policy" when it came to changing clothes. "We had a toilet but we only went No. 1 in it," Max said. "If you had to do anything else, you had to walk 300 yards up to the marina washroom. And we had to shower in the public showers in the marina."

After playing in the GTHL and being selected 252nd overall by the Ottawa 67's in the 2005 OHL Priority Selection, Max moved on to the United States Jr. Hockey League (USHL) to play for a team called the Green Bay Gamblers—an appropriate name given the gamble he and his parents made to play in Ontario—and his parents moved there with him. This time, they took an apartment instead of living on a boat.

But it was then that Max started to experience problems with his knee. It wasn't long before he dropped off the radar of the big schools with high-profile hockey programs. In fact, he didn't even secure a full scholarship at Mercyhurst, an upstart program playing in the Atlantic Hockey Conference. It's still Division I hockey, but the Atlantic Conference isn't on par with larger conferences such as the Western and Central Collegiate Hockey Associations, Hockey East, or the newly formed Big 10. And to be sure, the schools in that conference don't produce the same number of NHL players as the others.

So did the "investment" pay off? One thing is for certain: hockey isn't Max's ticket to university. In fact, Max is receiving more in academic scholarship money than in athletic scholarship money. His enrolment in intelligence analysis and Russian studies indicates he almost certainly has a brighter future in the Pentagon than the NHL. Maybe it wasn't the GTHL hockey that got Max started in life—maybe it was the home-schooling.

Strang blew out his knee in his first game as a freshman at Mercyhurst and was "red-shirted"—a process in which his freshman season was essentially taken off the books. He has had four surgical procedures done on his knee and as of the 2011–12 season had two years of college eligibility remaining and was hoping to earn the No. 1 goaltending job with his college team for the first time in his career. To that point, he had played only ten games as a varsity goalie in three years.

Meanwhile, the decision to head to Canada in search of elite hockey may look shortsighted in retrospect. From Max's birth year of 1989, there were four players drafted—James Van Riemsdyk, Eric Tangradi, Kevin Shattenkirk, and Colby Cohen—who originated from within ninety minutes of his hometown of Gilbertsville. In fact, the 1989 birth year was one of the strongest ever for players from that area. It may well be that Strang's enormous life decision did absolutely nothing for his hockey career.

Max's parents are still paying a price for what Scott calls a family adventure that was based around his son's hockey dreams. When Scott returned to the United States, he was in his fifties and found returning to a competitive job market in a recessed economy much more difficult than he had anticipated. He and his wife have since separated—largely, Scott said, because of her desire to move back east and his to live on the water.

He still lives on the boat by himself in Kenosha, Wisconsin, and works for a yacht-building company, while Shirley lives in Pennsylvania and has returned to working as a corporate travel agent.

"By the time we came back, I didn't have to deal with it because I was a kid, but I know we were in some financial trouble as a family," Max said. "I'm not really sure how my parents made the finances work, but I'm pretty sure we borrowed some money from my grandparents."

Both Scott and Max have a remarkably optimistic outlook on the situation, though. For the Strangs, it was more about the journey than the destination and they point out that if everyone always knew what lay ahead of them, nobody would ever be courageous enough to make a leap of faith like they did.

And as far as Scott is concerned, the cost of the adventure was far less than the cost of *not* doing it.

"The biggest factor was we never wanted to live with regret," Scott said. "We never wanted to regret the fact that we didn't allow Max the opportunity to pursue his dream. And little things like selling your business, selling your home, moving onto a boat, living a different lifestyle, those are relatively small things when you consider that the alternative is you and/or your son regret not having done it.

"The world is full of kids who, in one way or another, may have some animosity toward their parents because their parents held them back or didn't encourage their dreams. And we never wanted to be those parents."

There's holding kids back and there's not encouraging their dreams. We get that. But then there's quitting your job, selling your house, and living on a boat for three years so the child can pursue them. Surely there's some middle ground here, isn't there?

Max said that even if the game "tells me to get the hell out" after he finishes his collegiate career, he will never regret living on a boat in a harbour for three years while he played minor hockey in Toronto.

"I can say I've chased the dream," Scott said, "which is a lot more than a lot of people can say."

Sitting in a Tim Hortons on a lovely Sunday summer morning, Carlo Cimetta tried to explain his philosophy on life: You can tell how someone lives his life by looking at the state of his backyard. Not that Carlo has a problem with shabby backyards. It's when the expectation level is here—one hand elevated above his head—and the commitment level is here—the other down around his waist—that he has a problem with people.

He is also guided by the example of his father, who came to Canada from Italy in 1951 and got work in a foundry in Sarnia. The main staple of this foundry's business was making engine blocks for American Motors. This was long before the era of environmental consciousness and before the employees showered at work after their shift, so his father would always come home black with dirt and soot. The smell of the foundry has been indelibly etched in his memory.

Cimetta's father had the equivalent to a Grade 2 education, but his dream was to give his children the best education they could get. He paid Cimetta's way through university and law school and did the same for his daughter, who went to university and teachers college.

"If I do for my kids what my dad did for me, based on what he had to work with versus what I had to work with, I'll have done a good job," Cimetta said. "But if I don't, shame on me."

And that quest to give his children the best started early in life. In Matthew's second year of house league, when he was just six, Cimetta would drive an hour to London once a week so his son could have power skating instruction. But that was child's play compared to what would come later. Carlo Cimetta got involved in coaching his son's teams early in his minor hockey career, and Matthew showed promise as a AAA player with the Lambton Jr. Sting atom team in the Ontario Minor Hockey Alliance Pavilion League. But Carlo Cimetta found that the expectations of the parents involved in hockey in Sarnia didn't exactly mesh with his.

"Half of the people bought in, but some are just inside that box. I would say, 'Guys, why do you want to aspire for great things and you're not prepared to give of yourself?'" he said. "I had parents say to me, 'Well, you didn't expect to win, did you?'

"Damn right I did. That's why we're working our asses off. Just because we're from Sarnia we don't have to have some preconceived notion we're not good enough, that we will fall short because we're this and we're that.

"Bullshit! People want to talk about great things, but are you there when it comes to doing what needs to be done? I don't want to be one of those guys. I don't want to be a dreamer."

In the summer of 2005, Carlo Cimetta found in Toronto a bunch of people who thought the same way he did when he brought his son to a hockey camp run by Pro Hockey Development.

We met this organization in a previous chapter. Run by Jim Hofford, Pro Hockey Development puts together a super-elite team for the annual Brick Tournament held in Edmonton each summer, which features the best all-star teams of ten- and eleven-year-old players in North America. It was on that team that Cimetta met and played with several players from the Toronto Red Wings. It was also there that the seeds for his participation with the Red Wings were sown.

Cimetta first had to receive his OHF AAA waiver from his home AAA hockey association (Lambton), which proved to be easy. But in order to play for the Red Wings, he also had to secure a waiver as well from every minor hockey association with a AAA program between Sarnia and Toronto—and there were thirteen of them.

Bo Horvat from the nearby town of Rodney joined Cimetta on the Red Wings, and their year of travelling to Toronto began. The weekend would typically begin on Friday afternoon, when Cimetta would take Matthew out of school a half-hour early. They would then begin their trip to Toronto, usually picking up Bo Horvat along the way.

They'd arrive by about 4:30 at a hotel in the west end of Toronto where they were able to secure a rate of $89 per night including parking, have a quick snack, and head to the rink to be there at 6 P.M. for a 7:30 game. The game would end about 9:15; they'd go for dinner and go to bed.

Practice would be Saturday afternoon before playing another league game Sunday afternoon or early evening. Depending upon how late the game was and the location, they would arrive back home in Sarnia anytime between early evening and midnight.

That's a long way to go for a couple of ten-year-old kids.

And every Wednesday, Horvat's father, Tim, would drive his son to the Germain Arena in Sarnia, where the ice was rented for $125 for the hour. There, he and Cimetta, who also served as an assistant coach with the Red Wings, would put the two boys through all the drills and skill work they would have experienced if they had been practising with their teammates in Toronto.

The Red Wings were a powerhouse that season, winning both the GTHL and Ontario titles—and Matthew Cimetta, who was an assistant captain of the team, enjoyed a banner year. But the team that Cimetta left to join the Red Wings, the Lambton Jr. Sting, also won its league championship and advanced to the all-Ontario final along with the Red Wings. Clearly, with or without Matthew Cimetta, the Jr. Sting team was good enough and dedicated enough to win a league championship. The same group of boys that would occasion-ally give up a hockey practice to go to a birthday party found a pretty good level of success themselves. Meanwhile, that season saw the Red Wings go through a marathon playoff final, splitting the first two games in the GTHL best-of-seven final and tying the next five, forcing an unprecedented eighth game that went to overtime before the Red Wings won. But Carlo Cimetta found the travel to be too much to endure, and not wanting to move his son to Toronto, decided to return to Sarnia.

A year later, the Cimettas were approached by the Honeybaked organization about playing for them. Along with Little Caesars and Compuware, Honeybaked is one of the pre-eminent minor hockey associations in Michigan and has produced a number of NHL players, including future NHLers Ryan Kesler, David Booth, Drew Miller, Jim Slater, T.J. Hensick, and Chris Connor. Matthew had been playing summer hockey with a number of the Honeybaked players since he was young and had attended power skating and stickhandling schools in the Detroit area.

Once again, Cimetta was faced with the monumental task of making this opportunity work without sending his son off to live with someone else. So he came up with the idea to rent a home in Port Huron, which is just on the Michigan side of the Bluewater Bridge from Sarnia. That qualified Matt to play for a team in USA Hockey's jurisdiction and kept his family close enough together that they could see each other on his free nights of Tuesday and Thursday. Carlo lived across the river with his son in Port Huron and went back and forth to work in Sarnia, while his wife, Teresa, stayed with the couple's two daughters in Sarnia. They would get together for dinner twice a week at the home in Port Huron and travel to hockey games and tournaments together on the weekends.

Then there was the matter of getting Matthew to games and practices in Hazel Park, which was an hour from Port Huron. Honeybaked either practised or played five days a week, so that was a major challenge. Cimetta would pick his son up at the private Catholic school he attended and take him to practice, with Matthew finishing up his homework on the way. Practice was 6:00 to 7:30 and was followed by dryland training, meaning Matthew would get home and collapse into bed by about 10 P.M. before rising at 7:20 the next morning to do it all over again.

And as was the case with the Red Wings, Honeybaked was enormously successful. They won a number of tournaments over the next two years, including the Quebec International Peewee Tournament and an international tournament in Sweden. Once Matthew entered high school, though, the thought of continuing the arrangement for another four years proved to be too daunting and the Cimettas returned to Sarnia once again to finish Matthew's minor hockey career.

"I know what the optics might look like, might sound like," said Cimetta, a corporate lawyer who specializes in the buying and selling of businesses. "But we're not stereotypical fanatics who are one-dimensional, who are obsessed with some pursuit of some dream. That's not us. We're the furthest thing from that. I'm not one of these guys who is saying, 'My kid will beat the odds.' I'm a realist. I get it."

And if the frenetic pace of his minor hockey career took a toll on Matthew, you wouldn't know it. He made a verbal commitment to Cornell when he was just fifteen and was carrying an academic average of 95 percent in high school. He volunteered with charities in both Port Huron and Sarnia, ran track and field, was on the *Reach for the Top* team in high school, and in the eighth grade won first place in a Knights of Columbus essay contest with a piece titled "The Responsibility of a Catholic Citizen in a Free Society."

Who knows how Matthew Cimetta the player and the person will ultimately turn out? His father believes, though, that the character traits his son has displayed through his teenage years can be directly tied to his experiences playing minor hockey and making the sacrifices he made to do it starting at the age of ten.

"We weren't looking to enhance his career, we were looking to maximize his experience," Carlo Cimetta said. "We thought it would be demanding, we thought it would be an invaluable experience to take on this challenge and to teach him that with higher ground comes higher responsibility."

You just have to wonder if Matthew Cimetta, a young man of high moral fibre and character, wouldn't have picked up the same lessons had he stayed and played with his peers at home instead of spending countless hours on the highway and two years of high school in another country.

Despite the fact Cimetta likely would have been a fifth-round pick in the OHL draft in 2011 and there was a chance his hometown Sarnia Sting would have taken him earlier, Cimetta made it very clear that the plan for Matthew, at least for the time being, was to take advantage of his commitment to Cornell University, where he'll be able to register for the 2013–14 season. In the end the Sting waited until the eighth round to take him.

That's not the end of the world for a young player. What we've found in our research over the past thirty years is that about a third (31 percent) of the players who play a game in the NHL were selected after the third round of their CHL draft year. That is, one in three players who go on to careers in the NHL were not considered as top prospects after their bantam (age fourteen) or minor midget (age fifteen) seasons. That's good news for a kid who goes lower in the draft. But it also poses a challenge for all those kids and parents who give up so much in the hope of being picked higher. Not only does being a high pick not guarantee anything—it doesn't even mean much.

And if a scholarship were the end game, there's a pretty good chance Cimetta would not have stood for his son choosing Cornell, an Ivy League school with some of the highest tuition fees in the country and one that offers financial aid, not athletic scholarships, to those who qualify. Undoubtedly, having his son attend Cornell is going to cost him money, but not near as much as the hundreds of thousands he spent to help him get there.

So Cimetta won't play major junior, and his family's investment won't be paid back in the form of an education. So what exactly did all that sacrifice accomplish?

Both Cimetta and his old teammate and travelling companion Bo Horvat eventually returned home to Lambton and Elgin to finish out their careers. And both ended up being scouted and picked in the OHL draft several years later. In fact, that "inferior" Lambton Jr. Sting team that Cimetta said wasn't committed enough in atom hockey five years earlier included London Knights fourth-round pick Corey Pawley, who ended up being drafted higher and rated higher in his OHL draft year than Cimetta. The "inferior" Elgin-Middlesex Chiefs team that Horvat left home for eventually had nine other players selected in the OHL draft as well.

Natalie Zucker clearly remembers the day her son Evan left home. He was thirteen years old. He had travelled from his home in Las Vegas to Spokane to try out for a AAA peewee team there, and when he found out he had made the team there wasn't enough time for him to come back and gather his things before the season started. Evan remembers making billeting arrangements with the player in front of him in line. It was eight months before he would return to Las Vegas for the first time.

"He had actually only packed two days' worth of clothes," Natalie recalled, "and then they said they didn't want to send him home and I had to pack up his room and ship it to him. It was like he had died."

As difficult as it was for Natalie Zucker to let go, she knew she could not hold her son back from chasing the dream of playing in the NHL. Evan had started as an in-line hockey player and had become the best by far in Las Vegas, but the highest level he could play in the desert was Peewee A. In order to get better, he either had to go northwest or to the east coast. As difficult as it was, Natalie Zucker had a point of reference. Just when she was beginning to show promise as a competitive figure skater in her teens, her mother moved the family from Los Angeles to Oregon and there was no rink in their new city, so she had to stop skating.

"My mom regretted that every single day," she said.

That was the guiding principle for the Zuckers in allowing two of their five children to leave to pursue their hockey dreams before they were even old enough to have pimples. Evan left at the age of thirteen and his younger brother, Jason, essentially left home at ten to play for a AAA team in Los Angeles five days a week.

And while their boyhood choices were similar, things could not have turned out more differently for the brothers in terms of their hockey fortunes. Ravaged by shoulder injuries that he refused to allow to heal properly, Evan was forced out of the elite level of the game by his late teens and now can't raise his arms above his head without experiencing mind-numbing pain. Jason, on the other hand, landed a full scholarship at the University of Denver, was selected in the second round by the Minnesota Wild in 2010, and is an outstanding pro prospect. He has been a vital member of U.S. national teams that have won gold medals at the World Under-18 and World Junior Championships, and as a three-time member of the U.S.

national World Junior team he was captain of the American entry for the 2012 WJC in Alberta.

So Scott and Natalie Zucker have seen both sides of the dream. They remortgaged their home to allow Evan to play in Spokane and Colorado through his peewee and bantam years, yet did not allow his setbacks to deter them from making the same sacrifices for Jason, whose hockey travels have taken him from Las Vegas to Los Angeles, to Detroit, to Ann Arbor, to Denver in a few short years.

"What made us do it?" said Scott Zucker, who works as a construction project director for a major casino chain in Las Vegas. "It's dedication to our kids, wanting them to have everything we can possibly afford. I can't skate for them, but I can certainly give them the tools and talk to them and coax them along to help them succeed."

Like Matthew Cimetta, Jason Zucker received his break from participating in the Brick Tournament in Edmonton, only with a Los Angeles–based team comprising elite players from all over California. That led to a spot with the Los Angeles Hockey Club and a weekly regimen that would be difficult for a person twice his age.

Every Thursday night at 7 P.M., ten-year-old Jason would get on the Southwest Airlines flight for Los Angeles unaccompanied and arrive at his destination an hour later. His coach with the Los Angeles team would pick him up at the airport and he would stay at a teammate's house, a different one every weekend. The team would play games on Friday and Saturday and practise on Monday and Tuesday. After practice on Tuesday, Jason would spend Wednesday and most of Thursday with his family while completing his online classes. Then on Thursday night he would get back on the plane bound for LAX and do it all over again.

"Obviously, I didn't live a normal childhood," Jason said, "but I'm not a normal kid."

Neither was his brother Evan, whose talent level and passion for the game was renowned on the west coast of the United States. It was in Spokane that he was seduced by the opportunity to play in the WHL—and that, more than anything, might have been the reason why his career was derailed and Jason's flourished. In Spokane, Evan was inundated with ideas that the WHL, and not the U.S. college system, represented his best chance to play in the NHL someday. This prompted him to join the Spokane Braves Jr. B team, which was the only American team in the British Columbia–based Kootenay International Junior Hockey League. It was there that he began to have shoulder problems, and instead of having them looked at Evan insisted on playing—because he didn't want to be perceived as being weak, and he was desperate to prove himself to the WHL scouts who scour that league looking for major junior talent.

By his own estimation, Evan broke his collarbone seven times in one season and never allowed it to heal properly. He tore a joint in his left shoulder, chipped his rotator cuff in his right shoulder, and, in an injury that is as painful as it sounds, tore all the tendons off his breastplate on his right side.

"Evan was an absolute lunatic," Natalie said. "And I don't think he had the right coaches. They had the mentality of, 'You dislocate your shoulder and you're back out in the game in five minutes.' It didn't matter if you had broken your face, as long as your arm wasn't cut off, you were out there no matter what. He didn't care how much pain he was in, he wanted to play anyway."

As unfair as it might have been for him, Evan Zucker was the stalking horse for his younger brother. All the lessons they learned the hard way with Evan were applied to how they handled Jason. The first of those lessons was to steer him away from playing major junior hockey and more toward the college ranks. By the time Jason was fourteen he was on the move to Detroit, in part for the quality of the hockey and in part for the exposure to college scouts and the U.S. National Development Team Program, which hothouses the best sixteen- and seventeen-year-old American players in Ann Arbor, Michigan. Much of the success the Americans are experiencing in international hockey these days can be directly tied to their under-17 and under-18 teams.

Jason played two seasons for the Compuware program and excelled in an environment where hockey was a priority. The Compuware organization, one of the top in Michigan, was founded and is owned by Peter Karmanos, who also owns the Carolina Hurricanes and the Plymouth Whalers of the OHL. Compuware's program, like other top teams in the Detroit area, plays for keeps—it's run almost pro-style and its home base in Plymouth has all the amenities of an NHL team. The elite competition in Michigan is intense, all the more so considering the rival Little Caesars were established and are owned by Detroit Red Wings owner Mike Ilitch, with whom Karmanos has a long-standing rivalry.

But even there, Zucker faced challenges. He billeted with the family of teammate Jared Knight, a second-round pick of the Boston Bruins in 2010, in Battle Creek, which was about eighty minutes from Plymouth by car. But the hockey was better than anything to which Jason had ever been exposed, and he excelled. And his plan to be seen by as many hockey people as possible worked out perfectly—as a sixteen-year-old he was offered a coveted spot on the under-17 team with the USNDTP, which has led to international hockey opportunities and a full scholarship at Denver.

The way Scott and Natalie Zucker see it, all their sacrifices have paid off tenfold. They have opened doors for their children that caused them to live well beyond their means, but that is no longer the case. In fact, their desire to do the best by their children prompted Scott to build a 35-by-75-foot in-line rink in the backyard where Jason can hone his puck skills in the summer months and the other brothers can play whenever they wish.

It looks very much as though Jason Zucker will end up with the NHL career he and his brother grew up dreaming about. And Evan? Evan is now a low-voltage technician who runs a company that services the electrical needs of casinos in Las Vegas. Two stories of sacrifice and hard work: one brother with a real shot; the other living a good life of his own, but far from the rinks of the NHL. The lesson here is not that college is a better route to the big league than junior hockey—as we know, junior players are actually much more likely to make it. The lesson here is that while all that sacrifice may be necessary to fuel an NHL-sized dream, it's not nearly enough.

Not that Jason is complaining. Like his brother, he attributes his success to the life lessons he learned and maturity he gained from being separated from his parents at such a young age.

"The position I'm in right this second, I wouldn't trade for anything," Jason said. "If somebody said to me right now, 'Well, you could run a major corporation and be a billionaire,' I would rather be in the situation I'm in right now because I love doing what I'm doing. It's tough not being able to live a normal life, but it's something I needed to do."

It was mid-December of 2004 and Jarred Seymour was skating on the outdoor rink at Nathan Phillips Square in downtown Toronto with an ear-to-ear grin on his face. He had just been offered a spot on the defence corps of the Toronto Marlboros AAA team for the next season. He'd been hoping he might catch on with a house league team in Toronto when he first arrived.

That hardly made him an anomaly. After all, when you shake a tree in Canada, there's a good chance a number of gangly fourteen-year-old kids with dreams of making the NHL will fall out of it.

But how many of those kids would be from Sydney, Australia? How many of them would have fallen in love with hockey by watching *The Mighty Ducks?*—the movie, not the team. How many of them would have made the 16,000-kilometre trek from their home to a foreign land to chase the dream?

But that's exactly what young Jarred and his mother Tereise did in 2005. Six years later, Tereise Seymour was telling her story over lunch. The dream, in fact, had just recently died for her son when he was told there was no longer a spot for him on the hockey team at Cornell University. But on the flip side, Tereise and her son fell so in love with Canada that they decided to settle here. Tereise had met and married a Canadian man and planned to pursue citizenship, while Jarred was excelling in his studies at Cornell.

"It turned out to be a different dream," she said. "It has been a wonderful experience and there aren't any better places in the world to come and fulfill a dream than Canada. People can achieve so much here. It's limitless what you can do."

There are limits, however, to how far a hockey player can go, particularly one who hadn't received any elite coaching or faced challenging competition until he was fifteen years old.

When Jarred played in Australia, his mother compared him to the Pied Piper of Hamelin—the other players came up to Jarred's chest, and when he'd get the puck he would carry it around the ice and the other players would simply follow him. Both knew that if he was going to improve his game, he needed to move to Canada. Think of a beach volleyball player coming from Nunavut and you get an idea of how unlikely it was that a top prospect would ever emerge from Australia.

But when Jarred and his mother came looking for a team in Toronto in November 2004, they had no idea how things would unfold. As it turned out, Jarred had enough talent to be offered a spot—on merit, by the way—as a defenceman with the Marlies minor midget team, one of the top ten teams in Ontario.

Players come from all over North America to play in the GTHL and residency rules require them to do some pretty extreme things for the privilege. The next July Tereise and Jarred returned to Toronto to stay. Tereise immediately bought a house and enrolled her son in a private liberal arts high school.

A self-made millionaire who owned and operated a company that makes stainless steel pipes for many of the large food and beverage companies in Australia, Tereise was able to afford the luxury of running her business from the other side of the world so her son could play hockey. (She has since sold her business, and now that her son is in university plans to spend the harsh Canadian winters with her husband back home in Australia.)

It turned out Jarred Seymour was good enough to play with the Marlies and enjoyed a decent run with a Jr. A team in nearby Stouffville. And other hockey people saw the potential as well. He was drafted in the third round by the Ottawa 67's and had secured a family adviser to help him wade through the options of major junior hockey versus the OHL.

He didn't make the 67's, but was able to keep his U.S. college eligibility and managed to secure a spot with Cornell. But the hitch was that, despite being a hockey player, Jarred would have to pay his own way through university because he was turned down for financial aid. That meant a yearly bill of over $55,000, on top of the more than $10,000 his mother spent when he played for the Marlies and the tuition at his private school.

"To be honest, I wouldn't have been able to do it if I hadn't had the business and being very canny with my money because I couldn't work when I first came over here," she said. "And I wanted to pay my own way and not rely on the Canadian system. That cost me a lot of money and I don't regret it at all. It means I can open my mouth and tell people to take a running hike because I paid my own way."

Her son paid his dues as well, the same way any young

Canadian player would. After playing for the Marlies and at the Jr. A level, he earned a spot on the Cornell roster for the 2009–10 season.

But during a scrimmage in August he was slashed across his wrist and it broke in two places, requiring surgery. In fact, one specialist he saw told him he might never be able to play again. After consulting with the medical staff at Cornell, he saw a specialist in Syracuse who operated on the wrist and he was back on his skates in December. But by that time the season was already well underway and the roster had been set, so he asked to be red-shirted for the season.

Even when he was healthy the next season, it was just as difficult for him to establish himself. He played just one game on the varsity team before being told by Cornell coach Mike Schaefer that there was no spot on the roster for him. After that, his hockey was limited to scrimmaging with some of the security guards at Cornell who had seen him play.

Seymour's is a story that is all too common in university hockey in the United States. Players go there thinking their future is set for the next four years, but what few of them realize is that their spot—and, in many cases, scholarship—can be revoked at any time for any reason. (More on that in the next chapter.)

"You've got to kiss the coach's bloomin' ass because he has all the power," Tereise Seymour said. "I swear if Schaefer walked in front of me, I would run him down with my SUV if I could get away with it. He plays god more than God would play god. It annoys you."

Jarred Seymour, meanwhile, stayed at Cornell to pursue a business degree with an eye toward a career in financial planning, one he plans to pursue as a Canadian citizen. Tereise Seymour gave herself three years in Toronto and planned to return to running her business in Australia, but as she saw with her son's hockey career, plans change. She spent hundreds of thousands of dollars to chase a dream that didn't even result in a scholarship, but Tereise Seymour doesn't see herself as being much different than a lot of Canadian parents whose children play hockey.

"The boys chase their dream until they become not very viable and the parents just keep paying," she said. "That's what we do as parents. But I think when they get to twenty-one, they can start looking after themselves. I would have loved to have stopped paying for him at sixteen."

7

JUNIOR V. COLLEGE

If Joshua Ho-Sang hadn't been born in 1996, NHL commissioner Gary Bettman might have tried to invent him. The son of a Jamaican-born tennis pro and a Jewish nutritionist originally from Chile, Ho-Sang got his surname from his great-grandfather, who was born in Hong Kong. Imagine the marketing possibilities. His father, Wayne, bears an uncanny resemblance to Bob Marley, and Joshua is a gazelle on skates with speed so intense that his sweater luffs like a sail in its slipstream when he gets to his top gear. He is ebullient and celebrates goals with Alex Ovechkin–like zeal. And he has a penchant for on-ice flamboyance that, combined with his prodigious talent, makes it impossible for him not to be the centre of attention. During the championship game of a tournament involving his Toronto Marlboros team in early 2012, Ho-Sang slid across the ice on one knee à la Tim Tebow after scoring a goal on which he picked up the puck behind his net and stickhandled his way through the opposing team before powering his way to the goal. "Sometimes," his father, Wayne, said, "I think he can almost score whenever he wants to. He has always said, 'I don't want to be just another guy in the NHL. I want to be one of the guys, if not *the* guy in the NHL.'"

There are those who have watched the Greater Toronto Hockey League's minor midget league for decades who claim that Ho-Sang is the best they've ever seen at that level. And that's a group that includes the likes of John Tavares, Steven Stamkos, and Rick Nash. Ho-Sang was playing in 2011–12 at the minor midget level, the season in which the vast majority of players turn sixteen years old. It's a crucial year for them, since the next step for those who are good enough is major junior hockey. It can also be a confusing season full of stress and life-changing decisions. For many of the top players, it's also the year they're forced to decide whether they will pursue the option of playing major junior hockey and get on the fast track to the NHL or wait at least two years—since most are only in the tenth grade—to play U.S. college hockey. For Ho-Sang, the decision was already made years ago. His parents told him when he was nine years old that he could only play in the OHL if he was drafted in the first round. Otherwise, he'd have to play college hockey.

In the winter of 2011–12, Ho-Sang was one of the top prospects for the OHL draft, the annual exercise in which those who control major junior hockey in Ontario lord over more than 300 of the top sixteen-year-olds in Ontario and parts of the United States. It a process that's duplicated in both the Western Hockey League and the Quebec Major Junior Hockey League, the loops that run in tandem with the OHL to form a sixty-team behemoth known as the Canadian Hockey League, an entity that stretches from Cape Breton to Victoria and holds a virtual monopoly on the country's best teenaged hockey players.

For a number of years now, there have been examples of talented young players who have thumbed their noses at major junior hockey's draft rules. The most prodigious of them know that the leagues need them to sell tickets as much as they need the development opportunities junior hockey provides, so they dictate their terms. Many of them manipulate the process to get placed on teams where they can be closer to home or in situations they feel will be best for their development as a player. Some are more high-profile than others. Eric Lindros, for example, warned the Sault Ste. Marie Greyhounds not to draft him in 1989, but they did anyway and he refused to report to the team. The Greyhounds relented and dealt Lindros to the Oshawa Generals in exchange for three players, three draft picks, and $80,000. And now rarely a year goes by where at least one or two players don't "orchestrate" their selections by a specific team.

Apparently, Joshua Ho-Sang is not one of those players. From Grades 7 through 10, he attended the PEAC School for Elite Athletes in Toronto, where students are charged $15,000 a year in tuition fees alone for the privilege of being on the ice four more times a week and going to school with like-minded, driven, and affluent students whose athletic goals include scholarships and professional careers. An education and talent level like that would make Ho-Sang a shoo-in to attend any hockey-playing U.S. university he'd like, or at least give him an option that he could hold over the OHL to find himself the best landing spot.

Many players in that position would use their talent and

the fact they are being coveted both by junior hockey and the college system to dictate the terms of where they would play in the OHL. But that was never part of the plan for Ho-Sang, who went fifth overall to the Windsor Spitfires in the 2012 OHL Priority Selection. The way Ho-Sang has always viewed it, the prospect of playing hockey for at least two years for less than minimum wage is a minuscule sacrifice when it comes to the long-term benefits for his hockey career. That's why Ho-Sang is willing to play in a league that replicates the NHL in all but finances. Major junior players are paid, generally speaking, about $50 a week, which on a per-hour basis is less than their teenaged counterparts who are flipping burgers or working as summer camp counsellors for minimum wage. Still, it's a choice Ho-Sang is completely willing to make.

"He never talks about money. He just speaks about OHL, then NHL," Wayne Ho-Sang said. "He just wants to play hockey. That's all he's ever wanted to do. They can give him whatever they want, or nothing. He just wants to play hockey at the highest level. I think it's very humble, playing at the level he's playing at. Trust me, he knows he's a good player."

"I've probably thought about it since I was five," Joshua said. "I love playing hockey so much. Just to be doing what I love at the highest level that I can is my goal. It's all I want to do."

If that's the hold that major junior hockey has on a player such as Ho-Sang, one of the most dynamic on-ice players and charismatic personalities to come out of the Toronto ranks in years, think about how it might seduce the hundreds of other players who are chasing the dream and aren't nearly as talented or don't have Ho-Sang's options. If a player with

Joshua Ho-Sang's hockey talent and off-the-charts charisma isn't willing to take a stand, who will be?

In other words, when a kid like Ho-Sang is more than willing to sign on for years of indentured service, what might the players facing much longer odds be willing to pay? Some kids may be buying the dream, but far more are just renting it at this point in their careers, paying to hold on to something they will have to let go of soon enough.

Major junior hockey operators in this country sell the dream, perhaps more than anyone else involved in the game, because they sell it to the teenagers they employ, telling them it's the quickest and most important route to the NHL, and they sell it to their consumers. Be the first to see the future stars of the NHL while they're still pure and unjaded. And don't forget to stop by the tuck shop to pick up your big foam finger and a mini-stick.

It would be wrong to suggest that every major junior hockey operator in Canada is rolling in enormous amounts of money, although a good number of them certainly are. The thing with major junior hockey is it's a cyclical business model that performs financially based on the quality of the product on the ice, one that continually rolls over every couple of years. A team in the basement of the league might be a powerhouse within three years; conversely, a team that loads up for a Memorial Cup run often finds itself rebuilding one or two seasons after that. Generally speaking, but with a few exceptions, about one-third of the teams in the CHL make money, one-third break even, and one-third lose money—and those teams change almost on a year-to-year basis. There are some exceptions such as the London Knights, Quebec Remparts, and Vancouver Giants, but how the bottom line looks for each team in the gate-driven CHL depends on how many home dates it has in the playoffs.

But it would also be wrong to assume that money is not a paramount concern for each one of the CHL's sixty organizations. Some of them are run by community boards that are forced to watch every dollar, some others by civic-minded businesspeople who know having a junior team is good for the community but certainly aren't in the habit of losing gobs of money. "There are a lot of reasons why you buy a franchise," said OHL commissioner David Branch, who also serves as president of the CHL. "One of them is not to make money."

That's gilding the lily just a little. Not all junior owners are rolling in money, but they're not all hand-to-mouth paupers, either. Dale Hunter made just over $1 million in his last season in the NHL in 1998–99, which was also his most lucrative. Not long after, he and his brother Mark, also a former NHLer, along with former NHLer Basil McRae, bought the London Knights and the London Ice House for $3.8 million. Dale owns 75 percent of the team, while Mark owns 20 percent. In an effort to revitalize the downtown core, the City of London spent $52 million to construct the John Labatt Centre in 2002, which seats 9,090 for hockey games.

Construction giant EllisDon and leviathan arena management company Global Spectrum also have an ownership stake in the arena. Global Spectrum, which is part of the company that owns the Philadelphia Flyers, also owns Comcast SportsNet, Ovation Foods, New Era Tickets, and 3601 Creative Group, a full-service, in-house advertising agency. When the Knights were negotiating a lease with the John Labatt Centre, they used the Ice House as leverage, saying that if they didn't get a favourable deal they would continue playing in the Ice House. Global Spectrum, fearing it would have a building without an anchor tenant, gave the Knights a favourable lease and the Hunters sold the Ice House for about $1.8 million.

And if you do the math, they have been making gobs of money ever since. In 2010–11, the Knights averaged almost 9,000 people a game with an average ticket price of about $15. They played thirty-four regular season games and three home playoff games. (Which was a down year for them, considering they had averaged seven and a half home dates per playoff since their first playoff in the John Labatt Centre in 2003, and they hosted the Memorial Cup in 2005.) Based on those numbers, the Knights brought in almost $5 million in ticket revenue alone that season, along with getting a portion of concessions and rink-board advertising.

And what the cash-in, cash-out aspect of junior hockey doesn't take into account is that franchise values have risen dramatically in the past decade, even for the smaller franchises. For example, the late Ken Burgess purchased the Sudbury Wolves for $125,000 in 1986. They were a moribund, money-losing outfit that drew fewer than 2,000 a game and were known as one of the worst major junior hockey organizations in the country. To his credit, Burgess and his son Mark have built the organization into one that's very good on the ice and outstanding in its business model. They've poured $2 million into renovations to the Sudbury Arena and sponsor a number of minor hockey teams. The cash-in, cash-out performance varies, but little doubt exists that if Burgess were to sell his team he would get north of $5 million for it today.

The Knights, meanwhile, were recently valued between
$12 million and $14 million. In 1997, Hall of Fame goaltender Patrick Roy and two partners purchased the Beauport
Harfangs of the QMJHL for about $2 million and moved the
team to Quebec City to revive the iconic Quebec Remparts
franchise. In 2010–11, they averaged almost 11,000 fans a
game with an average ticket price of $15 in the Colisée, the
former home of the Quebec Nordiques. Andre Desmarais, the
co-CEO of Power Corporation, recently joined Roy and his
two partners, purchasing a 25 percent stake in the franchise
for $4 million, making the franchise worth $16 million.

"Have we hit the ceiling of franchise values?" Branch
said. "The business model does not support the value of the
franchises."

It clearly does in large markets or those with a devoted
fan base, but there are teams in the CHL for which survival
is a real challenge and meeting the operating costs of about
$3 million annually means they almost always lose money. In
fact, the CHL is not much unlike the NHL with respect to
the imbalances between the money-losing and money-making
franchises. One of those is the former Mississauga St. Michael's
Majors, a team that played in one of the biggest junior hockey
markets in Canada but still struggled mightily to get paying
fans. In 2010–11 the franchise was awarded the Memorial
Cup and was one of the top teams in the country, yet averaged
only 3,006 per game. Hoping to use the Memorial Cup as a
springboard, the Majors saw their attendance decline the next
season. One year after his team hosted the Memorial Cup
tournament, owner Eugene Melnyk essentially cut the organization down to the bare bones because he realized major

junior hockey was a money loser in that market; Melnyk sold the team in 2012 to local interests, who renamed it the Steelheads.

No organization has a greater hold on the best young players in Canada than the CHL. To be fair, the league has come a long way since the bad old days when junior hockey teams were essentially run by mini versions of Eddie Shore, the Hall of Fame defenceman for the Boston Bruins who operated the Springfield Indians of the American Hockey League and was notorious for treating pennies like they were manhole covers and holding the players' tenuous grip on their careers over them like a warlord. But as recently as 1999, former NHLer Bill Stewart was coaching the Barrie Colts and made headlines when he twice smuggled a Ukraine-born player over the Canada–U.S. border in the baggage compartment of the team bus.

But in large part, major junior hockey has become a professionally run entity. To prevent players from choosing the U.S. college ranks, the CHL has become much more focused on education and offers every player who goes on to post-secondary education a minimum financial package that helps cover some or all of the costs (more on that later). Their marketing and game presentation is much more sophisticated and leagues that were once havens for violence in the 1970s have become much more civilized. In fact, David Branch is one of the most progressive—and least tolerant—executives when it comes to dealing with on-ice violence. Branch has never shied away from meting out long suspensions, regularly giving out ten-game sentences for blows to the head, and has on a number of occasions suspended players (Marc

LaForge in 1987; Jesse Boulerice and Jeff Kugel in 1998) for the remainder of their junior careers. In 2012, Branch and the OHL announced stiff suspensions for players who get involved in more than ten fights in a season. Branch reasons that when parents send their teenagers so far away from home, they should expect a certain level of safety for them when they're on the ice.

If only that philosophy extended to all aspects of junior hockey. Teenage players can, and are, traded frequently and have been paid the same amount for the better part of the past two decades. In many ways, junior hockey has the same hold over young players as the tyrannical Shore did prior to the days of the formation of the NHL Players' Association. Young men such as Joshua Ho-Sang are selling tickets both for their home teams and on the road. Many of them go on to represent Canada in the World Junior Hockey Championship, which generates millions of dollars in revenues when it is held in Canada, but they receive poverty wages in return. And since the CHL bills itself as "the official supplier to the NHL," the options for players who have dreams of playing professional hockey are limited. Football, basketball, and baseball players are funnelled through the high school system and go to the university system in the United States, where they can choose among hundreds of schools. But in 2011–12, there were just fifty-seven schools that played hockey at the Division I level.

Junior hockey, meanwhile, has had a hold on Canadian players for more than a hundred years. In fact, the Ontario Hockey Association formed its first junior league for players under age twenty in 1896, and teams in Canadian junior hockey have been playing for the Memorial Cup since 1919.

Since then, junior hockey has become a rite of passage for the vast majority of Canadian-born players who have moved on to the professional ranks. While some former and current Canadian-born NHL stars played U.S. college hockey—such as Ken Dryden, Ed Belfour, Curtis Joseph, Paul Kariya, and Jonathan Toews—major junior hockey has almost always been the route of choice for Canadian players.

We've seen in previous chapters just how remote the chances are that a young man will play in the NHL, even after he has distinguished himself as one of the relative few that is good enough to play either major junior or college hockey. We also know that the road to either route is a difficult one that is reserved only for the truly elite teenagers of the world. Although it has happened in very rare circumstances—former NHLers Glen Metropolit and Steve Rucchin, to name two—it is almost unheard of for a young North American player to not apprentice in either major junior or U.S college hockey en route to the NHL. But with 60 CHL teams and 57 Division I teams in U.S. college hockey, that's just 117 teams—or just over 2,000 spots—for all the aspiring players in North America. History tells us that if you don't make it to one of those rungs, you might as well start planning your life without a career in hockey.

Neither route is lined with riches, relatively speaking, but each has its merits. For the players who are clearly special and so far ahead of their peers in terms of maturity and talent, pursuing major junior hockey is the quickest route to take to the NHL. Those whose hockey future isn't quite as certain and who are academically inclined might be better suited for the U.S. college route. But while the sense is that the CHL is something of a meat grinder and the NCAA with its paid education occupies a higher moral ground, the fact is both routes have their strengths and weaknesses.

And this is the first time in a player's career when the bottleneck really begins to tighten. At the age of sixteen, players who have aspirations of playing professional hockey are faced with the prospect of making a number of life-altering decisions. Do they decide to go all-in on a hockey career, knowing full well the singular dedication it takes to get to the NHL and the relatively minute chances of actually accomplishing the feat? What if they go the major junior route and turn down the opportunity to get a scholarship and things don't work out in junior hockey? Because the NCAA views major junior hockey as a professional league, players are not allowed to play college hockey after playing major junior.

For that reason, many players make verbal commitments to American universities, all the while knowing they can be broken at any time without consequences. But the time lapse between when they turn sixteen and qualify for major junior hockey and the minimum two years they'd have to wait to play college hockey is often too much to take, particularly for elite players who know they will be drafted by an NHL team when they turn eighteen. If they want to get to the NHL as quickly as possible, the best way for them to do it is to play major junior hockey right away. It results in college programs losing players constantly to the CHL, despite the fact they've already made a commitment to their programs. Because of that, the American universities are losing the hearts and minds of the best young Canadian players and, in many cases, their American counterparts.

But as former NHLer Steve Thomas points out, professional is a relative term. When he played with the Toronto Marlboros in the early 1980s, he was making $40 a week. Almost thirty years later, his son Christian plays for the Oshawa Generals and makes $50 a week, meaning the base salary for major junior players has gone up less than 1 percent a year over the past three decades. Go back to the London Knights and the Quebec Remparts. The great thing about owning those teams is that the standard player's contract in junior hockey doesn't allow them to—publicly, at least—pay their players any more than that even if they wanted to. (It is well known in junior hockey circles that some of the top players get extra money "under the table," but the vast majority of teenagers are paid the modest $50 stipend every seven days.)

"We're deemed by the NCAA to be professional to a certain extent," said the elder Thomas, now the player development coordinator with the Tampa Bay Lightning. "If you're going to be deemed professional, then let's be professional about it."

Nothing gets the back up of major junior operators more than the charge that they're complicit in child slave labour and are operating sweatshops on ice. But on the surface, the evidence looks damning. Teenage boys often having to play three games in three nights while enduring long bus trips and facing the prospect of possibly being traded for fifty bucks a week? In addition, players receive nothing when the league uses their likenesses in trading cards or video games. And since junior hockey is both transient and a crucial stepping stone to professional hockey, no agent or parent is about to get up on his or her hind legs to protest any aspect of it. There is no players' association the way there is for players in the NHL and the minor leagues, which gives operators something akin to omnipotent rule over their players. (In the fall of 2012 the loose formation of the proposed Canadian Hockey League Players' Association was announced, with former NHLer Georges Laraque appointed as its executive director. But the union quickly crumbled amid allegations that some of the people involved—not Laraque— were attempting to take advantage of the players they were supposed to be protecting.)

David Branch has been the OHL commissioner since 1979 and celebrated thirty-three years on the job in 2012. That's a long time, and even longer when you consider it's two years longer than Clarence Campbell ruled the NHL, three years more than Pete Rozelle presided over the National Football League, and five years more than David Stern has been at the National Basketball Association. Branch's authority is unchallenged in both the OHL and the CHL, but he prides himself on being a progressive thinker. And he is. Branch takes exception to the notion that junior hockey takes advantage of the dreams of teenagers, pointing out that players get much more than just $50 a week. He has worked hard to improve the overall benefits for players in junior hockey and speaks like a proud father about the education package players receive when they play junior hockey.

But there's a fair bit of justification in his words, too. One of the reasons, he says, junior hockey doesn't pay the players very much is that there's a concern young people would be walking around with too much money in their wallets. He also claims sports in North America has been built on people investing their time and effort to become Olympic athletes or professionals with few rewards until they hit the big time.

"If a young player can come into our league and doesn't play professionally, if he has his education paid for and along the way he's learned a lot of other things, I don't view it as exploitation," Branch said. "Others will view it as exploitation of young people, but I don't subscribe to that. We're not taking advantage of these young people in my view in any way, shape, or form. Absolutely not."

Branch points out that in addition to the $50 weekly sum, players receive room and board valued at $100 a week and every player who plays junior hockey has the opportunity to take advantage of a post-secondary education package that pays, at minimum, the cost of tuition, books, and compulsory fees for each season of service in the league. In addition, the league offers the truly elite players—essentially the ones they're afraid to lose to the U.S. college system—a "full ride" package that pays tuition, books, compulsory fees, and room and board at a Canadian university. The scholarship is for four years regardless of how many seasons the player performs in the league.

But a couple of catches exist. First, teams in the OHL are allowed to have only seven players on full rides at any time, so they're not available to everyone. Second, once a player signs a pro contract, the education package is revoked. The only exceptions to that are players who want to try to pursue a pro career in the minors after junior hockey; they have the option to play up to eighteen months in the minors prior to taking advantage of their education packages.

Perhaps, then, it's time to crunch some numbers to determine what kind of deal major junior players in Canada are getting these days. Are junior hockey players being taken advantage of unduly? Well, look at the numbers and decide for yourself.

Generally speaking, the junior hockey regular season runs from early September to the middle of March, a span of about twenty-nine weeks per year. We've added three weeks to each year to encompass training camp and playoffs. If the player's team misses the playoffs, the number is closer to twenty-nine weeks, but if his team advances all the way to the Memorial Cup, the commitment is closer to thirty-eight weeks.

But for the sake of argument, let's go with thirty-two weeks a year. Over the course of a four-year junior career, that means the player will work for his junior team for a total of 128 weeks. With a salary of $50 a week, that means the player will earn about $6,400 over the course of his career in salary and receive $12,800 worth of room and board.

In 2010–11, the average tuition fee for university was $6,640. Factoring in a 5 percent rise in fees each year, that means a four-year player would receive a total of $28,618 in tuition fees, plus about $8,000 to cover books and compulsory fees (estimated at $2,000 per year).

That puts the total amount of compensation at $55,518 for a four-year player in the OHL. When you total all the practices, off-ice workouts, games, travel, and public appearances, a junior hockey player spends about thirty-five hours a week working for his team. (That amount is more in the far-flung WHL, due largely to travel.) That means over the course of his career, a player can expect to work a total of about 4,480 hours. That would peg his wage at $12.69 per hour, which is about three dollars an hour more than the $9.60 per hour student minimum wage in Ontario.

When you frame the debate that way, it doesn't look so bad. But you also have to remember that learning to flip hamburgers or sell electronics requires very little sacrifice and no expense. And junior hockey players have virtually no time to hold down summer jobs, because most of them spend the off-season catching up on school and training.

And that's just for players who take advantage of the education package at the university level. Those who instead attend a community college in Ontario are faced with tuition fees of about $2,400, plus $2,000 in other fees. That brings the total compensation down to $44,518, which comes out to $9.93 per hour.

But let's go back to Christian Thomas, the son of former NHLer Steve Thomas. The younger Thomas was drafted by the New York Rangers and signed a three-year contract with the organization, meaning he forfeited his education package. Without any of the education money, he will have earned about $4.29 an hour, which is less than half the student minimum wage in Ontario. His contract calls for signing bonuses of $90,000 per year for each of the three seasons, but the point is that the players who usually are the ones who potentially will cost the most don't end up taking advantage of the most lucrative education packages.

When Thomas signed his deal, he lost his full ride and he was dropped from the list of full-ride players, which allowed the Generals to make that offer to another potential player. But since the full rides are offered only to the elite players—in other words, the ones who have the best chance of having a lucrative pro career—the chances of them actually taking advantage of it are significantly reduced.

Branch said his league does not keep track of how many players on full rides actually take advantage of their scholarships, compared to the numbers of players who abandon them after signing a pro contract. In the first semester of the 2011–12 season, the OHL said it paid out a total of $1.4 million in scholarship money. The WHL claims that more than 200 players receive scholarship money every year and that it has distributed more than $9 million to 3,000 players since 1993. (Unlike the OHL, the WHL does not have any full rides, but most schools in the Canada West University Athletic Association will match whatever a player receives from the WHL.)

Scholarships in junior hockey were once handled by the teams but are now administered by the league offices, who are billed by the university once the player registers; in turn, the league invoices the team. That happened after the OHL had the living daylights scared out of it by a run-of-the-mill journeyman by the name of Brody Todd. A big left winger with limited skill, Todd played for four teams in five years in the OHL and was never drafted by an NHL team. He was little more than a blip on the screen—until 2006.

That's when he went off to Acadia University in Halifax, only to discover that the Kingston Frontenacs, who originally drafted Todd in 2000 and agreed to an education that was valued at about $7,000 per year, balked at paying for his education, saying he quit the team for two weeks in his second season in Kingston. (Todd was later traded by the Frontenacs and went on to play three and a half more seasons in the OHL for the Sudbury Wolves, Ottawa 67's, and Sault Ste. Marie Greyhounds.)

Todd and his agent, Todd Christie, sued the OHL, the Frontenacs, and Branch for the education money plus an additional $150,000. And Todd and Christie threatened to advance it to a class-action lawsuit on behalf of every player who had played in the OHL since Branch became commissioner in 1979. Among other things, the lawsuit claimed the OHL's compensation of $50 per week represented restraint of trade and since the entry drafts in all three junior leagues were not collectively bargained, they also represented restraint of trade.

Predictably, the issue was settled out of court—and, while the results were never made public, Todd got his education money and then some. "Brody Todd and [*The Hockey News*, which reported on the lawsuit] made us better," Branch acknowledged. "It wasn't the best way to go about it."

One vehicle that serves to defray costs of the scholarship program is the CHL's share of revenues it receives when the World Junior Championship is held in Canada. It's an event that has grown to monstrous proportions in this country, and when it's held on home soil everyone involved seems to make gobs of money. It has proved to be a cash cow for both Hockey Canada and the CHL, which split the revenues 50–35, with the other 15 percent divided evenly among the host committee, the provincial amateur hockey association where the tournament is held, and the twelve other branches of Hockey Canada. The 2012 tournament put about $80 million into the Alberta economy, with a large portion of that going to Calgary, where Canada played its round-robin and medal-round games. The Sports Network, which has been as responsible as anyone for the growth of the tournament, is guaranteed a full roster of

advertising slots between Christmas and New Year's, a time
of year when business is slowest. "It's actually gone against
the traditional norms of television sales and sponsorship," said
Paul Graham, a vice-president and executive producer of live
events for TSN, one of the driving forces behind building the
tournament as a lucrative television property. "Even though
it may be a bit of a loss leader for [advertisers] in terms of
getting the money back right now—they're not going to sell
any stereos over Christmas because you've already bought
them. You've bought it before Christmas, but they've got to be
involved because there are so many eyeballs and there's such
a Canadiana to it that it has brought sponsors to a time of the
year where they normally wouldn't be around."

The tournament has become a holiday tradition in Canada,
one that tugs at the hockey heartstrings like no other. The teenagers who play for Canada are lionized for two weeks and
embody the Canadian mythology that surrounds the game.
These young men are, on the surface at least, playing for the
pure love of it, putting everything on the line to represent their
country. To a lesser extent, they're also showcasing themselves
and gaining an enormous amount of experience that will help
them when they reach the NHL. And they have delivered. The
national junior team has provided Canadians with a reason to
thump their chests with pride and some of the most compelling
on-ice moments they've ever witnessed. Of the top ten–watched
programs in TSN history, World Junior games occupy eight
spots, including the 2011 gold medal final between Canada
and Russia that attracted 6.23 million viewers. (When you add
in the numbers who watched on the francophone arm of TSN,
Réseau des sports, the number is actually closer to 7 million.)

Organizing committees mobilize thousands of volunteers for the event. In fact, former NHLer Jim Peplinski, who was the co-chair of the 2012 event in Calgary and Edmonton, marvelled one day at the fact that fans were helping arena staff pick up garbage when there was a quick turnaround between games at the Scotiabank Saddledome.

When the tournament is held in Canada or a border city in the United States, the centre that hosts it has a two-week windfall of intense economic activity. Everyone from hotels to cab drivers to waiters make money at a time of year when revenues are at their lowest. The players who perform in the tournament? Well, they get a sweatsuit, but not a single penny goes directly to the players who generate these millions of dollars for everyone else.

For years, the World Junior Championship was nothing more than a novelty to Canadians, owing to the fact that it barely registered on Hockey Canada's radar. From the inception of the tournament in 1974 through 1980, the Soviets won seven straight gold medals in the event, while Canada would send either club teams or all-stars from one of the three junior leagues. Not even a sixteen-year-old Wayne Gretzky, who scored seventeen points in six games and was named the tournament's top forward in 1978, could propel Canada any higher than a third-place finish. And when Canada, represented by the Cornwall Royals, finished seventh out of eight teams despite having future Hall of Famers Dale Hawerchuk and Doug Gilmour in the lineup, Hockey Canada began to take the tournament seriously and developed the Program of Excellence in conjunction with the CHL, which has supplied the vast majority of players for the team. When Canada won its first-ever gold medal in the event in 1982 in Rochester, Minnesota, organizers did not have a tape of Canada's national anthem so the players stood arm-in-arm along the blue line and belted it out themselves. The only broadcast of the final game was on CBC Radio.

From there, the tournament gained more and more momentum, but took an enormous hit in Canada when the 1987 team was kicked out of the tournament along with the Soviets for their parts in a brawl that prompted the referee to turn the lights off at the arena in Piestany in the former Czechoslovakia.

Anyone associated with the tournament pegs the true turning point for the event's popularity in Canada to the 1991 showing in Saskatoon. Led by a seventeen-year-old Eric Lindros, the Canadian team was 3-1-1, but looked to be doomed when it lost 6–5 to Czechoslovakia. But the Soviets, who had won their first four games, were stunned to tie Finland 5–5. That set up a showdown between Canada and the Soviets, with the Soviets needing only a tie, but Canada needing a victory. With the score tied 2–2, John Slaney of St. John's scored with 5:13 remaining in the game to give Canada the victory and incite euphoria from coast to coast. But what made it part of the Canadian hockey fan's consciousness was that it marked the first time TSN televised every Canadian game and provided blanket coverage of the tournament from start to finish. It was also the first time an organizing committee vying to hold the event gave Hockey Canada a financial guarantee. The Saskatoon organizers guaranteed a $1 million windfall for Hockey Canada if it were awarded the tournament, and it delivered more than that.

When Canada hosted the event in Winnipeg in 1999, the profit was in excess of $2 million; it was $3.7 million when it was held in Halifax in 2003. The tournament in Canada now fills NHL buildings, and the revenues have skyrocketed. Profits ballooned to $15 million in Ottawa in 2009 and in Saskatoon in 2010. The International Ice Hockey Federation, knowing a cash cow when it sees one, awarded the 2012 tournament to Calgary and Edmonton and the profits for that event were expected to be about $20 million. The hosting plan has been extended, with Canada scheduled to host the tournament in 2015, 2017, 2019, and 2021.

Who knows what the profits will be in a four-screen universe by that time? But the CHL will continue to get 35 percent of the take and Hockey Canada 50 percent. In addition, Hockey Canada has secured sponsorship from Esso, Nike, Molson, General Motors, and TELUS, and has crafted a deal where these companies each get four ad spots a game and opening and closing billboards. Not only does TSN not get any of that sponsorship money, it can't sell any advertising during the tournament to any of those companies' competitors.

So TSN picks up the slack by televising three pre-tournament games in that important pre-Christmas period and a preview show. The selection camp, meanwhile, is now known as the Sport Chek Selection Camp. In 2012, Hockey Canada dispensed with the selection camp in order to play a four-game series against the Russian national junior team to commemorate the fortieth anniversary of the 1972 Summit Series. Two games were played in Yaroslavl and the other two at the Halifax Metro Centre, where tickets were $43 for each game. With a seating capacity of 10,595, that brought in revenues of more than $900,000 for Hockey Canada. TSN, meanwhile, has become the host broadcaster for the event, and starting with the 2013 event in Ufa, Russia, Hockey Canada is the marketing partner with the IIHF for all World Junior tournaments, giving it broadcast and rink-board rights for every tournament inside and outside Canada. And with all those eyeballs looking on via TSN, no doubt advertisers will be lined up to continue supporting it.

So let's say, for example, the profits are conservatively estimated at $15 million for each of the next four tournaments. That would make the total take $60 million, of which the CHL would receive $21 million. That would conceivably give each team a total of almost $350,000 (assuming the number stays at sixty teams) to cover their educational commitments from 2016 through 2022.

The players? They'll continue to get nothing but a track suit and, perhaps, a medal.

There is no beast quite like major junior hockey in Canada. But there's also no beast quite like big-time college athletics in the United States. Just as nothing anywhere in the world resembles the CHL—namely, a multi-million-dollar enterprise built on the backs of players who are as young as sixteen years old—no other country has a system where institutions of higher education are used as a backdrop for big-time athletics.

University sports in the United States has become a multi-million-dollar business and, like junior hockey, universities and other corporations make money on the backs of young people who are not paid directly for their work. The NCAA's core values of inclusivity, the pursuit of excellence in both athletics

and academics, and the highest level of integrity and sportsmanship are noble and lofty ideals to be sure. The NCAA's
own website reports that the organization was formed in 1906,
"to protect young people from the dangerous and exploitive
athletic practices of the time." But over the years, it has become
so large and so lucrative that the lines between the amateur
ideals and exploitation have been blurred. That is especially
true with college football and basketball, but it also extends to
lesser sports such as what is known by the NCAA as ice hockey.

"They're all about amateurism and not paying their
athletes," said Paul Kelly, the former executive director of
College Hockey Inc., a marketing arm of college hockey in the
United States, "then you walk into a 12,000-seat arena and
you see two big college teams and they're bringing in hundreds
of thousands of dollars in ticket and television revenue and the
kids on the ice are the reason everyone is there. And they aren't
receiving anything other than a scholarship to the school."

It's interesting to note that a "full ride" scholarship, where
all school-related and living expenses are paid, has a sticker
price of between $40,000 and $50,000 a year, but Kelly
acknowledged the actual cost to the university is more like
$15,000 a year.

There are those who claim the NCAA's amateur ideals are
a sham and that the "student-athlete" is nothing more than
a provider of slave labour for universities. Martin Luther
King Jr. biographer Taylor Branch reported in *The Atlantic*
in 2011 that the Southeast (Football) Conference became the
first collegiate athletic league to earn in excess of $1 billion
in athletic receipts, with the Big 10 not far behind at $905
million. Taylor writes in the piece, "For all the outrage, the

real scandal is not that students are getting illegally paid or recruited, it's that two of the noble principles on which the NCAA justifies its existence—'amateurism' and the 'student-athlete'—are cynical hoaxes, legalistic confections propagated by the universities so they can exploit the skills and fame of young athletes. The tragedy at the heart of college sports is not that some college athletes are getting paid, but that more of them are not."

Hockey is not considered a big-time sport at most American universities, but the scholarship is something of a brass ring for players on both sides of the 49th parallel. Parents who view their spending on minor hockey as an investment simply hope their children can have their education paid for in return. Families who spend years in minor hockey pursuing the goal of having their son's (and now daughter's) education paid for often find that colleges are no different than junior hockey in some respects and that their spot is every bit as tenuous, perhaps more difficult to attain, and in some cases just as costly as playing major junior hockey.

Indeed, there seem to be a lot of misconceptions surrounding pursuing a college scholarship, not the least among them the ease with which they are attained. The fact of the matter is that only the best Canadian players—those who probably would have been star players regardless of which avenue they chose—get guaranteed, four-year "free rides" where all of their costs are covered. Many parents find that after years of pouring enormous amounts of money into a minor hockey career in the hopes of it paying off with a scholarship, the path to academic and financial security either isn't there or isn't quite as lucrative as they thought it would be.

"A lot of kids look at a scholarship like it's the consolation prize," said Christine Duchene, whose son Matt plays for the Colorado Avalanche and faced the junior vs. college decision when he was a teenager. "They don't realize those are hard to get, too."

In fact, they're probably even more difficult for a Canadian to get than a spot on a major junior team. In 2010–11, just 1,053 players were playing Division I men's hockey at American universities, and just 481 of those were Canadians. Those schools offered a total of just 822 full athletic scholarships. If you go on the assumption that 25 percent of a team turns over each season, that means only about 200 full scholarships are up for grabs among the thousands of players in North America vying for them.

Because of that, scholarships are often parcelled off into partial stipends so more players can be recruited with promises of at least having some of their schooling paid for. The reality is that only the truly elite players get all of their expenses paid. Combined with the much higher education costs in the United States, some families find that their son's or daughter's scholarship is *costing* them thousands of dollars.

"I know lots of parents who have paid more for their kids to go on a scholarship to the U.S., than to go to the University of Toronto," said OHL commissioner David Branch, who ironically was on a hockey scholarship at the University of Massachusetts Amherst. "That's because it's sexy. 'My kid's on a scholarship.' OK, if that's what you want."

Let's use the example of Michael Folkes, a young man from Burlington, Ontario, who accepted what he thought was a four-year scholarship at Ohio State University in 2008.

He certainly was not a star player, but he was probably good enough to play in the OHL at some point during his teenage years. Chosen in the fourteenth round of the 2005 OHL draft by the Mississauga IceDogs when he was a sixteen-year-old, Folkes played Jr. B hockey in 2005–06 and moved his way up to the Jr. A ranks by the next season. But he was also getting attention from Division I college programs, and despite having an offer to join the Mississauga St. Michael's Majors as an eighteen-year-old he opted to go to Ohio State in 2008.

But like most who are not star players, the scholarship was not the four-year full ride that so many have conceptions of receiving when they take their talents to an American university. In fact, it was far from it. All told, his scholarship barely would have covered half of his education expenses. He left Ohio State after two and a half years (more on that later), but here was how the financials looked for him and his parents, Paul and Diane:

2008–09: Scholarship set at 20 percent of the $35,000 fees for foreign students. That meant the Folkes family paid $24,000 in fees, plus a meal plan that cost about $1,500.

2009–10: Scholarship set at 80 percent of the $35,000 fees for foreign students. The Folkes family paid $7,500 of that, plus $560 per month in rent and $400 a month for meals. Michael was also accepted to the Fisher School of Business at Ohio State that year, which meant his parents had to pay $14,000 more in tuition fees. On the advice of new coach Mark Osiecki, Michael elected to stay in Columbus that summer to work out with the team and take summer courses, at a cost of about $2,000. The family also purchased a Jeep for Michael to get to and from practice.

2010–11: Scholarship set at 30 percent of the $35,000 fees for foreign students. The Folkes family paid $5,122 in September and Michael was released from the team about a month later. He left Ohio State at Christmas and transferred to Carleton University, which cost $4,500, plus about $3,200 in rent and food.

2011–12: Scholarship set at 90 percent of the $35,000 fees for foreign students, which Michael Folkes did not use.

Paul and Diane Folkes now attend hockey seminars all over Ontario, not to bash college hockey but to ensure people do their homework when they're weighing their options. And it has nothing to do with all the out-of-pocket money that having their son play at Ohio State cost them, but with the stunning manner in which he and two of his teammates were treated by the school.

The misconception has long been that a scholarship is a four-year agreement, but in reality it is a set of four one-year contracts that are renewed each season and can be revoked at any time for any reason, including performance on the ice. And that's precisely what happened to Folkes and teammates Taylor Stefishen and Erick Belanger—all Canadians—in the fall of 2010.

All three players were released by new Buckeyes coach Osiecki prior to the season. The players were all told their scholarships for the remainder of that season would be honoured, but none of the three was welcome on the ice or in the dressing room. Michael Folkes and his parents were stunned at the news.

"It was devastating to him," Paul Folkes said. "The first week after the release, he was just in a total depression. He didn't go to class. I don't think he even left his room."

The worst thing about all of it is that the hockey careers of all three players were in limbo. Belanger was a senior player who finished out the year at Ohio State and left hockey. Stefishen, a fifth-round pick of the Nashville Predators in 2008, joined the Prince George Cougars of the WHL for the 2010–11 season, then had his NHL rights traded after the season to the Washington Capitals for a conditional seventh-round draft choice in 2013. He joined the University of Calgary Dinosaurs in 2011–12. Folkes, meanwhile, transferred to Carleton University, where he plays for the varsity hockey team.

If that scenario had unfolded in junior hockey, the players at least would have had the opportunity to be traded or would have been released and free to sign with another team. But NCAA rules stipulate that when a player leaves a collegiate team, he cannot play for another university for a year, regardless of whether the decision to leave was the student's or the university's. Ohio State honoured the scholarships, but that was cold comfort for the players.

"They basically said, 'You know what, we'll honour your scholarships, but you're not going to play,'" Paul Folkes said. "Well, these kids are living with players on the team. Their whole social life is with the players on the team. And now all of a sudden you're no longer on the team. You're ostracized and you're going to pack up and go and that's exactly what [Ohio State] wanted. They knew those kids weren't going to stay. No kid goes to the NCAA just to go to school. They go there to play hockey. You take the hockey away and 99.9 percent of the kids are going to leave. And [Ohio State] knew that."

So by leaving early, Folkes and Stefishen opened up two more scholarship spots for the team to offer to other recruits. Michael Folkes is enjoying his experience at Carleton and still hopes to play some form of professional hockey one day, but the experience has taken a toll. The Folkes family contemplated taking legal action, but decided against it.

"Who are we?" Diane Folkes said. "We're just Diane and Paul Folkes against Ohio State University who pays its football coach $5 million."

Then there are players, such as Daniel Ciampini, who literally wait years for a chance to play college hockey. Ciampini finally made it in 2011–12 when he secured a spot at Union College in Schenectady, New York, three full years after finishing high school. Most of his peers are entering their last year of university education, but his has just begun at the age of twenty-one.

"It does suck because a lot of my friends who don't play hockey are graduating from university [in 2012] and I'm a freshman in college," Ciampini said. "It's pretty weird, but at the same time I'm not the first and I certainly won't be the last guy to do it."

In fact, fewer and fewer players are entering college hockey as true freshmen anymore, particularly in Ontario, which phased out the Ontario Academic Credit, or the equivalent of what used to be Grade 13, in 2003. Coaches have found over the years that there is little to be gained by having a young player in the lineup who can't contribute, so they have him hold off on playing college hockey until he is physically ready and good enough to handle the college game.

For Ciampini, that meant playing for the Jr. A St. Michael's Buzzers for three years after high school. Because he was restricted by NCAA rules to taking only two credits per school year, his days were filled with a lot of off-ice workouts and idle time. But that was what he had to do to fulfill his dream of one day playing college hockey. And even when he did make the team, he played a total of just fifteen of his team's forty-one games in his freshman season. Cracking a college lineup is difficult because there are always extra players on the roster and freshmen often see very little ice time. Regardless of all the waiting and so little ice time in his first season, Ciampini said he wouldn't change his course of action.

"At times I've said, 'What am I doing? What if it doesn't work out?'" Ciampini said. "But I love hockey and if I were to lose hockey, I'd lose a big part of my world. It takes up a lot of my life, a lot of my time. It was a decision I had to make and that's what I wanted. This is what a lot of kids dream about and I get to live it."

There are upsides to college hockey, too. A recent study by the NCAA revealed that hockey has the highest graduation rate of any intercollegiate sport, at 88 percent. Many others, players who leave for the NHL before graduating, often go back to finish their degrees in the summer. Kelly claims the university graduation rate for a player in junior hockey is somewhere between 16 and 20 percent. Branch said the CHL has never crunched the numbers, but finds that hard to believe. He said over 98 percent of junior players graduate from high school and many players go on to extend their careers at Canadian universities. In fact, of the 831 players on rosters of hockey teams in the Canadian Interuniversity Sport hockey league in 2011–12, 477 (or 57.4 percent) of them had some experience at the major junior level.

As a point of reference, 192 players in the OHL were born in 1987 and graduated from the league sometime between 2005 and 2008. Of those players, 41 (or 21.4 percent) embarked on careers in either the NHL or the American Hockey League, the top feeder league of the NHL. Only 18 of them (or 9.4 percent) signed contracts in lower minor leagues such as the ECHL, the Central Hockey League, the Southern Professional Hockey League, or the International Hockey League, and 9 of them (or 4.7 percent) signed with professional teams in Europe. Eight of the nine were European players who came to the CHL as imports.

But 77 of them (or 40.1 percent) played hockey for and attended a Canadian university and used the scholarship money that was allocated to them. Another 47 (or 24.8 percent) dropped out of competitive hockey altogether. Some of those players would have attended university or college and others would have used their scholarship money to take up a trade or become a police officer or firefighter.

Things often work well for players regardless of whether they play college or junior hockey, and sometimes they find out they've basically been kicked to the curb by having their equipment tossed into a garbage bag. It happened to Andrew Glass at Boston University and Christopher Beauchamp with the Sarnia Sting.

In December 2011, Glass learned he had been booted off

the team at Boston University when he showed up for the first day of practice after the Christmas break only to see his equipment sitting in a garbage bag in the middle of the team's dressing room. Glass had been late for two team meetings in December and had been warned to not let it happen again. Then, according to Glass, the team had one last practice scheduled prior to the Christmas break, but Glass could not make it because he had an exam scheduled for that time and said coach Jack Parker told him that was fine.

The practice was changed to a team weightlifting session—which, by NCAA rules, Glass could have done on his own time so as not to conflict with studying commitments. He did go to the workout later that day, but nobody was there to see him. He went home for Christmas thinking everything was fine, only to be dismissed from the team upon his return.

For Beauchamp, the end of his OHL career came just before the start of the 2009–10 season. He had finished the previous season with the Sarnia Sting after being traded from the Brampton Battalion and had struggled to create offence, but showed up to camp in the best shape of his life and was the team's fourth-leading scorer in the exhibition games. But two days before the home opener, he was called to the rink to meet with coach Dave MacQueen. When he arrived at the rink, he saw his equipment stuffed into a green garbage bag. "Never a good sign," he thought. He was told the team was rebuilding and that he was being released. He was too shocked to say much of anything, but did manage to mutter a few words.

"I said thanks," Beauchamp recalled, "but I don't know why I said thanks. They didn't do me any favours."

8

UNLIKELY NHLERS

When Regent Park was established as Canada's first social housing project in 1948, it was hailed as a progressive solution to the housing crisis for Canada's working poor in its largest city. The day it opened its doors was hailed by Toronto politicians as "an historic day, writing the first chapter in the story of subsidized, permanent, low-rental housing." Amassing a span of twelve city blocks, the twenty-three nearly identical low-rise apartments were intended to replace the squalor of the slum neighbourhood with a vibrant community for 10,000 people. It was meant to be a transitional community for those experiencing financial difficulties.

But mention the words "Regent Park" to anyone who lives in Toronto and you'll find that the utopia that was supposed to exist some sixty years ago is the furthest thing from the reality. Just a stone's throw away from the Bay Street financial district where billions of dollars flow every day, Regent Park has become a dead-end street for the disenfranchised. Just eight years after it was built, *The Globe and Mail* described Regent

Park as "the wrong place, for the wrong people in an erratic unplanned manner which cannot stand up to reasonable examination."

What was supposed to be a triumph for the disenfranchised has become a social disaster. Regent Park quickly degenerated into Canada's largest ghetto, described by many as "a hopeless slum." Perhaps the *Toronto Star* put it best when it once wrote in an editorial, "Living here is like getting kicked in the teeth." It has long been the poorest neighbourhood in Canada, with 76 percent of residents living below the poverty line. It has become a haven for violent crime, drug addiction, and prostitution. The City of Toronto announced a twelve-year plan in 2006 to gentrify the area and transform it into mixed-income housing, but the Regent Park legacy is one of desperation and hopelessness.

It was into this crucible that former NHLer Glen Metropolit was born in 1974. With the exception of a few brief periods, mostly when he was placed in foster homes, Metropolit spent the first eighteen years of his life in Regent Park. Metropolit figures he lived in more than half the buildings in Regent Park at one time or another, often with his grandmother and other relatives. There were times when things would be looking up and he and his mother and half-brother would get a little place far enough away from the development, but they never lasted very long.

"Things would go wrong and the next thing you know, we'd have to go back to Regent Park," Metropolit said. "We could just never leave it, I guess."

But Metropolit did leave Regent Park, and hockey was his ticket out of both the surroundings and the cycle of poverty. In fact, both he and his half-brother Troy managed to escape an adult existence in Regent Park, but they could not have taken more divergent paths out of the inner city. Metropolit did it by becoming one of the most unlikely NHL players in history, playing more than 400 games for the Washington Capitals, Tampa Bay Lightning, Atlanta Thrashers, Boston Bruins, Philadelphia Flyers, St. Louis Blues, and Montreal Canadiens before spending the final seasons of his playing career in Switzerland.

Troy, on the other hand, left Regent Park in handcuffs in 1999 after he was part of a group that kidnapped a prominent Toronto lawyer and his wife, holding them for hours in the trunk of their car before taking them to an apartment and beating them repeatedly. After making withdrawals from their bank, the two then ransacked their house. After receiving a fourteen-year sentence in 2000 for kidnapping, assault, and forcible confinement, Troy was charged with murder three years later in connection with the stabbing death of a fellow inmate.

Glen Metropolit readily acknowledges that things could have gone the other way for him quite easily. "If not for the grace of God, go I," is a popular saying for those who know they are lucky in life. And there might be something to that for him. Metropolit obviously had some God-given talents to play the game, but it was how he exploited those talents and how many results he squeezed out of so little opportunity that makes Metropolit a truly amazing case study. In fact, his story reminds one of a time when hockey truly was a meritocracy, when you couldn't buy your way into the game or be handed every opportunity to make yourself better because your parents could afford it.

And it is a story that is compelling, every bit as intriguing, unlikely, and inspirational as those of Michael Oher, the Baltimore Ravens lineman who came from similar circumstances to become a first-round pick in the National Football League, and Jim Morris, a high school baseball coach who broke into the major leagues at the age of thirty-five after attending a tryout camp because he lost a bet with his players. Both of their stories were made into big-budget movies, and if hockey were as popular as football and baseball are in the United States you can bet screenwriters and filmmakers would be lining up at Metropolit's door.

So how is it that Metropolit was able to make it to the pinnacle of his profession with so little guidance in his life on and off the ice? How was it that he had almost every obstacle imaginable tossed in his path, yet he persevered and played in the NHL while thousands of others in his age group had every opportunity to improve themselves and failed? Is the success of players such as Metropolit simply an anomaly or can it tell us something we might not want to hear about the hundreds of thousands of dollars we're spending on hockey careers?

It's true that Metropolit came through the system two decades ago, but things weren't that different then than they are now. Eric Lindros, who is a year older than Metropolit, was receiving one-on-one instruction and the best coaching from the time he was ten years old. The disclosure of player salaries, the Wayne Gretzky trade to the Los Angeles Kings, and the emergence of a far more militant NHL Players' Association under the stewardship of hard-liner Bob Goodenow was making pro hockey a very big business. Suddenly, the stakes were much higher and there was far more to gain than ever before.

That's about the time the insanity began in minor hockey, but Glen Metropolit was never a part of that. Perhaps he would have played more than 407 NHL games or been a big star if he had been given the opportunities many other kids received at that time, but it's likely Metropolit made it because he willed himself to play in the NHL. Perhaps that hunger would not have been there had he been handed opportunity after opportunity. Metropolit is certainly not alone. He's hardly the only player to rise from meagre circumstances to the best league in the world. John Madden, who won two Stanley Cups with the New Jersey Devils, grew up in a housing project every bit as gritty on the other side of Toronto. Tim Thomas, the Boston Bruins superstar goaltender and winner of the Conn Smythe Trophy in 2011, grew up in Flint, Michigan, one of the most depressed cities in the United States after the GM plant there closed its doors. He put himself through hockey by selling apples door-to-door and his parents once hocked their wedding rings in order to pay for hockey school.

If those players could make it, perhaps it has less to do with parents pulling strings behind the scenes than we thought. Perhaps if a player is determined enough and willing enough and resourceful enough, he's going to make it anyway. And conversely, those who don't have the hunger and God-given ability won't, despite the resources their parents are willing to pour into their careers. After all, are players such as Glen Metropolit and John Madden and Tim Thomas all that different from their peers, aside from their circumstances? There are barriers that cannot be overcome, to be sure.

Generally speaking, a player who maxes out at 5-foot-2 or 145 pounds is going to face enormous odds regardless of his ability level. Some players with skill simply do not possess the hockey sense or skating ability to keep up at the NHL, and others may not have received enough positive guidance.

But one thing is certain. There is no shortage of players out there who put to rest the notion that a hockey career is something to be nurtured, stage-managed by overzealous parents, and manufactured. Sometimes, as in the case of Glen Metropolit, they happen despite the odds.

The 1992 NHL Entry Draft was held at the Montreal Forum, the last time ever it took place in the league's most iconic building. Of all the NHL power brokers who gathered that day to divvy up the best eighteen-year-old hockey talent on the planet, it's possible not a single one of them had ever heard of Glen Metropolit. It was a very good draft—a solid crop of players was available, albeit one lacking in superstar quality. The best of them was Alexei Yashin, who went second overall to the Ottawa Senators that day, a player with a Hall of Fame skill level whom many observers thought frittered away his talent with a lack of commitment. That draft produced a number of serviceable players, seven of whom played more than 1,000 games in the NHL. Seven other players taken in that draft—Roman Hamrlik, Sergei Gonchar, Yashin, Sergei Brylin, Craig Rivet, Adrian Aucoin, and Nikolai Khabibulin— were still playing, scattered in the NHL, Europe, and the minor leagues, in 2011–12.

This would have been Metropolit's draft year if he had been on anyone's radar. The addition of the Senators and Tampa

Bay Lightning had increased the number of teams to twenty-four, meaning there would be about forty more jobs opening up for NHL players. Not surprisingly, Metropolit's name wasn't called, since scouts were not in the habit of scouring Jr. B leagues for talent.

What is surprising is that of the 264 players selected that day, 222 of them did not play as many NHL games as the 407 Metropolit did. A good number of them didn't play a single one, including Ryan Sittler, son of former Toronto Maple Leafs captain and Hall of Famer Darryl Sittler. The younger Sittler had played much of his minor hockey in Buffalo, where Darryl and his family settled after his retirement in 1985, in part because Darryl did not want to expose his son to the pressure of playing minor hockey in Toronto. Sittler was a phenom, though, and looked to have discovered the family genetic code for hockey stardom. The Philadelphia Flyers took Sittler seventh overall, and after two mediocre seasons at the University of Michigan he was rushed into the NHL, signed to a contract with a $400,000 signing bonus. Unfulfilled potential and injuries, including one where he suffered a broken cheekbone, a fractured orbital bone, and a crushed sinus cavity in a fight in the American Hockey League, took their toll until he retired in 1999. Sittler's best season as a pro was with the South Carolina Stingrays of the East Coast Hockey League, where he scored twelve goals and twenty-seven points in forty-four games in 1997–98.

By the time he retired from the game, Ryan Sittler had become hooked on the painkillers he had taken during his many injuries and required two stints in rehab to kick the habit.

Two players, two entirely different circumstances, two diametrically opposed hockey careers. Ryan Sittler had the pedigree from his father, all the best life could offer, every opportunity to rise up the ranks because of his family connections, enough money that his father could retire away from the pressure of playing in Canada's largest city, and a stable home life with all kinds of support from loving parents.

Metropolit, on the other hand, had a birth father with whom he had no contact and a stepfather who drifted in and out of his life depending on whether or not he was being incarcerated for criminal activity. "A lot of times the only time they'd see me was during [jail] visits," Glen's stepfather, Bruce Metropolit, told the *Toronto Star* in 1999. "It's pretty hard to support your family from there. I did some foolish things."

Metropolit's organized hockey through almost all of his minor hockey career consisted of Saturday morning games in house league where the quality of hockey was low and the teams were led by well-intentioned but unqualified coaches. When he finally did secure a college scholarship, it was taken away from him that summer when Bowling Green University deemed him academically ineligible.

No pre-season hockey schools existed in Regent Park, so Metropolit would stickhandle around the fallen leaves in the autumn, counting the days until the ice would be ready at one of the two municipally run outdoor rinks in the complex. The only dryland training available was to run the hills in the public parks, which he would do until he was ready to collapse— not because anyone told him to, but because he thought that would be one way he could gain an edge and become the best hockey player in his area.

Metropolit recalls sultry summer nights in the projects when drug deals would go badly and gangs would fight each other with baseball bats. He remembers taking the garbage out one night while living with his grandmother on the thirteenth floor of one of the buildings and seeing a man in the garbage chute doing crack cocaine out of a pop can. Where there was little but hopelessness, Metropolit found hope in his zealous pursuit of hockey, and in church. In Grades 5 and 6, he would go to a nearby Catholic church and pray to God that he would be good enough to make the NHL. Amidst all the chaos and uncertainty in his life, Metropolit never lost sight of his dream.

"With all this happening, all I had was my hockey stick," Metropolit said. "And thank God for that. Who knows where I would have been or what would have happened if I hadn't had that?"

Hockey school? Out of the question. One-on-one instruction? Well, if you include watching hockey with his mother's friends and his uncles while they drank beer and smoked weed as one-on-one instruction, then that qualified. "If my uncle was going to play men's league at night with all his buddies," Metropolit recalled, "I'd try to stay up and go play with them."

Metropolit's road to the NHL, as circuitous as it was, started on the outdoor rinks of the Regent Park projects. There were two city-operated rinks in Regent Park about 200 metres apart. One would hold public skating sessions and the other would have shinny hockey—and if you were ever looking for Glen Metropolit, the one with the shinny hockey was the place to find him. Human pylons everywhere was the way Metropolit described their outdoor games. Metropolit spent so much time on those rinks he thinks they should name one of them after him. When there was no ice, Metropolit always carried a hockey stick and a tennis ball, playing impromptu games of ball hockey and walking the maze of streets in the project with the ball on his stick. Between those two pursuits, he honed a skill level that was sublime.

He certainly didn't do it through organized hockey. In fact, he played house league hockey, the lowest level of organized hockey in Ontario, until he reached the bantam ranks. For most of the first thirteen years of his life, his structured hockey consisted of one game a week. No practices, no travelling, just an inordinate amount of time to work on his skills on his own without some well-meaning adult hovering over him and telling him how to use his edges or force feeding a defensive system.

"In bantam AA, that was the first time where I remember having a practice with a coach," he said. "Until then, it was like, 'Go play right wing or whatever.'"

Metropolit never played a single game at the AAA level in his life and was the last cut of the worst AAA midget team in Toronto. As was the case when his family had a setback and had to move back to subsidized housing, it was back to house league for Metropolit, then on to high school hockey, which wasn't much better. With no options in minor hockey because he was too old, Metropolit played Jr. B for the Barrie Flyers for a year and, after getting a tryout with the Jr. A. Richmond Hill Riot at the age of eighteen, he was the last player to make the team. Over the next two seasons, Metropolit scored 163 points in 92 games and led the team in scoring.

It was then that Metropolit made his most significant life decision. He could see himself falling into bad habits, partying too much and not taking anything but hockey seriously. He would go to school, sign out, and basically skip the rest of the day. If he was going to earn a scholarship, he knew he had to go far, far away. So that's what he did, by joining the Vernon Vipers of the British Columbia Jr. League—the best Jr. A league in Canada—as an overage player, where he scored 43 goals and 117 points. After flying to Bowling Green, Ohio, to meet with coach Buddy Powers at Bowling Green University, Metropolit finished his high school credits in June and was preparing for his first year at university when the school called to tell him he was academically ineligible.

"I had no agent. I had nothing," Metropolit said. "I was twenty-one years old and I still wanted to play hockey."

So he played in the East Coast Hockey League as a free agent and continued to work his way up through the minors, playing roller hockey in the summers, until he finally signed a contract with the Washington Capitals in 1999. His first year in the NHL, in which he shuttled up and down between the NHL and the minors, his paycheque was for $18,000 after taxes. From there it was a journeyman's existence between the NHL and Europe, but a charmed life nonetheless. Ironically, one of his best seasons in the NHL was his last, when he scored sixteen goals and led the Montreal Canadiens power play with ten goals. Metropolit has never been without work and had established himself as a solid Swiss-league player in his late thirties. He watches his son, Max, who plays in the Zug minor hockey system where he spends two hours on the ice twice a week, then trains off-ice for an hour.

"It's pretty intense for a seven-year-old, but that's how they do it in Switzerland," he said. "You have kids who are almost like robots when they play hockey. There's no hockey sense. It's just skate down the wing, shoot, and don't be creative, instead of letting them just go out and play. That's where you get your creativity."

Metropolit plans to continue playing as long as the game will have him, and then take the money he earned in hockey to open an organic food bistro near Pensacola, Florida, where he met his wife, Michlyn, when he was playing in the minors.

Metropolit's tale can tell us a lot about how we develop hockey talent. That's because Metropolit himself fully acknowledges that he wasn't even the best player in Regent Park growing up. There were plenty of other players with skills and gifts every bit as good as his, some with better. But it's almost impossible for one player to come out of an environment like that one, let alone all of them. Perhaps if we took all the money that's going into elite hockey in this country and directed it to grassroots areas where it's really needed, we might be surprised with the result.

Philadelphia Flyers GM Bob Clarke approached the podium at the 2006 NHL draft at GM Place in Vancouver to announce the twenty-second overall pick. For Claude Giroux, it should have been the proudest moment of his career, particularly since, unlike the vast majority of the teenagers on display, he had never been drafted by a major junior team. Clarke approached the microphone and said, "With the twenty-second selection in the 2006 draft, the Philadelphia Flyers are proud to select ..." After an awkward pause, he turned to his assistants and said, "What was that kid's name again?"

It should come as no surprise the Flyers forgot Giroux's

name. Legend has it they were determined to take New Jersey–born defenceman Bobby Sanguinetti with that selection, but became discombobulated when the New York Rangers unexpectedly took Sanguinetti with the previous pick. The Flyers could not have known it, but it was one of those franchise-altering strokes of luck. Giroux has developed into one of the premier playmaking forwards in the NHL, while Sanguinetti appears destined for a career in the minor leagues.

After playing almost all his minor hockey career in obscurity, Giroux had become accustomed to being overlooked. Even though his hometown of Hearst, Ontario, is a hockey-mad place, it's a little difficult to find elite hockey players there. In fact, the small lumber town has produced just three players—Claude Larose, Rumun Ndur, and Giroux. Hearst does, however, bill itself as the Moose Capital of Canada. Once a bustling forestry town that boasted the most millionaires per capita in Canada and three family-run sawmills, Hearst is now home to just 6,000 people. Situated along Highway 11, the one that runs from the foot of Yonge Street in downtown Toronto to the Minnesota–Ontario border at Rainy River, Hearst represents the last McDonald's for 500 kilometres going west. It was there that Ray Giroux raised his family, working as an electrical contractor.

Although his son showed talent in hockey, Ray Giroux was never a controlling stage parent. He never looked for a better opportunity for his son because the one he had was perfectly acceptable. The highest level of hockey Claude Giroux ever played prior to moving to Ottawa when he was fifteen was the A level, which he played almost exclusively at home and in the small towns surrounding Hearst. There was very little competition for spots and the range in abilities was usually immense. Not exactly the typical breeding ground for an NHL star.

"Pretty much everybody who would show up for the tryout would make the team," Claude said. "We were able to just play and have fun."

The lack of competition never seemed to bother the Giroux family. Some years Claude would have quality coaches and other years the coaching would be lacking. But there was not much Giroux could do because there was really nowhere else to go, unless he wanted to move three hours away to Timmins, the closest centre that had a AAA organization, and that was out of the question.

"No, we never thought about that," Ray Giroux said when asked whether he ever considered moving his son to a bigger city for hockey. "He was too young to do stuff like that. That's too young. It's stupid. Sorry, I shouldn't say that, but I think it's too early. I think it's important to have all the good values for the kids. You take the chance of missing giving the kids some values when you send your kid to another town like that. But that's me, it's the father talking, you know? Besides, all those players who played in Timmins AAA, we don't hear about them these days."

And you might not be hearing about Claude Giroux if he had moved to another city as a youngster to find better competition. We've already told you about a few who did so, some of whom were hugely successful and others who were not. You'd have to think that all this running around looking for a higher level of competition at the novice, atom, and peewee levels could easily be avoided if players and parents simply embraced the opportunities they had where they lived. Nothing says Giroux would not have made it had he chased the dream elsewhere, but how much better could he have possibly become? He's already one of the top young players in the game today.

By staying in his small town, Giroux was able to, in fact, exploit his talents more. Had he played for a AAA team, he might have been stuck on the third or fourth line because he was so small and he wouldn't have developed the confidence he got from being a go-to player for his team. He also wouldn't have been put in situations where he could challenge himself, and rise to the challenge. And he would certainly not have had access to the Claude Larose Arena in Hearst, the two-pad rink in town that he and his friends could rent for $20 an hour. Between that and the outdoor rinks—remember, this is a place that regularly reaches minus-forty Celsius in the dead of winter—Giroux was on the ice working on his skills every bit as often as a player who is playing AAA.

But there is also something to be said for the life experiences Giroux had while playing hockey. He and the same group of kids played together every season and the friendships he made have endured into his NHL days, even though none of his other friends made it out of minor hockey. The kids who move around, well, you can't help but think they have one person, and one person only, in mind. If it weren't about individual pursuit, why would they go through all the trouble and move to a place where they have no roots, no civic pride? It's almost as though they're minor hockey mercenaries, travelling to where they can find the best competition.

"When you play hockey with people you care for, I think you play better and you play harder," Claude said. "Back in

Hearst there's only 6,000 people so you know pretty well everybody in the town. You're in a small town and you don't really know any better. It was always my dream to play in the NHL, but I never thought I would do it because only one in a million makes it. And it's not like a big city where you're separate from your team, where you play your game and then everybody goes their own way. For us guys, it was like a family."

Playing in a small town like that, too, it's impossible to act like a prima donna. No matter how good you are, there are always going to be people around you to set you straight. Playing in Hearst did not afford Giroux the opportunity to set himself apart, and even if you're having a bad season it's not as though you can simply ask for your release and move to another organization the way you can in larger centres. When you have only one team in town and everyone who plays hockey is on it, it's not as though you're brimming with options. You have to make the best of it and it's that kind of character that often defines whether or not a player is going to have the intestinal fortitude to be a pro. Ray Giroux provides a very good example:

"Sometimes you don't like your coach, but you have to put that aside and do what you have to do," he said. "Claude had some bad coaches and I would tell him, 'It's just for one year. Have fun, go out there and have fun with your friends and do what the coach asks you.' If I would have said, 'I know he's no good. Don't do this and don't do that,' I would have started to coach in the background and that would have been the worst thing I could do for the kid. I saw so many people talking in the background and it's not good for the kid. It's terrible."

Hearst is so small and remote that, in fact, it's not even required to play A-level hockey. Its population actually affords it the status of being a B team for the purposes of rep hockey competition, but Giroux's teams were always good enough to play at a higher level. Long gone are the days when little northern Ontario towns such as Hearst supplied a bountiful crop of players for the NHL. Back in the 1950s and 60s, places such as Kirkland Lake, Timmins, and Sudbury were gold mines, literally and figuratively, when it came to producing players for NHL teams, far more than Toronto and the other large centres in Canada. Take, for example, the Toronto Maple Leafs dynasty that won three Stanley Cups from 1962 through 1964. Of the twenty-five players who played at least twenty-five games in one season for the Leafs during that run, just two players—Billy Harris and Carl Brewer—were actually born and played their minor hockey in Toronto. All of the others, with the exception of Calgary-born Ron Stewart and Andy Bathgate of Winnipeg, were born in small-town Canada, with a mind-boggling twelve of them hailing from northern Ontario or northwestern Quebec.

George Armstrong, Eddie Shack, Al Arbour, and Jim Pappin were all from the Sudbury area, with Frank Mahovlich, Bob Nevin, Allan Stanley, and Tim Horton from Timmins and the surrounding areas. Dave Keon (from Rouyn-Noranda, Quebec), Dick Duff, Kent Douglas, and Larry Hillman all hailed from the former hockey factory known as the Kirkland Lake area.

Times have certainly changed, however. Kirkland Lake has not produced an NHL player since goalie Daren Puppa, whose career ended in 1999. Places such as Toronto now yield far more major junior players than the small towns do, but it's also home to the biggest minor hockey association in the world, with twelve AAA teams and a far larger population base. In 2011–12, there were eighteen NHL players from Toronto with its population of 2.48 million, which equates to one player for every 137,778 residents. Sudbury, meanwhile, had Todd Bertuzzi and Andrew Brunette in the NHL ranks—and with a population of 160,274, that comes out to an NHLer for every 80,137 people. Timmins had just Steve Sullivan, meaning that city produced one NHL player for every 43,311 people.

However, that does little to stop the Max Strangs and Matthew Cimettas of the world, or at least their families, from making huge financial and lifestyle sacrifices to expose their sons to what they believe is a higher level of competition and the well-oiled machine that is the GTHL.

In 2010, fourteen-year-old Nikita Korostelev came to the GTHL from Moscow to play for the Vaughan Kings AAA minor midget team. Now the GTHL has had American and European players in its league before, but Korostelev represented a new breed of player, one who was essentially recruited by the Orr Hockey Agency, which in turn helped expedite his entry into the GTHL.

Prior to the 1980s, there were almost no Soviet Bloc players in the NHL, but the trickle that began then became a flood throughout the 1990s. Young players wanting to seize opportunities in North America and make the adjustment to Canadian hockey and the NHL grind at an even younger age began showing up wanting to play for major junior teams. That led to the richest teams in the three junior leagues getting the best European talent until the CHL introduced the import draft in 1992, which regulates the flow of players to North America.

Now, if Korostelev is any indication, that effect is trickling down to minor hockey. He is represented by the Orr Hockey Group, which paid his expenses to live in Canada and play for one of the top organizations in the GTHL. Korostelev's Canadian-based representative, Alex Belopolsky of the Orr Hockey Group, said there are many other young Russians who are destined to follow in Korostelev's path. Even though most North Americans see Russian hockey as a factory that produces nothing but highly skilled players, Belopolsky paints a much bleaker picture. He said ever since the collapse of the Soviet Union in 1991, Russia has become a cesspool for corruption and greed and that has trickled down to its hockey system.

The Orr Group held a camp in Toronto for players from Russia and Ukraine in the summer of 2011 and it attracted twenty-three participants, many of whom Belopolsky said want to leave Russia. He said parents have told him stories of players drinking and carousing, of having to pay 120,000 rubles (about $4,000) just to be named to some of the elite teams, and a system that is rife with an every-man-for-himself mentality.

"When communism fell in the 1990s, everyone did what they had to do survive and if that meant taking and stealing, that's what they did," Belopolsky said. "The people who were in their twenties during that time are now in their forties with their own kids. What are they teaching to their kids?"

But it goes even further than that. The days of minor sports being a propaganda tool for communist regimes ended decades ago. And with that came the infrastructure and resources for sports that were provided for largely by the government. If hockey has become a game for the rich in Canada, that notion is even more prevalent in Russia. And those with the resources are increasingly looking for better opportunities for their children.

"Why do you think there are three million Russians the ages of eighteen to twenty-two who are studying abroad? Why do all the government officials send their kids away?" Belopolsky said. "As for the reasons Russian kids want to come over, it's the same reason they want to come to the CHL. For development purposes. The 2010 Olympics showed it, the system is in bad shape."

When Claude Giroux finally did leave Hearst at the age of fifteen, it had little to do with hockey. Because if it had, Ray Giroux would have probably moved his family to Toronto instead of Orleans, a francophone enclave just east of Ottawa en route to the Quebec border and Montreal. The Ottawa District Minor Hockey Association didn't even have AAA hockey at the time, although ODMHA AA teams competed against AAA teams across Ontario in tournaments and provincial championships on equal footing for years.

Ray Giroux wanted to leave Hearst for a number of reasons, not the least of which was that his daughter was attending the University of Ottawa. As an electrical contractor he was seeing his business opportunities dry up in Hearst, and he wanted to be closer to a higher quality of medical care for his wife. Claude, in fact, was upset that he had to leave all his friends.

And it's not as though going to a bigger centre was the key that opened all kinds of doors of opportunity for Giroux, either. After playing minor midget for the AA Cumberland

Barons based in Orleans, Giroux was not even drafted by an OHL team in the 2004 priority selection.

So he decided to play a season with the Cumberland Grads Jr. A team, and when he started putting up some very good numbers he caught the eye of scouts in the Quebec Major Junior Hockey League, something that turned out to be the most fortuitous development he could ever hope for. Still ignored by OHL teams, including the Ottawa 67's, Giroux signed as an undrafted walk-on with the nearby Gatineau Olympics. Since he was already fluent in French the adjustment to the league was no problem, and he still had the opportunity to play near his home. He was also coached by up-and-coming coach Benoit Groulx, who later left the Olympics to coach the Montreal Canadiens farm team.

But by being bypassed by the OHL, Giroux could go to a less physical league where a player of his talent level would have a better chance to excel. By NHL standards, Giroux is not a big man, although he seems to be able to take care of himself. But the success of his game is predicated on having the room to make plays, to draw checkers to him when he has the puck and set up open teammates for good scoring opportunities. The chance to do that presented itself immediately in Gatineau, and it wasn't long before Giroux was rocketing his way up the prospect list with the NHL's Central Scouting department.

"I might have gone to the OHL and maybe they wouldn't have liked the way I played and maybe I would have sat out a little bit," Giroux said, "but that wasn't the case in Gatineau. I went to Gatineau and the coach really liked the way I was playing. At seventeen, I was playing on the top line playing against the best players on the other team. I proved myself there and it was the best thing for me for sure."

After going twenty-second overall to the Flyers in 2006, Giroux found himself competing for a spot on the 2008 Canadian national junior team along with the likes of Steven Stamkos, John Tavares, Luke Schenn, Kyle Turris, Drew Doughty, and P.K. Subban. But there was an interesting contrast to Giroux in that camp in a player by the name of Angelo Esposito. Unlike Giroux, Esposito grew up a star in Quebec and at a young age was drawing comparisons to some of the greatest players the province has ever produced. His career had been stage-managed from the beginning and because of his talent he was receiving some of the best training available on and off the ice. He was a star in the world-renowned Quebec peewee tournament, and by the time he had reached his teens had every high-profile agent in hockey lining up to represent him.

"His father asked me straight out, 'What can you give me?'" said an agent who did not end up representing Esposito. "When I wouldn't give him any financial compensation, that ended our conversation pretty quickly."

After declaring that he had not decided between the QMJHL and U.S. college hockey, Esposito landed with the Quebec Remparts in a deal that some say was worth hundreds of thousands of dollars. The Remparts gave up a package of players and prospects to draft Esposito in the first round in 2005 and were prepared to pay for it. Even his father said at the time that his son received "a deal he couldn't refuse." It represented a huge windfall for the son of a man who owned a modest grocery stand in Montreal. His path to the NHL seemed assured and paved with riches, especially after he scored ninety-eight points in his rookie season of major junior hockey.

But Esposito's development stalled, and by the time the Canadian junior team was being chosen Giroux made that team and Esposito was cut for the second straight year. (Esposito, however, would make the team the next year.) Two players, two wildly divergent paths; four years later, Giroux is a bona fide star in the NHL and almost certainly will be wearing Canada's colours in the 2014 Winter Olympics if the NHL decides to continue participating.

Esposito, on the other hand, was traded by the Pittsburgh Penguins to the Atlanta Thrashers before ever playing a game for them. By 2010–11, he was in the Florida Panthers system, then was traded to the Dallas Stars organization in the middle of the season. By 2012–13, he was playing for the Lahti Pelicans in Finland on a one-year contract. Three NHL organizations with not a big-league game to show for it, bouncing between the AHL and ECHL, Angelo Esposito is destined to become one of those players who never made it.

There isn't even a hockey rink in Salmo, British Columbia—just a curling rink that opens its doors two weeks before the curling season begins and allows families to take their kids skating. It was there that a three-year-old Barret Jackman first put on skates and started twirling around the ice with his mother MaryJane.

So now when MaryJane sees her son on television playing for the St. Louis Blues, she still has a difficult time getting over the shock of it all, even though her son has played more than

600 career games in the NHL. This was never supposed to happen. Son of a single mom playing all his minor hockey for a tiny town in the B.C. interior makes it to the NHL? Incredible. Wins rookie of the year in 2003? You've got to be kidding. Has career earnings in excess of $13 million and counting? Preposterous.

MaryJane has some theories on why that happened, including one that makes you think. You see, Barret's father and MaryJane divorced when Barret was a child, and he was never a big part of his son's life. That left much of the heavy lifting to MaryJane when it came to raising a rambunctious boy and his two younger sisters. MaryJane knew nothing about hockey, but learned it along with Barret by watching his practices in the Beaver Valley Minor Hockey Association, which runs out of the small town of Fruitvale in the heart of British Columbia's West Kootenay region.

When you see NHL players these days, not too many of them are raised by single moms. More and more, the parents in general and the fathers in particular are taking active roles in managing their sons' hockey careers. And of course, the results are mixed. But the soft-spoken MaryJane Jackman thinks that her son might have made the NHL *because* he didn't have a steady father figure in his life, not in spite of it.

"I think a lot of things that go wrong for boys is the fault of fathers these days," she said. "They take the joy of the game out of it for them. They don't enjoy what they're doing and they're just pressured to do better."

That pressure was virtually non-existent for Jackman growing up. Although his mother suspects he always had a burning desire to be an NHL player, it was nothing that was ever a constant topic of conversation, never mind an obsession with him or his family. Playing at the lowest level of competitive hockey in the province will do that to you. The one concession MaryJane did make for hockey was that she moved when her son was twelve from Salmo to Fruitvale, which was a forty-minute drive away. The purpose of that was so she wouldn't have to sit through her son's practices and spend more than an hour on the road, which gave her more time to devote to her daughters.

Barret would attend the Trail (B.C.) hockey school every summer, but other than that he remained a well-rounded kid who excelled at baseball in the summer and hockey and skiing in the winter. The travel was basically limited to other small towns in the B.C. interior such as Castlegar, Nelson, and Grand Forks, and the occasional tournament. Unable to afford a hotel room for herself, MaryJane would often sleep in the motel parking lot in her car while Barret stayed with another family. "It was where I wanted to be," she said. "So I never had a problem with it."

There were sacrifices, to be sure. By the time Jackman was sixteen, he was old enough to play for the Regina Pats of the Western Hockey League, but not rich enough to play for the Team Pacific entry in the 1998 Under-17 World Hockey Challenge that runs each year in conjunction with the World Junior Championship. It is there that future NHL talent often first surfaces in a tournament that has an alumni list that would form about a half-dozen NHL all-star teams. More importantly, though, it's one of the first steps on the ladder of Hockey Canada's Program of Excellence, which identifies the best young players in the country for future international competitions. But the problem for Jackman was not talent. In fact, in his first year in Regina he was establishing himself as a force in the league. At one point he confronted a nineteen-year-old teammate whom he felt was not carrying his weight with the team. "He was like the new dog on the playground," Pats GM Brent Parker, who provided a strong male influence for Jackman, told *Sports Illustrated* in 2003. "He went out and pissed on every tree he could."

If making that team had been based on merit, Jackman would have been a shoo-in. But the problem was that the cost of each of the selection camps for the team was up to the player and his family to cover, and MaryJane simply couldn't afford it. So instead of participating in what is supposed to be a crucial stepping-stone tournament, Jackman had to decline.

"One of my biggest regrets was that I wasn't able to do that for him," she said. "But he hasn't missed any of his other opportunities to represent Canada."

It certainly didn't deter Jackman from becoming one of the most coveted young players in the country. Not only did he go on to play for Canada in the 2001 World Junior Championship, he was a first-round pick of the St. Louis Blues, and after just one season in the minors made the NHL permanently in 2002–03.

MaryJane, meanwhile, was about the furthest thing from a stage mother that you could possibly find, but her son managed to make the NHL because he had the talent and desire to do it. One hockey school per summer was all that he did outside of playing a fairly modest level of competitive hockey as a youngster. There was no inclination, or means, to have him move to a larger centre such as Vancouver to expose him to better competition. MaryJane simply allowed him to progress at his own pace, and by the time he was old enough to play Jr. B hockey for the Beaver Valley Nitehawks at age fifteen, he had become a player who was physically and mentally prepared for the challenge. (Ironically, Jackman would not have been able to play Jr. B hockey at fifteen if today's Hockey Canada rules were applied. In 2005, Hockey Canada instituted a rule that barred all players from playing any level of junior hockey as fifteen-year-olds unless they received an "exceptional player" designation, which is awarded by a handpicked panel appointed by Hockey Canada. It's known as the Tavares Rule, because John Tavares was the first player granted the status.)

After her son left to pursue his hockey career, MaryJane Jackman continued to billet players for the Nitehawks for twelve years and was the team's trainer for five seasons. And during that time, she saw countless examples of the sense of urgency so many young players seem to have when it comes to their hockey careers. Rather than embrace the experience they're having and using it to improve and learn, players seem to see levels such Jr. B as a pit stop en route to bigger and better things. It's not the Beaver Valley Nitehawks they're playing for, because they're playing only for themselves.

"I just saw a lot of kids coming in and out and they don't think they should be here, they should be somewhere else at a higher level," MaryJane Jackman said. "They're not appreciating what people are doing for them at this level. They're not even learning because they're thinking, 'I don't belong here. Next year I'll be where I'm supposed to be,' sort of thing. They're just looking too far into the future and not embracing what's in front of them."

He'll probably describe it differently to his grandchildren—
gilding the lily a little bit, of course—because Joel Ward's first
point in the NHL was hardly the stuff of highlight reels. The
struggling Minnesota Wild were visiting the equally struggling
Toronto Maple Leafs on Boxing Day 2006 in one of those
games where many of the 19,355 in attendance were using the
office tickets their company was only too happy to give away.
But it gave Ward the opportunity to play in front of family and
friends, and in particular for his devoted mother, Cecilia, for
the first time as a bona fide NHL player.

The Wild were working the puck deep in the Maple Leafs
zone and it squirted out to the right faceoff circle, where Ward
made a lunge at it. He and Leaf defenceman Hal Gill slapped
at the puck simultaneously before it squirted back to Wild
defenceman Kurtis Foster, whose seeing-eye slapshot somehow
made it through a maze of bodies, off the goalpost, and past
Toronto goalie Andrew Raycroft at 2:35 of the first period.

It was Ward's fifth NHL game, which was five more than
almost anyone ever thought he would play. Anyone, that is,
aside from Randall Ward, an auto mechanic who emigrated
to Canada from Barbados in the 1960s and married Cecilia,
who had also left Barbados and made her way into Canada the
same way many Caribbean women did, by being a nanny for
a rich white family, before working her way through nursing
school.

It was Randall who would encourage his younger son
in hockey, bribing him with the chicken wings he loved at
Chesswood Arena in Toronto or with a trip to McDonald's
in exchange for going to hockey practice. Perhaps Randall
saw the same thing another parent once saw in Joel, when his

mother was sitting within earshot and heard the parent predict that the Ward kid was going to make it to the NHL someday.

"He was the one guy who truly believed I would make it one day," Ward said of his father. "I remember he would tell family friends that I would be playing in the NHL one day. Sometimes I didn't even believe it. But I think he knew I had the tools to do it and I needed a swift kick in the rear end to get going."

Each season, NHL teams allow the fathers of all the players on a road trip with their sons, known colloquially as the "Dads' trip." Those are especially difficult for Joel Ward, whose father never got to see his son realize his dream and fulfill his own prophecy. Joel had barely turned thirteen and was playing at the venerable St. Michael's College Arena in Toronto when Randall collapsed in the stands during one of his games. Joel was told after the game by one of the other parents on the team that his father had suffered a stroke and had been rushed to hospital. Fifteen days later, on January 18, 1994, Randall Ward died when the embolism that had caused the stroke struck his brain.

We'll never know what twists and turns Ward's hockey career would have taken had his father been there to guide him, encourage him, and provide him with the kick in the pants he occasionally needed to put in the extra work it takes to get better. Perhaps Ward would have made the NHL more quickly. Perhaps his father would have pushed him hard enough that he'd have been good enough to get drafted. But there is no denying the fact that when Randall Ward died, his son found his refuge in hockey—and that, in turn, spawned a renewed desire to improve and be the best hockey player he could be.

And despite setback after setback—after setback—Joel Ward finally did make it to the NHL, taking one of the most circuitous routes possible to the best league in the world. Ward did not establish himself as an NHL regular until he was almost twenty-eight years old, but hit the jackpot when the Washington Capitals, looking to add grit to a talented lineup that had consistently come up short in the playoffs, signed him to a four-year deal worth $12 million in the summer of 2011.

He managed it in part because his mother worked two nursing jobs in order to help pay for his hockey. Nurses often work four consecutive twelve-hour shifts, then get five days off. It was during those periods when Cecilia Ward would take work at other hospitals, running herself between jobs and taking her son to his hockey games. There were days when Joel didn't see his mother, because she was working nights and wouldn't get home until after he had left for school and then be gone to work another shift by the time he got home.

"Sometimes she would just come home, scoop me up, and take me to the game," he said. "I would sometimes have to sleep at the hospital with her while she was working. She would find me a little bed on the side somewhere when she was working nights. In the morning she would take me home and then drop me off at school and catch a [nap] before taking the evening shift. Lots of times I would take the bus to practice and I had a lot of parents help me out in a big way."

Cecilia Ward still works as a nurse, though not as much as she did after her husband died, and lives in the same house in the east end of Toronto. Ward grew up in Scarborough, a working-class enclave that is home to 600,000 people, about 400,000 of whom are visible minorities. It represents an enormous mixed bag of socio-economic levels, from the gritty crime-ridden areas to the opulent million-dollar homes along the shores of Lake Ontario. And it has produced its share of NHL players—among them Hall of Fame defenceman and four-time Stanley Cup champion Larry Murphy, Mike Ricci, Rick Tocchet, Anthony and Chris Stewart, Kris Draper, Anson Carter, Kevin Weekes, and Devante Smith-Pelly.

Almost all of them came from either unprivileged or working-class backgrounds, while many other kids who played in the Greater Toronto Hockey League who had all the privileges and everything handed to them did not make the NHL. Jeff Ware, a first-round pick of the Toronto Maple Leafs in 1995 who played just fifteen games in the NHL, came from a well-to-do family of high achievers, but never managed to make the cut as an NHLer. At one point in his career, one of his coaches in the minor leagues told him, "Jeff, you have to decide whether you want to be a lawyer or a hockey player, because you can't be both."

It's a lament often heard by hockey people in Canada's largest city, that the kids in Toronto are generally so well off and so pampered that they don't have the intestinal fortitude it takes to withstand the rigours of playing in the NHL. Sweeping generalization? Perhaps, but it's one that is out there. In fact, *Toronto Sun* sports columnist Steve Simmons, a long-time and outspoken fixture in minor hockey in the GTHL, believes that sense of entitlement exists.

That has changed somewhat with a renaissance of Toronto hockey players, but they're certainly not coming out of places such as Regent Park and working-class areas such as Scarborough. Most of them are now making their way through minor hockey on teams that require $10,000 to $15,000 a season to play for them. Many are going to the hundreds of skill development coaches who have set up shop in the city. Claude Lemieux, who forged a career as one of the best big-game players in the history of the NHL, was raised in Quebec and played his NHL hockey in Montreal, New Jersey, Colorado, Phoenix, Dallas, and San Jose, but settled in Toronto after his playing career so his son, Brandon, could be exposed to the best hockey possible. Brandon also attended The Hill Academy, a private sports school that costs about $28,000 a year to attend. Max Domi, the son of former Maple Leaf enforcer Tie Domi, spent summers as a minor hockey player training with Sidney Crosby.

But for every one of those players, countless ones from Canada's largest city excel as minor hockey players but fail to go beyond junior hockey. Perhaps that's just the natural order of things when players move up hockey's food chain and find more competition for fewer jobs at each level, but Simmons thinks there's more to it than that. To illustrate, he brings up the names Michael and Adam Henrich, both of whom were stars as minor hockey players in Toronto. Each went on to play in the OHL, Michael for the Brampton Battalion and Adam for the Barrie Colts. Michael was taken thirteenth overall by the Edmonton Oilers in 1998 and Adam went sixtieth overall to the Tampa Bay Lightning four years later, but neither one ever played a game in the NHL, and after years of bouncing around the minor leagues in North America they were playing in the Italian League.

"They were from a privileged family in the suburbs," Simmons said. "What happened when they got to the next highest level? They didn't know how to compete. They weren't able to compete at that level. They were able to compete at eighteen or nineteen when they were better, more skilled, bigger, faster, stronger. But when they had to compete with an equal, they weren't able to do that."

Former NHL goaltender Kevin Weekes, who grew up in the same neighbourhood as Ward and at one time during his NHL career underwrote the Skillz Hockey School that Ward and many inner-city Toronto kids attended, said when he was growing up and playing in what was then the Metro Toronto Hockey League (MTHL) the players who made it were the ones who came from hard-working families such as the Wards, largely because those families had the work ethic and attitude that an NHL player requires. He also notices that seems to have changed with the costs of competitive hockey gradually eluding the financial grasp of those in the working class.

Just off the top of his head, Weekes can rhyme off a host of players from Toronto during his days in minor hockey who came from working-class backgrounds. Brendan Shanahan was the son of Irish immigrants who lived in a middle-class area called Mimico. Steve Thomas, Michael Peca, Anson Carter, Paul and Gino Cavallini, Sean Burke, all sons of blue-collar parents, many of whom were first-generation Canadians who came to this country and forged their way by getting their hands dirty. Weekes, the son of an electrician, was typical of the player growing up in Toronto in the 1980s—not poor by any stretch of the imagination, but not financially advantaged either.

"The only guy I can remember who was in a financially advantaged position—but his work ethic never reflected that—was Eric Lindros," Weekes said. "He was always the hardest-working guy around. He wasn't the kind of guy who said, 'Hey, my dad's an accountant and my mom's a nurse and we live in [the well-to-do area of] Forest Hill, so I don't think I need to run hills today.' That was never his attitude.

"But I honestly think for us, that was a strength because nothing was handed to us. We had to scratch and claw for everything. A lot of people in hockey look at a guy from Fort Saskatchewan and they equate that with a hard-working, down-to-earth guy, but what about Shanny's [Shanahan's] parents who came from Ireland and started from scratch?"

Those players tend to have more perseverance, a character trait Joel Ward has in abundance. But he also combined that with a pragmatic attitude, and while he did not allow his setbacks in hockey to crush his spirit, he was not so singularly focused that he lost sight of perspective. And the setbacks were many for Ward.

Take his draft year, for example. Ward went to Boston in 1999 to the NHL draft with his best suit packed and his family with him, and the full expectation that he would be chosen at some point by one of the twenty-eight teams in the league. Keep in mind that the 1999 draft is considered to be the worst one in history in terms of the quality of players who were selected. It started with Patrik Stefan going to the Atlanta Thrashers, a player who is generally regarded as the worst No. 1 overall pick of all time. After Henrik and Daniel Sedin went second and third overall, it was a long parade of either middling or marginal NHL players—with the exception of Barret Jackman and Martin Havlat in the first round. Some stars were taken later—namely Ryan Miller and Henrik Zetterberg—but it was generally known as a very weak draft.

A total of 272 names were called that day in Boston and Joel Ward's was not one of them. He went back to the Owen Sound Attack of the Ontario Hockey League and became the team's captain and one of the most popular players in franchise history. But along the way he was cut by the Atlanta Thrashers and the Detroit Red Wings, twice. But instead of going to play in the ECHL for the Toledo Storm, as the Red Wings had requested, he decided to pursue his educational opportunities to play at the University of Prince Edward Island. He played there for four years and was the team's MVP for three of them, picking up a Bachelor of Arts in sociology along the way. It seemed a prudent move at the time for Ward, but not one that had a lot of NHL potential. Even though the Canadian Interuniversity Sport hockey league is chock full of former major junior players, it is generally known as the place where NHL aspirations go to die. Players use the education packages they get from their junior teams—Ward got $2,000 per year—and play out their careers at a decent competitive level while still having fun enjoying the game.

The list of CIS graduates who have played in the NHL is small, but there have been some success stories. Randy Gregg won five Stanley Cups for the Edmonton Oilers after playing at the University of Alberta and becoming an orthopedic surgeon. Mike Ridley, Steve Rucchin, Charlie Bourgeois, Stu Grimson, Claude Vilgrain, and Cory Cross all enjoyed productive NHL careers after playing Canadian university hockey. Among current NHLers aside from Ward, Jody Shelley and Mathieu Darche are products of the Canadian university system.

"It does give me pride knowing I controlled my own destiny," Ward said. "There are some things I wish would have turned out differently. It would have been cool to be drafted, and maybe play for Team Canada at any level."

How does one quantify the struggles of people such as Glen Metropolit, Barret Jackman, and Joel Ward and the effect it had on their NHL careers? Would they have been even better NHLers if given access to the best coaching and competition, to one-on-one instruction, to summer hockey programs? Or was it the struggle that made them stronger and gave them the fortitude they needed to continue their careers to the highest level? It's hard to believe Claude Giroux would have developed into an even better NHL player had he grown up in a place bigger and less isolated than Hearst, Ontario.

But maybe the exceptions help prove the rule. One thing all these guys have in common? Something hockey parents should take notice of: all these players grew up without a parent barking at them like a drill sergeant, motivating them and "developing" them. Sure, the Walter Gretzkys and Carl Lindroses have their place in hockey lore, but it may well be that if a kid has what it takes, maybe the best thing a parent can do is get out of the way and let the kid have fun.

That might not be easy, though, in the financial landscape that has taken shape around the game. As Glen Metropolit said, there's a lot of talent in housing projects such as Regent Park that goes untapped because of a lack of opportunity. But there are those who believe it goes beyond the ones in need and is stretching its tentacles into the middle class. As we've said in a previous chapter, it seems that it takes one of two things to be able to make it in the NHL: a family that either is financially well off or is willing to make enormous financial sacrifices.

"It's become almost about haves and have-nots," Weekes said. "It has become so financially prohibitive for so many people. And it's not just one sector. I know a lot of people will think, 'Because you live in the inner city and you're Glen Metropolit or you're Anthony Stewart ...' No. Whether you're Mike Ricci or Shanny or Dave Bolland or Dave Clarkson ... if this was now, I don't know how our parents would be able to pay for us to play. I really don't know. Are you going to contribute to your RRSP, are you going to pay your mortgage, or are you going to rent a house because you have a son or daughter who plays high level minor hockey?"

9

CANADIAN ROULETTE

Standing on the front steps of his family's home in Ajax, Ontario, in the spring of 2011, fourteen-year-old Matthew Kostuch was preparing himself for a ten-kilometre training run. As he pulled his heel up to his buttock and balanced himself on one leg, he used the moment to take stock of how he felt. It was a usual ritual with the usual result. His head was pounding just as intensely as it did the day before … and the day before that.

"I have a headache as we speak," he said. "On a scale of one to ten, it's probably a nine. It's really bad."

Not bad enough to deter him from running, though. His doctors tell Matthew exercise is the best thing for him. Plus, it takes his mind off the pain for a little while in ways even the strongest drugs have failed to do. So off we went, talking about young Matthew's plans for the future, one that will never again include a game of competitive hockey. He talked excitedly about coaching and refereeing because he's unable to shake his love for a game that has been so cruel to him over the past couple of years. One of his favourite quotes, attributable to nobody in particular, goes something like this: "Strength is nothing more than how well you hide the pain." Matthew Kostuch has had mixed success hiding the pain since being drilled into the boards in 2007, but being able to run 10K with a headache measuring nine out of ten—from somebody who knows a headache when he experiences one—indicates that, at least for this day, he will not allow the pain to rule him.

"If you had a video camera here on him ten minutes before you arrived, he wasn't the same kid," said Matthew's father, Jim. "Then he was like, 'OK, let's run!'"

For the vast majority of hockey players, the end of a career is not something that is voluntary. Almost always, the game, and not the player, dictates when a player will no longer play at a competitive level. For all but a very select few, that thinning of the herd takes place relatively early. The best players are usually segregated from the others at a young age and players drop from there as the competition gets more intense. Most players have been told by the game they're not good enough by their early to mid-teens, while the others forge on at the junior and college levels, only to be culled and weeded out as the truly elite players sort themselves out. From there players go one of three routes—to the NHL, to any number of minor leagues in North America, or to Europe. Very few ever end their careers the way players such as Jean Béliveau, Mark Recchi, and Ray Bourque did, as Stanley Cup champions who left the game on their terms still with something to give. Most, regardless of the level, limp away from the game after being told they can no longer contribute.

But at the other end of the spectrum, so few of them are forced to retire before they get the braces off their teeth. But that's exactly what happened to Matthew Kostuch, who has suffered from post-concussion syndrome every bit as much as players such as Eric Lindros, Paul Kariya, Keith Primeau, and Pat LaFontaine, and ultimately suffered the same fate as those NHL stars. Kostuch, though, never had the opportunity to chase the NHL dream. It had nothing to do with his ability— he was playing AAA at the time, the highest level of competitive hockey available—and everything to do with a devastating hit he took along the boards in December 2007.

Matthew Kostuch was just ten years old when he was playing for the Ajax-Pickering Raiders AAA major atom team in a game in Kingston. Kostuch went deep into his own zone to retrieve the puck, turned up-ice and was carrying it with about eight feet of ice between him and the boards. Then into the picture comes a black sweater. The young player is churning at full speed and has Kostuch directly in his sights. As he makes impact, the Kingston player brings up both his arms, coming into contact with Kostuch's head before drilling him into a Pizza Pizza board advertisement. Not only was the referee, who didn't even call a penalty on the play, able to see what happened, but he had to let up along the boards to avoid the collision himself.

Since then, Matthew Kostuch's life has been turned upside down. Doctors later said that it's likely he suffered two concussions on that hit, one on the right side of his brain from the initial contact and one on the left side of his brain as a result of being slammed into the boards. Not only has he had to retire from hockey, he'll never be able to play soccer, football, lacrosse, or rugby because the danger of suffering another serious concussion is far too great. More than three years after the injury, he was still ravaged almost daily by intense headaches, mood swings, and an inability to sleep. Dr. Karen Johnson, regarded as one of the leading experts on concussion in Canada, was the one who ordered Kostuch to the sidelines, and while she is confident his pain and misery will end one day, even she can't tell him how much longer he'll have to endure it. And there's not a drug in the world that can mask the pain, even temporarily. But it was the loss of hockey for the rest of his life that is the most difficult for him to accept.

"The game he loves the most," said Jim Kostuch, "took him out of the game he loves the most."

And this is a family that did everything right. They kept him out of hockey for the rest of the 2007–08 hockey season and took every precaution imaginable to ensure their son was getting the best treatment they could find. They took far longer than everyone told them to before they allowed him to go back on the ice—nine full months, in fact. They only allowed him to return to playing when he was fully cleared by a doctor and, unlike many other parents of young players, did not rush the process. And when Matthew's headaches began to resurface again in 2010 with a vengeance for no particular reason, they shut him down again. Only this time, it was permanently.

Thousands of players are injured every year playing minor hockey in Canada. In 2009–10, Hockey Canada reported 11,755 injuries, which is 2.03 percent of the 577,000 who were registered that year. But that number represents only a tiny fraction of the number of players who were actually injured that season because it reflects only the injuries in which an insurance claim was made. That usually means an ambulance was called or further treatment was required that is not covered by a provincial health plan. Nobody knows how many more players are injured in a typical season and to what extent they are hurt, but even Hockey Canada acknowledges the number is much, much higher than that.

For example, nobody called an ambulance, nor was an insurance claim made, when Matthew Kostuch suffered his concussion.

Of those injuries, a total of 1,543 (or 13 percent) of them were concussions, which was by far the malady most reported to Hockey Canada, significantly more than the reported broken arms (1,162) and, shockingly, more than three times the number of broken legs. The only problem is that unlike broken arms and legs, no finite healing time exists with concussions. Anyone who has followed hockey in even the most peripheral way has realized that the game has reached a crossroads when it comes to concussions: They have become a major concern at every level from peewee to professional. The long-term effects are just now being realized, and even those in the scientific community acknowledge that they are only beginning to scratch the surface when it comes to understanding a concussion.

Dr. Michael Cusimano, a neurosurgeon at St. Michael's Hospital in Toronto and a leading authority on concussion, estimates that 15,000 to 20,000 young players sustain a concussion in hockey each season. He also thinks his numbers are conservative. The great majority of them will recover, return to play after some time off, and continue their minor hockey careers. In fact, concussion expert Dr. Charles Tator estimates that 95 percent get over one concussion. The other 5 percent end up like Matthew Kostuch, or worse.

So little hard data on concussions exists that we're going to have to make some assumptions here. Let's assume that Dr. Cusimano is right with his estimate of 20,000 concussions. If we apply Dr. Tator's math to the equation, that's 1,000 kids a season who get concussions so traumatic that they have to stop playing the game and suffer life-altering consequences. One thousand players, assuming all of those 20,000 concussions are first concussions. Those with cumulative concussions are more susceptible to future concussions than those who have not been concussed and the recovery time is often longer, as is the potential for more damage.

"I see those kids all the time," said Tator, a renowned neuro-surgeon and the founder of ThinkFirst Canada, an organization dedicated to the prevention of brain and spinal cord injuries. "In other words, it's a regular occurrence in my practice to have to tell young people they can no longer pursue their dreams."

If nothing else, you must understand this if you are ever in a situation where your hockey-playing child is suspected of having a concussion. There is not a doctor in the world—at the moment—who can definitively tell you when he or she will be ready to return to playing. In fact, when Matthew Kostuch first suffered his concussion in December 2007, the first doctor he saw in the emergency room at the hospital told him he would be back on the ice in a couple of days. He didn't play the rest of that season, missed fifty days of school, and caused his mother to break down into tears on one occasion when, as a straight A student, he couldn't perform the simple task of converting grams to kilograms.

"I was trying to explain it to him and he couldn't get it and he was getting frustrated because he realized he couldn't get it," said Matthew's mother, Christine Kostuch. "It was then that, as a mother, I realized my son's brain has been injured."

Concussions as severe as the one suffered by Matthew Kostuch are rare to be sure, particularly at that age. But it does bring into focus the lack of uniformity in Canada when it comes to the notion of bodychecking. There are constituencies that allow body contact right from the age of ten, while Quebec doesn't allow body contact until bantam hockey, when the players are fourteen. It has provided a long-running debate in Canada: Are children better served by learning the proper way to give and receive a bodycheck—and grasp the notion of respect—as early as possible? After all, there are those who believe bodychecking is a skill that is every bit as important as passing, shooting, and stickhandling.

Dr. Lauren Sergio, who is doing some interesting concussion research at York University in Toronto, thinks any branch of hockey that allows bodychecking at the age of ten and under is doing its players a disservice. Hockey Canada's rules state that bodychecking is not allowed in the atom division and below, but some branches do allow it at that level. Which is a mistake, according to Sergio.

She maintains the developing brain of a ten-year-old is not adequately equipped to process all the cognitive tasks it is required to on the ice and be mindful of avoiding a bodycheck from someone out of their line of vision. As soon as you throw thinking into moving, it's going to slow down the cognitive process. The truly gifted players will always be able to multitask and make marvellous moves without being hit, but it's the more ordinary players who have a problem with it.

"You can't keep them all," she said. "The kid is going to let cognition go. If you have anything else that takes precedence, say stickhandling, you're going to focus way more on that than you will on positioning."

There is no such thing as a "severe" or "mild" concussion, and like DNA, no two concussions are the same. Some players can receive a half-dozen concussions over the course of their careers, and others like Matthew Kostuch can be forced out of the game by just one or two. So taking the concussion Sidney Crosby suffered in 2011 and comparing it to those sustained by players such as Max Pacioretty, Nathan Horton, or Marc Savard is pointless. In fact, even those at the medical ground zero of concussion research admit there is so much about it they don't know.

"Recognition of concussion in the past has been dreadful," Tator said. "And the missed diagnoses have been due to practitioners like myself who have been uninformed about concussion, and also the entire sporting world of coaches, trainers, parents, players, leagues, and referees have been just as unaware that the problem is so great."

This is a book about the sacrifices players and families make to chase the opportunity to play professional hockey— and what sacrifice could be greater than abruptly having to stop playing permanently because of a catastrophic injury? And it's not only concussions we're talking about. Even though spinal injuries have declined in the past decade due to more awareness and greater penalties for hitting from behind, catastrophic spinal injuries still occur in hockey. Sports medicine doctors see impact injuries from hockey players regularly, and some at the professional level believe the spate of hip and groin ailments we see at the pro level is a direct result of overuse, a trend that starts now in younger and younger players with the advent of spring and summer hockey.

Michael Clarfield is the director and co-founder of Sports Medicine Specialists, the largest sports medicine clinic in Canada. The walls of his Toronto clinic are adorned with pictures and sticks from a Who's Who of glitterati in professional hockey. He worked with a gangly Eric Lindros when regular growth spurts were causing him knee problems as a teenager, and was the team doctor for the Toronto Maple Leafs for sixteen seasons. Currently the company physician for the National Ballet of Canada and the team doctor for the Canadian national tennis team, he said about 40 percent of his clientele is made up of young hockey players. Clarfield has seen a spike over the past decade in two types of injuries— concussions and groin/hip injuries. Fifteen years ago, he might have seen one hockey player a month with a concussion. Now he often sees more than ten a week. As far as hip and groin injuries go, Clarfield said he didn't see many of them until the 1990s. Like concussions, the spike has something to do with the medical community's ability to better detect them, but also because kids are playing more hockey than they ever have. It's not uncommon for an elite tyke team to have as many games a season, with tournaments, as an NHL player does. And with elite players taking only a few weeks off in the summer instead of the entire off-season, all that strain on hips and groins is going to lead to injuries.

Most of them are adductor strains, an injury that, in and of itself, is not a terribly serious one most of the time. They generally occur when the adductor muscles contract to deal with the forces that push against it when the athlete has to shift direction suddenly and push off. How many times does that happen in a typical hockey game or practice? Just about every time the puck is turned over, that's how many. So a player is doing it dozens of times a game, and if that's happening almost every day, the wear and tear on the tendons and muscles is going to be tremendous. That's why, Clarfield said, we shouldn't be surprised if we see a future generation of elite hockey players hobbling around in arthritic pain as adults needing surgical hip replacements. The sooner and more often you expose your body to that type of injury, the more cumulative stress you're putting on your body and the more likely you are to develop arthritic conditions.

"The hip and groin area is probably one of the prime areas where I rarely saw injuries in kids and now we see them all the time," Clarfield said. "Injuries we were seeing in pros years ago that we never saw in kids, we're seeing working its way down to the kids as they're playing more and exposed to more. You're exposing the same muscle groups to the same stress over and over again and they're not getting a rest. And with the pressure on kids to play through things, sometimes you see they've already progressed to a level where it's more difficult to treat."

Dr. Michael Stuart, who is the chief medical officer for USA Hockey, says one of the most difficult concepts for young hockey players and their parents to understand is that a young body needs rest, the kind of rest some of them never seem to get. Hockey has become a twelve-month-a-year pursuit for many elite young players, often at the expense of playing other sports that can enhance a player's balance, aerobic/anaerobic fitness, and strength through cross-training. Stuart, whose three sons played professional hockey, said most elite young hockey players are on the ice in the off-season more than professional players, who are working on their balance, overall fitness, and strength. And then there's the possibility of burnout, the psychological effects of too much, too often. How is a player supposed to get excited for the start of another hockey season when he's had his equipment on through most of the summer?

"Why would a young player who's trying to get to the highest level skate more and play more games and have their blades on more than these pro athletes?" Dr. Stuart said. "Often times, that's driven by parents. I see players going into training camp with muscular-skeletal problems that are not related to an eighty-two-game season. They're related to the way they're getting ready for an eighty-two-game season. If you think about it, it doesn't make much sense."

Hockey always has been, and always will be, a risky game to play at any level under any set of rules. The game is played on a slippery surface and the ten players on it are guiding themselves on a blade of steel that is just one-eighth-inch thick. They are carrying sticks that sometimes can be used as weapons, but most others are intended to shoot a frozen piece of vulcanized rubber as hard as possible. At the highest levels, players are travelling up to 50 kilometres per hour when they're at top speed. And unlike soccer, football, and basketball, there is no out of bounds, only hard and unforgiving boards.

"I just don't know of a sport that moves as fast and as full-throttle as hockey does," said Dr. Richard Ginsburg, the co-director of the sports psychology program at the Massachusetts General Hospital and co-author of the book *Whose Game Is It Anyway?* "Hockey is one of those sports where you are going 90 miles per hour all the time and that, to me, is unique."

Just as players at the highest levels have become better, stronger, faster, and bigger than ever before, so have those all the way down the hockey food chain. So it only stands to reason that there would be more violent collisions and more serious injuries among young players than there were before. And just because there's a rulebook doesn't mean everyone is going to follow it. The truth is, hockey has been surrounded by a culture of violence for more than a century. Teams at all levels are encouraged to stretch the limits of the rules as far as they can and the players who are most celebrated at any level are those who not only play through the pain, but ignore it. To do anything otherwise would be to admit weakness.

And just because there are leagues with no body contact doesn't mean unintentional collisions won't occur. It doesn't mean players won't trip over an errant stick and fall awkwardly headfirst into the boards. And just because hockey cracks down on hits from behind and many have sewn STOP patches onto the back of hockey sweaters doesn't mean those dangerous and catastrophic hits are not going to ever occur. Dr. Charles Tator said his research indicates that the issue of spinal cord injuries has become "a good news story," because people have been convinced to take it so seriously. Spinal cord injuries continue to decline, to the point where Tator said there are at least twenty brain injuries for every spinal cord injury, thus putting concussion and brain injuries at the forefront.

It would be difficult, though, to convince Marc-Andre Emond and Andrew Zaccardo that spinal injuries are on a precipitous decline. In the fall of 2009, Emond and Zaccardo were promising players with the Montreal Blitz midget "espoirs" team, both trying to impress scouts in an effort to get drafted into the Quebec Major Junior Hockey League. Less than a year later, however, cruel and calamitous twists of fate would see both of them paralyzed and unable to play again as a result of separate incidents.

Emond was playing in a game in the Montreal suburb of Pointe Claire on November 27, 2009, when he tried to swing around a defenceman in order to get a clear path to the net. Had he been able to, there's a good chance he would have scored, since he was leading the league in scoring at the time. As he was making his move, the defenceman dropped his stick and Emond stepped on it and stumbled. At precisely the same moment, knowing he was in trouble, the defenceman gave Emond a desperate push in the back, sending him flying into the boards.

The collision resulted in Emond fracturing the fifth and sixth vertebrae at the base of his neck, leaving him temporarily paralyzed from the neck down. One of the first players at his teammate's side that afternoon was Andrew Zaccardo. He didn't know it at the time, but eleven months later he would find himself suffering an almost identical injury with almost identical results. By this time, Zaccardo was playing for the Laval Patriotes midget team at the Martin Brodeur Arena in St-Léonard when he was hit from behind on a similar play and sent into the boards. Both young men suffered fractured fifth and sixth vertebrae, with doctors using bone from Emond's hip to replace them. As of 2011, both were moving with the aid of a walker after years of difficult rehabilitation.

"I really think it was an accident," Emond told the Montreal *Gazette*. "The same thing could have happened to anyone."

And therein lies the conundrum when it comes to catastrophic injuries in hockey. Yes, they are rare, but they do happen—and as Emond cautioned, they can happen to anyone. It's also worth noting that unlike every other jurisdiction in Canada, bodychecking is not allowed in Quebec in competitive hockey until the bantam level when players reach the age of fourteen. But, critics will argue, that's also precisely the time players begin to develop testosterone, grow into their bodies, and become more innately aggressive when they compete. ("Just when they get hair on their balls," said former NHLer Ray Ferraro, "that's when they start allowing them to run around and hit people.") And if they have been unfamiliar with the concept of safely giving and taking a hit, it is going to be foreign to them.

Emond and Zaccardo aside, catastrophic spinal cord injuries are on the decline. But the same cannot be said for concussion, which continues to make its impact felt more intensely with every passing season. And while a vast body of knowledge and an enormous amount of resources are going into concussion research, there remains much people don't know about concussions, which often leads to the wrong diagnosis or, even worse, players being sent back into play in a contact sport far too early. Not only does that increase the possibility of subsequent concussions, but every young player who returns to play and sustains a second concussion before the first has resolved exposes him- or herself to the prospect of second impact syndrome, a malady that in a best-case scenario causes irreparable brain damage and in worst-case scenarios causes death.

It, too, is rare, "although it is more common than previously expected," according to Dr. Paul Echlin in an editorial he wrote for *Neurosurgical Focus* in November 2010. And what is even more disturbing is that while the developing brain seems to be able to develop alternative pathways that prevent them from developing the chronic traumatic encephalopathy (CTE) that has plagued multiple concussion victims as older adults, teenagers are almost exclusively susceptible to second impact syndrome. It is precisely in this age group that players at an elite level are trying to establish themselves as players and are often more likely to hide or downplay the seriousness of their injury. Perhaps they have an important prospects tournament to play that weekend, or they've taken a blow to the head in the semifinal of an important tournament with the championship game only hours away.

That leaves the player open to the possibility of a second hit with far more devastating consequences. In second impact syndrome, the brain loses control of its auto regulation of blood flow, which in turn results in swelling and brain damage that can bring on respiratory problems, brain damage, and death. Virtually all the cases have occurred in athletes aged twenty or younger—athletes such as Max Conradt of Waldport, Oregon. A seventeen-year-old senior quarterback at Waldport High School with a 3.95 grade point average—which made him an A-plus student—he was planning to attend college to study sports journalism. In a game in 2001, he suffered a concussion in a helmet-to-helmet hit wearing a twenty-year-old helmet that had been reconditioned three times. He finished the game and was diagnosed with a concussion the next day, but was in the lineup eight days later when he hit his head on the ground after being sacked. He collapsed on the sideline and was rushed to hospital with an acute subdural hematoma. He underwent three surgeries, spent four months in hospital, and now lives in an assisted living facility for people with severe brain injuries. He suffers short-term memory loss, is prone to violent outbursts, and has never held a job.

In 2009, Conradt's home state of Oregon passed "Max's Law," which requires all coaches to receive concussion-recognition training and states that any athlete who is even suspected of having suffered a concussion must be immediately removed from play and cannot return without the written permission of a health care provider. Now more than half the states in the U.S. have similar legislation. Sadly, a private member's bill calling for the same kind of legislation died in Canada's House of Commons in 2011, and none of the provinces has introduced any kind of sports concussion legislation.

"There is definitely something about the teenage brain," said Dr. Lauren Sergio, who is heading a study on the long-term effects of concussion at York University and leads the baseline testing for all prospects at the NHL's draft combine. "I'm not sure—and as far as I know, nobody has figured out the fine brain physiology of why auto regulation in teenagers isn't working as well or able to deal with the second impact, other than the obvious which is the brain isn't developed yet. It's not finished. You don't finish until your early twenties."

So why do hockey players continue to get concussions at almost all ages? Well, the nature of the game has something to do with it. And the fact that concussions are more readily identified and understood accounts for some of the higher numbers. But even with more information, those in the medical field claim we have a long way to go to overcome our lack of understanding about the severity of concussion and the cultural resistance to acknowledging the injury. The fact is, a concussed player often ignores or hides the symptoms he or she is experiencing, largely because there is pressure— either internal or brought on by outside forces—to continue to perform. Competitive athletes learn at a young age to please those who support them, such as parents and coaches. By not admitting to an injury or playing through one, they might think it would please their coaches and parents and not only keep their place on the team secure, but result in more playing time. It also doesn't help that concussion is largely an invisible injury that exhibits no outward effects, so the player often has a difficult time explaining to teammates and coaches why he or she is not able to play.

Athletes, as a rule, are far more likely to follow the advice of their coach than they are a doctor. That often creates a push and pull between the coach and the doctor where both can be coming from opposite perspectives. Coaches, even at the youngest levels of elite hockey, are under pressure to win and that sometimes conflicts with the well-being of a player. Studies have shown that young players predominantly obtain their information concerning concussions and returning to play from their coaches and teachers before medical personnel.

"I'm struck with the influence the coach has on a hockey player," said Dr. Richard Ginsburg. "All athletes are affected by their coaches, but the power of a hockey coach, the intensity of a hockey coach, the political position of a hockey coach ... It seems to me the player's position is very fragile."

But more than anything, society and the hockey community continue to ignore concussion and look at it as a benign and temporary image that doesn't necessarily need medical attention. Or as Dr. Paul Echlin put it in his editorial in 2010, "cultural and societal obstacles may prevent the seriousness of this brain injury and its long-term effects from being appropriately recognized."

Dr. Echlin, in fact, spearheaded the Hockey Concussion Education Project (HCEP) in 2009 because of that very attitude. A sports medicine specialist in London, Ontario, and a former team doctor for the London Knights and Plymouth Whalers of the Ontario Hockey League, he decided to embark on the groundbreaking study after a junior coach overruled him on a return-to-play decision involving a player with a concussion. When confronted by the doctor, the coach responded by saying, "Who needs a doctor anyway?"

Michael Clarfield has seen that sort of attitude at levels much lower than junior hockey. As one of Canada's foremost sports medicine experts, he has treated some of the biggest stars in the NHL, but he's also involved in minor hockey in Toronto. In a game several years ago, he could clearly see that one of the players on his son's team, of which he was an assistant coach, had suffered a concussion. He strongly suggested to the coach, the trainer, and the player's parents that the boy stop playing, but was met with nothing but vociferous resistance from all parties. One of them even said they would let the child play if the doctor wasn't there to diagnose a concussion, so why not let him play? Then, Clarfield said, the player's father told his son that if he were to get hurt in the future not to tell Clarfield about it because the doctor would tell him he couldn't play.

"This is single-A hockey and this is the mentality of some of these parents," Clarfield said. "The dad was, I don't want to say an idiot, but this poor kid has to listen to his dad tell him, 'If you're hurt don't talk to Clarfield because he'll make you sit out.' You wouldn't believe the flak I got for not letting this kid play. It was unbelievable."

In his concussion study, Dr. Echlin reported that when it came to parents, "in many of the concussion cases during the HCEP, the athlete's health did not seem to be a priority." He also went on to write that the father of a fourteen-year-old player with a concussion told him that he could understand parents of players with concussions choosing to ignore their children's injury, even after it has been medically diagnosed. "He said that parents had a significant amount of time and money invested in the child and if there was nothing visibly wrong, he should be on the ice with his teammates," Echlin wrote.

Dr. Charles Tator, one of the sport's leading authorities on concussion, reports that he often sees parents who are shopping around from doctor to doctor to get the answer they want rather than the truth. And the problem is that so many doctors are so uninformed about concussion that there's a good chance if a player and his parents look hard enough, they'll find someone who will clear him or her to play. Echlin wrote that on two separate occasions, players diagnosed with concussion by a doctor attending the game refused follow-up and instead got a return-to-play note from their family doctors. When the doctors were told about the original diagnosis, they said both the players and parents deliberately deceived them about the nature of the injury. The management of the team and league were made aware of the deception and took no action against the players.

So why is it that the same parents who will seemingly do anything for their children when it comes to their minor hockey careers are willing to place it all in jeopardy by ignoring the dangers of concussion? We've already established that many parents of elite hockey players in this country are willing to go to almost any length to enhance their children's hockey experience, including spending thousands of dollars and placing an enormous emotional investment in their careers. But when it comes to a legitimate medical diagnosis that results in the player being forced to sit on the sidelines, they sometimes put on blinders.

"There are multiple people who come to my office and say, 'I just spent $200 on a hockey stick,'" Echlin said. "And you tell them, 'Look, your son is symptomatic. He has a brain injury.' And you never see them again."

And that attitude often originates from the same place that prompts parents to spend money on private instruction, and forces others to place their own lives on hold while their children pursue their dreams and make financial and emotional sacrifices that clearly go above and beyond the call of duty as parents. According to Dr. Richard Ginsburg, parents of elite athletes often get tossed into a whirlwind of expectation and intensity that spirals out of control. As a result, they often lose perspective.

"Everyone is looking for that competitive edge, everybody is playing in that extra tournament," Ginsburg said. "The stuff that kids are doing in hockey ... You have kids in boarding schools who are travelling from Maine all the way to Boston for a game on a Sunday and they spend four or five hours in the car to watch their kids play for two hours on their day off. How do you behave normally in a culture that behaves this way?"

Mark Hyman can certainly relate. A sports dad, coach, and award-winning journalist, he wrote about his experiences in his book *Until It Hurts: America's Obsession with Youth Sports and How It Harms Our Kids*. The book was born out of the mistakes he made with his own son, Ben, a promising pitcher who had a talent level to match his passion for baseball. In the book, he admits to teaching his son a pitch akin to a curveball, a pitch that places an enormous amount of stress on a young arm. When Ben was thirteen years old, he confided in his father that his right shoulder, the one that anchored his prized pitching arm, didn't feel right. After being told by his son's athletic trainer at school to be examined by an orthopedic surgeon and lay off pitching for a month, the first question he asked was whether or not Ben would be able to pitch the next Friday. Despite the advice, he sent his son out to pitch in the league championship game three days after that meeting. That was the start of injury woes that not only derailed his chance at a scholarship, but also resulted in his son having Tommy John surgery, an operation in which a tendon from the patient's wrist or leg is used to take the place of a useless elbow ligament. Hyman's book points out the reason why 3.5 million athletes in the United States under the age of fifteen require medical treatment for sports injuries is that parents such as him have engineered a hostile takeover of youth sports.

"I hadn't pushed him in front of a speeding car, nothing like that," Hyman wrote in his book. "But what I'd done was silly bordering on reckless and above all narcissistic. The irony of the situation was that if another mom or dad had used such terrible judgment at my son's expense, I would have been livid."

It's that kind of attitude, among other things, that prompted Echlin to launch the Hockey Concussion Education Project (HCEP) during the 2009–10 season, a study that turned out to be groundbreaking work in hockey concussion research. The study followed sixty-seven Jr. C players for one season, tracking the number of concussions that were suffered as well as how quickly players returned to the ice. The study contained a number of shocking revelations—namely that the incidence of concussion is seven times higher than was previously reported—but came to the even more pertinent conclusion that when it comes to serious brain injuries and Canada's national game, passion often wins over common sense and good judgment.

In fact, one team that had originally agreed to take part in the study pulled out of it halfway through the season at the insistence of a team executive, who said he would allow his team to return to the study only under the condition that the protocol be changed to prevent the doctor attending the game to examine a player suspected of having a concussion until after the game and only with the permission of the trainers, coaches, and players. Think about that for a second. Here you have a team executive preventing his player from being evaluated immediately by a qualified and experienced physician as to whether he might have a concussion. The remaining two teams, Echlin reported, had ongoing resistance to the project as the season progressed and one GM said he feared a "mutiny" among his players concerning the post-injury testing that was being done and that his team would lose players as a result of it.

Echlin approached a men's hockey team from a major Canadian university about the project and it was accepted by the school's athletic director, athletic therapist, and team doctors but the coach of the team refused to participate, saying he didn't think he could fit the three-hour testing period into his team's schedule. Rather than overrule the coach, the school's administration and medical staff supported his decision. At a university. You know, an institution that's supposed to be devoted to higher learning. That kind of thinking doesn't surprise Toronto concussion expert Dr. Michael Cusimano, who approached thirty minor hockey coaches with a hockey safety video designed to prevent concussions, only to be rebuffed by twenty-two of them because they thought it would make their players less aggressive.

Echlin also reported that one player in the study, upon suffering his third concussion of the season in a hockey fight, said the brain injury was causing him to have difficulty in his university classes and feared he might not get good enough grades to go to graduate school. He said he felt pressure from a team executive who promised him a letter of recommendation for graduate school and, even after his diagnosis, continued to feel pressure from the team to return to play. Another player admitted to failing to report a concussion one week before suffering another one and returned himself to play against the direct medical advice of those doing the study.

"The pressure to win the next period, game or series is an important and overriding factor that blinds many of those who should be protecting our young athletes," Echlin wrote of his study. "Hockey and other contact sports should always be respected as a game, not a life-and-death battle that places the participants at needless risk for future disability."

A study done in Edmonton for the *Clinical Journal of Sports Medicine* in 2001 concluded that hockey accounted for 21 percent of all sports-related head injuries, with the largest numbers coming in the fifteen- to nineteen-year-old age group—well ahead of cycling, which was second and accounted for just 12 percent of all sports head injuries. In Canada, at least, there is not an athletic pursuit out there that produces even close to the number of head injuries that hockey does. The study concluded that just 7 percent were caused by soccer, and football—by far the leading cause of concussion among young athletes in the United States—accounted for just 5 percent of all sports-related head injuries.

That should be expected, really. With the exception of soccer, hockey has the greatest number of players taking part in the game. But it simply cannot be discounted that the fact young players play so many games over the course of the season accounts for some of that total. Hockey Canada puts no restrictions on how many games a team can play, and it's common for minor hockey teams to play more than eighty games a season including tournaments and playoffs. Elite young major junior players are seemingly always on the ice. Once they're drafted, their summer starts with a prospects camp with the team that drafted them, followed by a rookie camp and rookie tournament, which usually follows training camp for their own junior teams. Then comes main training camp in the NHL, followed by a sixty-eight-game schedule, plus playoffs. If the player is good enough to be considered for the World Junior Championship team, he'll play two extra games as part of a Russian team tour of Canada, then take part in the selection camp and the World Junior tournament itself. There's usually a league all-star game to be played, and if his team is good enough to make the Memorial Cup that means four rounds of playoffs, plus the tournament that stretches the season into late May.

After a firestorm of criticism, Little League Baseball established maximum pitch counts in 2010. Not only are young players not allowed to throw curveballs, which is lethal to developing arm tendons, there are also strict limits on the number of pitches a player can throw. Players aged seventeen and eighteen, for example, are limited to 105 pitches a day and must have four days' rest if they throw more than 75 pitches. Players who pitch more than 41 pitches in a game cannot go back into the game as a catcher.

But despite a loose guideline that mandates teams hold two practices for every one game, Hockey Canada seems perfectly content to allow elite young teams to travel and play as much as they see fit. And that doesn't include spring and summer hockey, over which Hockey Canada has no control.

Dr. Michael Stuart, the chief medical officer for USA Hockey and the vice-chair of orthopedic surgery at the Mayo Clinic in Rochester, Minnesota, has a unique perspective on the game. His three sons, Mike, Mark, and Colin, have all appeared in the NHL after playing college hockey and his daughter, Cristin, played for the women's team at Boston University. Despite knowing the risks of playing too much hockey, Stuart said his son Mark played ninety-two games when he was thirteen, the year his team won the Minnesota state championship. He also allowed his children to play summer hockey, despite the fact that he was part of a study of hockey injuries in 1995 that led him to the conclusion that more games means much more chance of injury.

"We found there's a twenty-five times higher risk of sustaining an injury in a game compared to a practice," Stuart said. "So one way to make the sport safer is to practise more and play fewer games."

And the greater the position the player has on the team, the greater the chance of him being injured. So that means the star players who play the power play, kill penalties, and play every other shift are far more susceptible to injury than the third- or fourth-line player who gets out for fewer shifts and the ones he does play are usually shorter. The probability of injury also increases exponentially with the level of play, meaning those who are playing bantam and midget with spots on junior teams and scholarships on the line are going to be far more likely to be injured than a ten-year-old playing atom in a non-contact league. Dr. Lauren Sergio, who does the baseline tests for hundreds of NHL draft prospects each year, said five years ago, one or two prospects might have reported a history of concussion, but now she estimates one in four draft prospects she sees has had at least one concussion during his hockey career.

Part of that, at least, has to come from more diligent reporting. Most teams now have concussion tests that can be administered on the bench or sideline after a suspected concussion, and if a player is suspected of having a brain injury he can be pulled out of the game. There was a time when that player would have been asked what day it was and sent back out to play as soon as the initial fog cleared. Dr. Stuart, for one, doesn't believe an enormous number more concussions are being suffered now than in the past. It's simply that they're now being recorded. Stuart calls it "historical controls" and compares it to those who claim they never wore a seat belt, but don't take into account the fact that the cars didn't go nearly as fast and there were only a fraction of them on the roads compared to today.

"I remember being knocked out and sitting on the sidelines and not knowing where I was and finally coming to on the bus on the way home," Stuart said. "And I would be playing the next day. That's ill-advised nowadays, but back then it was seen to be part of the game."

Perhaps times haven't changed so much after all. The most pressing problem when it comes to concussion is having players admit to having suffered one and having those around the athlete—largely coaches and parents—back them up when they learn of the injury. Dr. Cusimano notices that he regularly sees the parents of young players in his clinic who are pushing their kids to return to play before their symptoms have healed. Perhaps what is most disturbing, though, is that the parents are often doing so despite the fact that their child is expressing doubts about his or her own well being.

"I've had players come into the clinic when the child is sitting there and clearly the pressure is coming from the parent to get back in," Cusimano told a concussion conference in 2011. "You ask the father or the mother to leave. This is with both boys and girls. And they'll say, 'I don't really want to play anymore. It's not fun for me anymore. I don't want to get hurt.' But the parent comes in and it's, 'OK, you're OK, play, play, play.'"

So we've established that the players, parents, and coaches are the last people we should be relying on for accurate information when it comes to injuries, concussion in particular. But when the coach and the parents are the most important people in the sphere of influence, that can be a problem. And the player himself will almost always do or say whatever it takes to get back into the lineup as soon as possible. The prospect of lost playing time and status in the lineup resulting from an injury is a common fear among athletes. Players often put themselves at risk of further injury by either ignoring the injury or playing through it to maintain their spot in the lineup. We saw in a previous chapter the story of Evan Zucker, whose shoulder problems knocked him out of the game. They drove him out in large part because he refused to ever take himself out of the lineup and give his body proper time to heal.

And remember Mitchell Davis, the child scoring phenom who failed to live up to his Gretzky-like numbers as a seven-year-old? Just days before leaving for training camp with the Erie Otters in 2009, he was told by his doctor that he had a pilonidal cyst in his tailbone that needed to be lanced. Despite the surgery, he went to Erie's camp and confided in one of the members of the training staff that he was in constant pain. When the first round of cuts was announced by then-coach Robbie Ftorek, Davis learned that he had made it to the next round.

"On the one hand, I was excited," he said, "but on the other hand I was thinking, 'Am I going to be able to take another hit out there without collapsing?'"

He ultimately didn't make the team and had to have major surgery with a two-month healing process by February 2010. Again, he rushed things after recovering from the surgery and discovered he had torn his cremaster muscle, the muscle that surrounds the testicle. Whatever slight chance he had of playing major junior hockey was basically destroyed because of his injuries.

A patient of renowned concussion specialist Dr. Paul Echlin knows exactly the kind of pressure a player faces to stay in the game after an injury. Echlin outlined the case of a twenty-year-old goaltender who suffered a concussion after he was run by an opposing forward and hit his head on the goalpost and then the ice. There were ten seconds remaining in the second period at the time of the collision, and while he sat out the remainder of the period he went back in for the third period after his coach and trainer asked him if he was all right to play.

"I decided to return to play in the third period after becoming very emotional telling my team to protect me," the player wrote. "Any competitive athlete questioned if they are OK to play will always say 'Yes.' I wish I was either given no option or was more in tune with how I felt."

Another hockey player treated by Echlin wrote that the one constant throughout his career, from the time he was four years old, was the basic idea of playing through pain. Hockey players learn, usually at a very young age, that if they're not prepared to play through injuries and adversity, they're not going to have the character and fortitude it will take to advance very far in the game. For that reason, he avoided doctors constantly because he knew they were almost always the bearers of bad news. But the multiple concussions he suffered left him debilitated, in part because he ignored his previous concussions and each subsequent one got more serious.

"This [playing through pain] is an awesome ideology for life in general because we learn to push through the hard times," he wrote. "The only problem is, pushing through head pain and acting like it isn't there doesn't make you stronger. It gradually breaks you down."

Part of the problem is that concussion is a largely invisible injury. There are often no outward symptoms, which in many cases just encourages people who have never suffered one to tell those who have them to suck it up and play. Concussions cannot be picked up on an X-ray and the majority can't even be detected on magnetic resonance imaging (MRI) tests or CT scans. When people see someone in a sling or a cast or hobbling around on crutches, they never question his ability to play. But when it's an injury to the brain, there are times when nobody but the closest people around the athlete know anything is wrong with him.

But the effects, both long- and short-term, of concussion are very real. Consider what some of Dr. Paul Echlin's patients, made up of both male and female hockey players who have sustained concussions, have said of their ordeal dealing with the injury:

> "Depression was there and thoughts of suicide crossed my mind on a few occasions. This was a scary time in my life. I had never lost touch with my emotions and thoughts to such an extent. I also had headaches so bad I couldn't sleep. I was put on sleeping pills, which slowly became addicting. These were some of the darkest days of my life."

"Removing sports from my lifestyle has been extremely difficult. It feels like I completely lost my identity as a person. The hardest part through all of this is the fact that as much as people can try to understand, no one knows what it's like until they go through it."

"It has been almost a year and a half now of headaches. I am slowly losing hope of a 100 percent recovery."

"My concussion set me back a year, causing me to miss my high school graduation with all of my friends and class-mates, a moment I will never get to relive."

"When I listen to people speak or when I try reading, it is very frustrating because by the second sentence, I have already forgotten the first. I am in pain with bad headaches almost every day and jaw pain that is getting worse. There is often numbness in my legs that makes it very difficult for me to walk properly or stand for very long. I have also been suffering from insomnia. I would be past the point of exhaustion, but I can't sleep. My anxiety is debilitating and I have a dizzy nauseous feeling most of the time. When I shut my eyes, my head spins and my body almost falls sideways. I can't take a shower without holding onto some-thing or I will fall."

"I went from being a hard-working student and athlete to someone that couldn't be either."

"After I had to quit hockey, the headaches and lack of physical activity led to depression. Since I couldn't play the

sport I loved, I felt like I no longer fit in. Since I wasn't able
to work out or do any physical activity for a long time, I
put on weight, which made me feel even worse. I began
to no longer find joy in hanging out with friends or being
social. It made tasks at school and work much harder to
deal with. The years I should have been having the most
fun, I was dealing with this problem."

Matthew Kostuch can feel their pain, both literally and
figuratively. In the years following his injury, different doctors
put him on naproxen. Others advocated the use of amitripty-
line and nortriptyline, powerful antidepressants that are also
used to treat migraines, tension headaches, anxiety attacks,
and schizophrenic symptoms. Doctors at the chronic pain
clinic at the Hospital for Sick Children in Toronto suggested
that Matthew take the highest dose of Advil, along with the
highest dose of Tylenol, all at the same time. Another broached
the prospect of acupuncture. They even tried craniosacral
therapy and massage therapy. They tried to take dairy out of
his diet for a while. Not a single thing any one of them did
made one iota of difference in the level of pain Matthew was
suffering.

Sometimes all his helpless parents can do is give him a hug.
They have a little wire head massager they use at nighttime
when they're trying to put him to sleep. They find the constant
pressure of the massage helps calm him down and distract him
from the pain. Like a toddler who often needs his parents by
his bedside, Matthew requires help to get to sleep about five
out of every seven nights. He goes to bed by about 9:30, and
if his parents can get him to sleep by 10:15 that's considered a

good night in the Kostuch household. Many nights he doesn't shut his eyes until well after midnight.

Matthew Kostuch doesn't miss so much school anymore, except to go to doctors' appointments. But there are still times when he has to tell his teacher he wasn't able to complete his homework assignment because his head was pounding so heavily the previous night that he simply couldn't concentrate. He's a smart kid with a bright—but non–hockey playing—future ahead of him. Dr. Johnson has assured him that he will be pain-free someday, and the lucky thing is the concussions have had no lasting effect on his intellectual capacity.

He's a teenager who needs his brain for the rest of his life. There is the relief that he stopped playing before any further damage could be done, but there is also the lament that the hit that sidelined him shouldn't have even been part of a game involving ten-year-old players. He was hit by an individual player, yes, but he was also the victim of a culture of violence that surrounds hockey at every level of the game. There was a time when the purpose of a bodycheck was to separate your opponent from the puck. But somewhere along the line, it transformed into an attempt to separate him from his senses. Every bodycheck must come with a message that if you're going to carry the puck, you had better be prepared to pay the price for doing so.

The same young man who used to be on the ice six days a week playing the highest level of competitive hockey possible now spends his nights dealing with headaches and trying to steal a decent night's sleep. His parents are proud of the way he has handled the ordeal, and they should be. Rather than allow his pain and his injury to define him, he stands up to it and tries every day to wrestle it to the ground, or at least run it out of his system. Some days are more successful than others on that count.

And there is always the underlying realization that he will never, ever, play hockey again.

"What makes you sad is that he's not playing hockey," his father Jim said. "What he loves to do ..."

"... is gone," said Christine.

The cruel irony is that not playing hockey is the price that Matthew pays for playing hockey in the first place. What that suggests is that hockey is not the problem. Hockey itself is one of the things we have to save when we look for ways to protect kids.

Certainly, none of the saddening stories here should be taken to mean that kids shouldn't play hockey, or that the risks are too high. And while we don't want to point fingers in any particular case, it is important to note that the sense of what we can expect to get out of hockey affects the way we play it. It will affect the way we coach it, and; the way we talk to our kids in the car on the way home.

If you think of minor hockey as an investment, then the possibility of catastrophic injury is probably part of the equation. Earlier, we suggested that making it to the NHL is akin to winning the lottery, but that leaves out the downside. In some ways, it's more like Russian roulette—there is a cost to losing that corresponds to the dream of winning.

But childhood is *not* an investment. At least not intrinsically. The kids who play the game certainly don't see it that way. They dream the dream, and they're inspired by it. That hasn't changed in generations. But as we've seen, something has changed. Something has corrupted the dream we started with: kids playing shinny on the windswept ice of a frozen river, far from parents and referees, sports psychologists and nutritionists.

There was a time when kids just went to high school after graduating from the eighth grade. Generally speaking, it basically involved showing up at the secondary educational institution that was closest to your home. While that still can happen for a typical student, there now are myriad high school programs and specialty schools that require students to apply and be vetted in order to determine whether they belong. It seems as though it's no longer acceptable to go to high school and concentrate on chemistry, physics, and biology. Instead, the best and brightest now attend schools that specialize in science instruction. Where students at one time simply explored and honed their performing arts skills by taking part in high school productions, the most promising now attend secondary schools devoted to the performing arts.

Like high school and almost every other pursuit that involves young people now, the stakes seem to have risen exponentially ... and so has the pressure on young people. Former NHLer Ray Ferraro saw it when his son Landon, a prospect in the Detroit Red Wings system, was a teenager. "I said, 'Look, now it's really unfair, but let me give it to you this way,'" Ferraro said. "'You can have a buddy who can be a smart kid, a relative screw-up, drinks, probably smokes pot, hangs out on weekends, screws around through his first three years of college, gets serious, six years later he's a doctor. But when he was a teenager he could do whatever he wanted. If you do that as a teenager, you're done.'"

But amid all of this, there is something much more important at stake here: the very future of the game itself. As we've seen previously, the number of players playing minor hockey is dropping, along with birth rates in Canada. Go into many elementary school classrooms in Canada's large cities and there's a good chance you won't find more than a handful of kids who play organized hockey.

And somewhere along the way, the spirit of the game has been lost. There is something perverted about the fact that many kids now treat the game as work, while adults play it for fun. That's what the game is supposed to be. Don't kids deserve the same from the game as the forty-year-olds who enjoy it so much now? The irony is that the game has never been better at producing superstars, but is its exclusivity preventing us from producing another generation of beer league players?

And, invariably, almost all of us get caught up in it. I have worked in this business for more than a quarter of a century and know full well the pitfalls of single-minded focus when it comes to hockey. We like to think we're above it all, but in the end it seems we're all overconsumed and insecure about our children's endeavours on the ice. We talk the talk about it being all about fun for the kids, but do we walk the walk?

Even in the latter stages of writing this book, after interviewing hundreds of people and coming to the conclusion that hockey needs to be saved from itself, I succumbed to it as well. It was the summer of 2012 and my twelve-year-old son was preparing for the season. He has always been a house league player, but two years previous he had an opportunity to play at the Select level, which is basically a rep level for house league.

After playing as a skater, he switched to goaltender as a minor peewee.

Worried he would be cut by the Select team, we embarked on an off-ice training regimen. By mid-August, I was looking at on-ice options and we settled on an instructional facility outside the city that housed two 40-by-60 rinks with square corners in what was probably once a warehouse in a nondescript industrial strip. It was about as far from grassroots hockey as you could possibly get.

We walked into the office, which was adorned with medals and trophies from spring and summer league championships. On the shelf was a plaque that read,

PERSISTENCE
Nothing in the world can take the place of persistence.
  Talent will not; nothing is more common than unsuccessful men with talent.
  Genius will not; unrewarded genius is almost a proverb.
  Education will not; the world is full of educated derelicts.
  Persistence and determination alone will bring success.

Places such as this one are where young hockey players bring their patience and persistence, with their parents dragging a hockey bag in one hand and carrying a chequebook in the other. Two pads: one for individual instruction and the other for a small group of goaltenders. Along one wall is the Endless Ice skating treadmill and not far away from that is the Rapid Shot Hockey Training System. OVER 10 MILLION PUCKS SHOT! the sign near the machine says.

In one corner, a teenaged boy is slumped in a chair. His hair is still wet and he's wearing the bottom parts of his hockey equipment and an Under Armour T-shirt. He has just endured a one-hour training session, only to be reminded he has to drive across the city to be back on the ice within the next hour.

A mother comes in to speak to one of her instructors. She tells him her son needs some work on shooting and defensive play and that he's a little lazy picking up his feet when he skates backward. If the instructor needs any visual proof, she has her iPad with footage of one of her son's games from the previous season. After the session, she declares herself pleased and works on making an appointment for Sunday afternoon, which has to be worked around his pre-season practice with his club team.

Over at the goalie instruction pad, one of the boys turns on his skate and heads toward the boards, where his mother dutifully opens the door and squirts water into his mouth.

It's all craziness. When the hell did we get so overindulgent? Then I realize I'm there too. I tell myself and my son my only goal is for him to enjoy the game, but how enjoyable is this? Is this what we really want for our children out of hockey? Is this what they want? But more importantly, are we at a point from which we can't return?

10
SOLUTIONS

In the past five NHL seasons, the average age of a fifty-goal scorer has been 23.7 years, thanks in part to the fact that Steven Stamkos of the Tampa Bay Lightning accomplished the standard when he was 20 and again when he was just 22. It's undeniable that Stamkos has been blessed with some very high-end natural gifts, along with a sense of determination that is almost without peer. When he was born in 1990 to the son and daughter of immigrants from Greece and Scotland, there was nothing in his family history to suggest he would become one of the most dynamic offensive producers in the NHL.

But Stamkos was set on his career path early in life by a father who realized the benefits of specialized instruction and exposure to the best competition. By the time Stamkos was nine years old, he was working regularly with renowned skills coach Jari Byrski, who counts NHL stars Jason Spezza, Brent Burns, Michael Cammalleri, and Rick Nash among his disciples. From very early in his hockey career, he played for the Markham Waxers, a minor hockey juggernaut that also featured future NHLers Cody Hodgson, Michael Del Zotto, and Cameron Gaunce. He played spring and summer hockey on powerhouse teams that had some of the best players in Ontario. And early in his career, he became a disciple of nutrition and conditioning guru Gary Roberts.

You could certainly argue that Stamkos's career was, if not manufactured, helped along the way by other factors as much as it was born of natural talent. Even his coach with the Lightning, Guy Boucher, refers to him as "the new generation of machine"—players so well prepared to play in the NHL at such a young age that they've established themselves not only as full-time players, but in many cases superstars, before blowing out even twenty-five candles on their birthday cakes.

Using Stamkos as the template, where do we go from here? After all, it can be difficult to find fault with the culture of minor hockey when it regularly churns out players of his ilk. Not long after Canada finished eighth (behind Kazakhstan!) at the 1998 World Junior Championship and failed to medal at the Nagano Olympics two months later, the stakeholders in the game convened for the Open Ice Summit where much of the debate centred around where all the skilled players had gone and why Canada seemed to no longer be producing them. Almost a decade and a half later, such navel gazing is no longer necessary. Canada is at or near the top of the world at all levels of international hockey, its production of high-end NHL talent remains brisk, and if you go to any arena on any given night in any part of the country to watch minor hockey, chances are you'll be treated to some very special players with breathtaking skills and a maturity level to match.

As we said, it's kind of difficult to suggest we need to fix something that might not necessarily be all that broken. But not to do so would be to suggest that it only matters how many elite hockey players we produce. There is no worry there, because there will always be enough übertalents from Canada and around the rest of the world to fill the NHL and keep us all entertained, even if the league expands over the next decade. This has never been about those players. It has been about the hundreds of thousands who chase a dream abiding by all the rules of minor hockey culture, no matter how demanding or what price they exact, both financially and emotionally. If this book has done anything, we hope it has provided something of a reality check. Even with all the sacrifices and expenses and missed opportunities, the chances of making a professional career in the game are remotely small. That doesn't mean players shouldn't keep chasing the dream, but to the exclusion of almost everything else? Does any of that really make sense?

Should we be hothousing our elite players and singling them out as special talents as soon as they're able to tie up their own skates? Does it really help a player to move to a bigger city with more teams simply to improve his hockey prospects? Is there any way we can make this wonderful game more accessible to families of all socio-economic circumstances to give them a chance to chase the dream, too? Do we really need our top players playing hockey eleven or twelve months a year?

No easy answers to these questions exist but there are alternatives, both systemically and personally. Here are some of them:

NO ELITE HOCKEY BEFORE
THE PEEWEE LEVEL

In February 2010, just a few minutes after the Ajax (Ontario) Knights Tykes skated off the ice after losing the championship final of the Three Rivers Cup, the roof of the Rostraver Ice Garden in suburban Pittsburgh collapsed. The Knights lost by one goal and narrowly missed tying the game on a breakaway with two minutes left in the game. Had the player scored, the game would have gone into overtime and the main arena would have been filled with players and parents. There is no doubt a major tragedy would have resulted, since that was where the roof collapsed.

One question that needed to be asked was, How can any arena be in such disrepair that its roof would collapse after a couple of snowstorms? Another question that needed to be asked was, What in the world was a team of seven- and eight-year-old kids doing travelling six hours across an international border to play in a tyke hockey tournament?

Canada has never been reticent to throw its youngest players into the frying pan of competition. There was a time when players would stumble out onto the ice before they could even stand up, let alone know where to line up for a faceoff. The Initiation Program established by Hockey Canada has done a good job of providing the fundamentals of the game in a non-competitive atmosphere, but it seems once our children learn the basics of the game, there's a rush to make sure they get into the best programs and face the best competition right away. Some jurisdictions have the AAA or "rep" designation for teams as young as tyke and novice.

This is driven by a number of factors, not the least of which is the increasingly professionalized approach to youth sports. But is there credence to starting our young kids playing in hyper-competitive situations as early as possible, or is it more the product of a herd mentality that suggests more is better and that getting started that young is a matter of competitive survival? If there is one thing that many of today's parents fear, it's that their children will fall behind the others. The pressure to keep one's children on track and competitive with their peers is enough to fluster even the most balanced parents. So we put our children into preschools that lead to better elementary schools, that lead to better high schools, that lead to better universities. And as a result of this thinking, parents over-schedule their children and send them on their way with back-packs heavy enough to make them collapse. In fact, researchers have determined that children today have eight fewer hours for free, unstructured playtime per week than they did twenty years ago. Despite mountains of research that shows children learn best through active, unstructured play, we continue to take that away from them and replace it with activities run by adults and with rules made by adults.

And hockey is no exception, at least at the elite level. It is not uncommon for an elite team of nine- and ten-year-olds to be on the ice five nights a week. Every parent with a child who does this has a common response. And that is that the child is so passionate about his pursuit that he insists on doing it. But exactly who is driving the bus here?

It is, in fact, possible to resist the urge to have children playing a hyper-competitive level of hockey at a young age without losing the competitive edge. One of the most successful minor hockey associations in Canada has proved it, as has the country that has supplied the NHL with some of the most skilled players it has ever seen.

The Thunder Bay Minor Hockey Association does not allow its teams to have AAA programs until the peewee level; this means the earliest any player can play at that level is eleven, but the vast majority of the players are twelve. The rationale is simple—that playing at the AAA level is an enormous commitment for both the parents and the player and a certain level of physical and emotional maturity is required to handle it. And the people who run minor hockey in Thunder Bay have decided that kids under the age of twelve are generally not prepared for it.

"The feeling here in this community is that peewee is plenty early to get into AAA hockey," said Al Tennant, president of the Thunder Bay Kings, the only AAA organization in the northwestern Ontario city of 110,000. "It's a huge commitment for the kids and a really big one for the parents, both from a financial and time standpoint. The thinking here is, 'Let's make sure these kids have that fire burning in their belly, that they are living and breathing hockey and then let's get them into the AAA level.'"

All that philosophy has done is create a minor hockey association that, per capita, produces the most NHL players of any city in Canada. Having his kids wait until peewee to play AAA hockey certainly didn't stop Henry Staal from seeing three of his four sons—Eric, Jordan, and Marc—make it to the NHL. (The fourth, Jared, was drafted in the second round of the NHL draft in 2008 and is playing in the minor leagues.) Patrick Sharp, Alex Auld, and Taylor and Tom Pyatt all played for the Thunder Bay Kings. A total of fifty-two players from the organization have gone on to play Division I college hockey in the U.S., and an additional thirteen have played Division III. Twenty-eight former Thunder Bay Kings have played hockey in the Canadian Interuniversity Sport (CIS) league, and many more play in professional leagues in both North America and Europe.

As far as results are concerned, since 1989 the Kings have won four all-Ontario bantam championships, two national midget championships, and two national Jr. A championship titles. That would be an impressive accomplishment for any city, let alone a medium-sized centre that is an eight-hour drive away from the next major city. And not one of those players was exposed to AAA competition until peewee.

But the strategy of waiting doesn't only work in Thunder Bay. In fact, Sweden waits substantially longer to get its players involved in the elite stream of hockey. Players there must wait until they're at least fourteen years old before they're exposed to the equivalent of AAA hockey in Canada. And what might even be more important, there is virtually no level of competition at all for players under the ages of ten. What they do have is something called the Three Crowns Hockey School, which focuses largely on fundamentals. The way the Swedish system works, sports clubs sponsor teams from the professional elite league right down to the Three Crowns Hockey School. The only games they play prior to the age of ten are cross-ice games, which allows four teams to use one ice surface and saves on costs.

"On a Sunday afternoon, four clubs get together and they set up two teams each, so they have eight teams, and they play mini-tournaments," said Tommy Boustedt, the development director for the Swedish Ice Hockey Federation. "There is no league. They count the goals when they're playing, but they don't report the results to a league or anything."

The benefits of directing a player into an elite program are many. First, parents don't incur enormous expenses and time sacrifices while their children are young. Al Tennant estimates that the difference in playing at the AA level in atom and the AAA level at peewee is about $3,000 a year, with the higher level costing about $4,500. It also produces more well-rounded athletes because they have time to pursue other sports. But most importantly, it keeps all players on an even playing surface, which allows late bloomers to catch up and can minimize the impact of what's known as the "relative age effect," a factor many in hockey believe provides an unfair advantage to players born in the first six months of the year.

Boustedt points to players such as Peter Forsberg and Henrik Zetterberg, two of the most successful NHL players Sweden has ever produced. Both were small for their age until their teens and both were late to hit puberty. Had they been dismissed as elite players at a young age when they could not possibly compete with their more physically developed peers, there's a chance they both would have dropped out of hockey to pursue something else.

"I started working as a coach in the 1970s and I still find it very hard to see which one is going to be the best player when I watch twelve- and thirteen-year-olds," Boustedt said. "The big risk of choosing elite players very early, you choose the big ones who are early in puberty and you miss all the late bloomers. In a big hockey country like Canada, there are ten players for every position so they can afford to lose some.

But we are such a small country and the numbers are so low in Sweden, we can't lose so many because then we won't be competitive."

ALL HOCKEY, ALL THE TIME
IS NOT A GOOD THING

One by-product of our obsession with having children directed into elite streams of hockey so young is the growing phenomenon of early specialization. After all, how else is someone to get the 10,000 hours of dedicated practice that the Malcolm Gladwell disciples have been led to believe is needed to become an expert at something?

And once again, it's largely a product of our insecurities. That kind of effort often requires a singular dedication that excludes almost everything else. After all, it's difficult to make a commitment to soccer or baseball when you're playing hockey throughout the spring and summer and your winter season starts sometime in mid-August.

As a result, not only does the hockey season take up most of the calendar, it doesn't allow for too many pursuits during the season either. What often ends up happening is you're developing one-dimensional athletes and one-dimensional people along the way.

Again, we use the example provided by Sweden. One of the reasons they don't allow elite hockey until the age of fourteen is they want their young athletes to experience as many different sports as possible. As a young person, Mats Sundin played bandy (basically a form of field hockey on ice), tennis, soccer, and golf along with hockey—and was very good at all of them—before deciding to pursue a hockey career when he was fourteen. The Swedes have studied this phenomenon extensively, and whenever they ask their elite NHL players about the major factors in their development they always point to the fact that they experienced a number of sports as youngsters. Not only did they not get burned out by hockey, they also gained muscle memory and skills they might not have been able to pick up on the ice surface. In fact, the Swedes are so insistent on this they have made it part of their curriculum for developing players.

"You need to be so good at so many different things to be a hockey player," Boustedt said. "If you do a lot of sports, you get a broader base to stand on when you get on with much more hockey at age fourteen."

And really, isn't one of the pure joys of hockey digging into your equipment bag and putting your skates on for the first time in the fall? For many elite players, that day has become just another day on the never-ending hockey calendar.

"I hate spring hockey," said former NHLer Ray Ferraro. "I think at its worst, it's nothing more than a money maker."

There is enough evidence out there to support the theory that early specialization isn't necessarily a good thing. Some who have done research on the subject claim it gives no competitive advantage, while others have concluded that singular devotion to one activity at too young an age can actually hurt development more than help it. Robert Malina, a professor emeritus in the department of kinesiology and health sciences at the University of Texas, has done extensive research on early specialization and thinks it can be a bad thing not only from an athletic development point of view, but also from a social standpoint.

"Early specialization in sport has social consequences for children and adolescents," Malina wrote in the *Journal of Exercise Science and Fitness* in 2009. "Given the time commitment to a single sport, the young athlete often faces potential for social isolation from age and sex peers, especially during adolescence, and altered social relationships with parents and family."

So in other words, you may (or may not) be churning out the next great athlete, but at what cost to the athlete and society?

THEY CALL IT "HOME SWEET HOME" FOR A REASON

In the summer of 2011, Hockey Canada announced a plan to "create mechanisms in player movement to facilitate flexibility within the game reflecting the needs of the modern player and family." Simply put, you can expect Hockey Canada to loosen, not tighten, its residency rules in the future.

And that's all well and good. Parents and players who want to move to another jurisdiction because they think it will expose them to better teammates and competition and make them better players should be permitted to do so. After all, if someone from Peterborough, Ontario, has the intellectual capability to attend Harvard, he or she shouldn't be forced to go to Trent University. And if a young dancer has enough talent and his or her parents have enough money, he or she should have the flexibility to attend the National Ballet School in Toronto rather than be required to take ballet instruction from the elderly lady in town who rents the church basement every Saturday.

But before players use those residency rules to beat a path to cities such as Montreal, Toronto, Vancouver, Calgary, Edmonton, Winnipeg, and Halifax because there are more players and more arenas, they should be aware that if a player is good enough, he will be found wherever he's playing. They should also be aware that, according to the numbers, it's actually more advantageous to play hockey in a mid-sized city rather than a large one.

Jean Côté of Queen's University studied NHL rosters from the 2002–03 season and came up with some very interesting findings when it came to NHL production relative to the size of a city. We already know that Thunder Bay produces more players per capita than any other city in Canada and that's consistent with what Côté found in the NHL. In fact, Côté found that very big cities and very small towns did not produce players even close to their relative size. In fact, it suggests that the best kind of city to produce an NHL player is one that has a good number of rinks, but is not so large that the demand for ice time outweighs the opportunities to use it.

Côté found that cities of 500,000 or more people make up 33.2 percent of the population in Canada, but represented only 15.7 percent of the Canadian players in the NHL. Cities of 100,000 to 500,000, meanwhile, account for 13.3 percent of the population, but punch at more than double their weight, with 33.2 percent of the NHL players. Cities of 30,000 to 100,000 also did well, accounting for 7.6 percent of the population, but 15.8 percent of NHL players. Cities of 10,000 to 30,000 make up 7.3 percent of the population, but 10.4 percent of NHL players. Cities of 5,000 to 9,000 account for 3.4 percent of the population and 7.7 percent of NHLers, while cities of 2,500 to 5,000 make up 3.3 percent of the citizenry and 6.2 percent of Canadian NHLers. Towns of fewer than 2,500 people, meanwhile, make up 28.5 percent of the population, but only 5.1 percent of NHL players.

Jack Birch has been in the scouting business for more than thirty years and has analyzed the science behind scouting more than anyone in the world. In fact, his Ph.D. dissertation at the University of Waterloo in 1987 investigated ascribed variables versus achieved variables in the selection of elite players. Ascribed variables are those that have nothing to do with the game, such as height, body type, family background, hometown, and relative age effect.

And Birch has found that players who come from smaller cities and towns, in fact, have an advantage over those who play in large cities. He uses the example of municipal politics. A city with a million people and one with 50,000 people can have only one mayor each. And that's how things often work when scouts are looking for the top players. There are only about 180 scouting nights in a given year and those who make the decisions rely on "bird dog" and regional scouts, each of whom has a territory to cover.

Let's take a major junior head scout or general manager, for example. He relies on his area scouts to provide him with a list of the top players from each region, and those are the players who receive the most attention. The worst thing for a GM is to walk into an arena on a scouting mission where there are no prospects, so they need to know who the top players are in every region.

"You're typically skimming the top," Birch said. "So what happens is players [from smaller cities] end up getting overrepresented a little bit relative to the size of their community. By virtue of its population, there could be fifteen players who were better in a place like Toronto than the top three kids in Woodstock, but they're not getting the same type of viewing. There's not enough time or energy or thoughtfulness that goes into, 'Well, there could be seventeen players on this team that are better than the five players who are in Woodstock.'"

Henry Staal of Thunder Bay, who has had three sons star in the NHL and a fourth in the minor leagues, notices another advantage of playing in a smaller, more isolated place rather than a large city that is far more accessible to the power brokers in hockey. Elite players in Thunder Bay get plenty of exposure by travelling to tournaments and showcasing their skills, but those who hold the levers of power in the game are hardly beating a path to their city.

"First, I guarantee you that our kids practise more than any AAA team in the country," Staal said. "They get bored of it, but in the end they become better players. And there are no agents kicking around our rinks, so the kids realize nothing is going to be given to them. I think there's a bit of an inferiority complex that drives them, but they don't really have any sense of entitlement."

WHAT TO DO ABOUT ARENAS

One of the most prominent barriers to grassroots participation in hockey has to do with access to ice, from both an availability and an affordability point of view. Canada has about 3,000 indoor arenas, which works out to one for approximately every 10,000 people. That sounds fairly reasonable, doesn't it?

But there are those who feel a crisis is looming in Canada when it comes to rinks. By far, the two biggest expenses for hockey players in this country are equipment and ice time, and that ice usually goes to those who can most afford it. Take Calgary, for example. In that city, the minor hockey associations pay $150 an hour for ice time, while non–minor hockey groups pay $225 per hour, which means that budget-conscious rink operators are squeezing minor hockey in favour of giving more ice time to adults.

"There's an ever-increasing desire for the rink and facility managers to be topping up their capital reserve funds and aging facilities are requiring more capital expenditures," Hockey Calgary president Perry Cavanagh told *The Hockey News* in 2010.

That's because the majority of the arenas in Canada are wearing out and either have to be refurbished or replaced. A study by the Canadian Recreation Facilities Council in 2005 found at the time that the majority of the arenas in Canada were in the thirty- to thirty-five-year-old range for buildings that are supposed to have life expectancies of about thirty-two years. There was an enormous infrastructure boom in the 1970s, but since then the building of publicly funded arenas has slowed to a trickle. In the survey, of the 1,857 arenas that supplied construction dates, 1,350 of them were built prior to 1980 and 594 of them were built before 1960. It was estimated that it would cost somewhere in the range of $3.7 billion to renovate those rinks.

"The information shows that arena infrastructure is at a point in its life cycle where within the next few years, massive amounts of funding will be required to maintain and sustain this infrastructure," the report said. "The burden of funding will be with municipal governments as they are owners of 86 percent of the infrastructure."

There has not been a publicly funded arena built in Toronto since the 1970s. Private operators have stepped in to fill some of that need and they will charge what the market will bear, which is usually somewhere in the $300 to $400 range for prime time ice. So you can see how those who are selling the dream pass on their costs to their customers. That's partly why minor hockey rates are so high and some minor hockey associations charge admission for the games, for everyone attending, including the player performing in the game!

It certainly doesn't make for much inclusiveness. If players are restricted from participating because they can't even step on the ice, it's difficult to imagine they would ever be able to have access to the game. And if you're cutting an entire segment of the population out for that reason, then it stands to reason that only those with the financial resources to pay are going to be the ones who excel. It may come as a surprise to some people that just one in six boys in Canada actually plays organized hockey. In 2006, there were 2.1 million children aged ten to fourteen in Canada and by 2016, that number is expected to plummet by 300,000 to about 1.8 million. Hockey Canada has a 9.5 percent retention rate in that age group, which means if it holds that number, it will stand to lose 30,000 players at its most crucial age group in the next several years.

Access to ice is a pivotal issue. Cash-strapped municipalities seemed to get out of the rink-building business a long time ago, and many have cut the number of outdoor rinks they operate. Even if they did keep those up, they would have to deal with a changing climate. A recent study done by Concordia University determined that most areas in Canada have experienced a significant decrease in the number of days in the outdoor skating season. Really, they actually came up with a numerical figure for that based on the notion that it requires three consecutive days of minus-five-Celsius temperatures to form a base. The study found that the worst-hit areas were British Columbia and southern Alberta, which had seen a decrease of 20 percent in their outdoor skating season, while Ontario and Quebec were not far behind.

As long as both public and private entities insist on building multi-pad facilities with restaurants, the situation isn't about to change. It is very expensive to build an indoor rink, with a single-pad structure costing upwards of $20 million to construct. Then there are the costs associated with running the facility.

But it doesn't have to be that way if we can learn to live with rinks that are, well, just rinks. The fact of the matter is that basic rinks that are enclosed by basic structures can be built now for under $6 million and can be completed within six months. But they are as barebones as can be. There are no seats for spectators, they're rather cold, there are limited washroom and shower facilities, and spectators who don't bring their own coffee and aren't willing to stand along the boards are out of luck. Not only do those who go this route save on construction, but maintenance costs are about 20 percent less.

If it costs $6 million to build one of these rinks and $20 million to build a conventional rink, wouldn't most municipalities in this country prefer to build three indoor ice surfaces instead of one? And while we're doing that, why are we not examining the possibility of playing more hockey outdoors?

To that end, a venture capitalist by the name of Graeme Roustan has a dream. He wants to build 100 outdoor rinks that can withstand the unpredictability of Canadian winters in the next ten years. His project is called Rinks Across Canada. Among many other things, Roustan owns a company that can build an outdoor rink complete with a refrigeration system for about $2.25 million. As of early 2012, he had teamed up with the Montreal Canadiens and Ottawa Senators, with plans to build twenty outdoor rinks in each city.

The way it works is this: Roustan's company pays $500,000 for the site preparation and refrigeration systems and pays for the construction work, which, combined with the lost profits, adds up to about $1 million. Then the Canadiens or the Senators, usually through their charitable foundations, pay the remaining $750,000 for materials, which Roustan purchases and sells to them at cost. The rinks are built on municipal land that is donated and once they're completed, the rinks are turned back over to the municipalities.

Roustan does have a vested interest in all of this, despite the fact that his rink-building company does not make any money on the venture. First of all, he's the largest single share-holder of the hockey equipment giant Bauer, and the more people he can get playing hockey, the more potential consumers his company will have. (But, as he points out, so will Bauer's competitors.) And he has also been a finalist to purchase two NHL teams and very much wants to be in the club. In fact, he's also building an NHL-sized rink in the Toronto suburb of

Markham in the hopes of luring a second big-league team to the Toronto market.

But he's also one of the only people in Canada building rinks these days. And if anything is to be learned from his venture, it's that people who want their facilities can no longer depend on the public sector to build them, because municipal governments are too preoccupied with keeping libraries open, schools running effectively, buses running on time, and roads being repaired to focus on building new arenas. Clearly, this is something that will have to be driven by two groups—private citizens and corporations.

It's difficult to prove a negative here. Exactly what effect would more outdoor rinks have on the hockey land-scape? Well, first of all, it creates a connection to the game that can last a lifetime. And by putting those rinks in more economically disadvantaged areas, the way Roustan and the Canadiens are doing, it provides access to a group that had been until then shut out of participating. Roustan said one of the rinks in Montreal services about 20,000 children. Is there a rule that says all hockey leagues must play indoors? Almost anyone over the age of forty-five who grew up in a northern climate will tell you his or her first connection to the game came from playing outside, on a backyard rink, a community surface, or a pond. It is there that kids are free to play in an unstructured way, free of a minor hockey system that is run by adults and that promotes the values and expectations of adults.

And we go back to former NHLer Glen Metropolit, whom we met in a previous chapter. Metropolit developed the skill set he needed to play in the best league in the world for one reason. He did it because he had free access to two publicly funded and city-operated outdoor rinks in his Regent Park housing project, not because he played a high level of minor hockey. In fact, until his mid-teens his organized hockey was limited to rudimentary house leagues that practised once a week under the tutelage of volunteer parents, if at all.

The question is, How many Metropolits are we missing out on by not giving them access to good, free ice? "There's so much talent down there," Metropolit said of Regent Park. "If they just had an agency or the right person to get down there and train these kids and support them, but you can't do it all. I wish I could, but I can't."

AND FINALLY, A LITTLE PERSPECTIVE, PLEASE?

Remember Jack Birch? His son, Braden, is playing at Cornell University and was taken by the Chicago Blackhawks in the sixth round in 2008. Birch thinks one of the reasons for that is that he has been socialized into the game. He was attending Florida Panther development camps when he was fourteen years old.

As part of his research, Birch found that 30 percent of the likelihood of a player getting into the NHL was based on ascribed variables, those that are outside a person's control. He also found that 15 to 20 percent of players in the NHL had some kind of previous connection to the NHL through a family member, and Birch suspects that has far more to do with socialization than it does bloodlines.

"So if you can say that 30 percent of the correlation can be

explained by something that is not under the player's control,"
Birch said, "I felt that was a significant thing."

With those kinds of odds, you'd wonder why any parent
or child would dare to chase NHL dreams. But thousands of
them do, and some of them succeed. As the father of one minor
hockey player we spoke to for this book said, "Hey, somebody
has to make it. Why not my kid?" The dream of playing in the
NHL, or even major junior hockey or the college game, is one
worth pursuing. Walt Disney once said, "All our dreams can
come true if we have the courage to pursue them."

Courage? Absolutely. But it takes a lot more than that to
realize the hockey dream. And it seems to be getting more difficult as the stakes get higher and the elite are identified and
nurtured at younger and younger ages. There are those who
worry that hockey has become a rich man's game, and their
fears are not unfounded.

The rewards are high, but so are the costs. That doesn't
mean we should stop chasing the dream. It means we should
do so armed with perspective and balance. It's then that we'll
get what we want in life, whether that comes with an NHL
career or not.

ACKNOWLEDGMENTS

A former publisher at *The Hockey News,* the late Mike Lawton, once said that new magazines are not born, they are "beaten to life." The same could certainly be said for a project of this magnitude. And it was impossible to "beat to life" this book without the help of a multitude of people.

The first words of enormous thanks must go to my research partner Jim Parcels, whose 2002 study titled *Chances of Making It in Pro Hockey* provided much of the initial grist for the mill. Jim's guidance, along with his contacts and experience navigating the complex waters of minor hockey, was absolutely integral to the project.

Thanks also must go out to two very special people. The first is my agent, Arnold Gosewich, for taking me on as a client and displaying an inordinate amount of faith in me and the project. The second is my editor at Penguin Books, Nick Garrison, who narrowed the focus and helped craft the words into something much better than they were when he received them.

My eternal gratitude also goes out to my colleagues at *The Hockey News,* most of all to editor-in-chief and true friend Jason Kay for his patience with me during the process. Kudos also go to Brian Costello, Edward Fraser, Ryan Kennedy, Rory Boylen, Erika Vanderveer, Ronnie Shuker, Matt Larkin, Adam Proteau, Ted Cooper, Carlie McGhee, and Alyson Young.

I interviewed literally hundreds of people for this book and I owe each and every one of them a debt of gratitude. There are too many to mention, but I would like to single out a few of them: Matthew Kostuch for his frankness and kindness in the wake of having his dreams taken away from him; Mitchell Davis and Pierre Dupuis for sharing their stories with me; and all the other published authors for allowing me to access their work.

Most of all, I would like to thank my friends and family for standing by me with unwavering support and love while I toiled away at this project. My most heartfelt thanks go to my sons, Connor and Lukas, and my wife, Lucie, for, among other things, allowing me a couple of hours a day to myself to write during our family trip to the Dominican Republic. All three of you are my inspiration and nothing I do means anything without you.

INDEX